BRITISH TRADE UNIONS

BRITISH TRADE UNIONS

by

N. BAROU
Ph.D.(Econ.), Lond.

LONDON
VICTOR GOLLANCZ LTD
1947

PRINTED IN GREAT BRITAIN BY RICHARD CLAY AND COMPANY, LTD.,
BUNGAY, SUFFOLK.

PREFACE

I SUPPOSE THE main reason why my friend Dr. Barou asked me to write a Preface to this book is that I was responsible for the only large-scale study of British trade unionism that has been published since Mr. and Mrs. Webb made their great contributions half a century ago, and that my study, in which I had the aid of a number of leading experts on particular industries and problems, was made shortly before the Second World War. As I compare his book with my own, I am naturally led to think above all else of the changes which the past eight years have made in the position of the trade union movement, in the tasks facing it, and in the measures needed for tackling these tasks in a sound and effective way.

There is, indeed, a quite extraordinary difference in the situation which underlay my description of eight years ago and that which underlies the present study. Then trade unionism was slowly recovering from the serious setbacks it had suffered, first in the failure of the General Strike of 1926 and thereafter in the great world depression. Membership was picking up; but the situation was still one of heavy unemployment in the depressed areas and industries and of weak organisation in many of the newer trades which were taking on additional workers. Under such conditions, the trade unions needed all their strength to secure any concessions; and their strength, especially in the basic industries, which were the most depressed, had very narrow limits.

To-day, the conditions are entirely different. The trade unions could, if they chose, demand almost anything; and in a great number of industries at any rate, no power could resist them, if their members were really determined to have their way. They are, however, rank and file as well as leaders, taking up an attitude of undeniable moderation: indeed, that is a very mild way of putting the case. They are, in instance after instance, deliberately refraining from pressing demands which they know could not be refused. They are observing a most scrupulously moderate wage-policy: they are refraining from insisting on the concession of the forty-hour week, even though this forms part of the official policy of the entire movement. There are, no doubt, from time to time unofficial strikes, which cause great perturbation in high quarters and are assiduously written up by reactionaries who would dearly love to attack the entire trade union movement if they dared. But the astonishing thing about these unofficial strikes is not their frequency, but their fewness; and even unofficial leaders have been careful in most cases to put forward only moderate demands.

The reasons for this change of temper and attitude are not far to seek. In the period before the war moderation was not voluntary: it was enforced by the weakness of the trade unions' bargaining position in face of heavy unemployment. To-day, on the other hand, trade unionism is moderate in its demands, despite its accession of power, because it is conscious of its responsibility. Not only do ordinary trade unionists, as well as trade union leaders, understand perfectly well that it can be of no use to force up wages generally, except to counter rising prices, until there are more goods available for consumption: they are also well aware that their chance of getting more goods, and even of maintaining their present standards of living, depends on British industry's power to export enough to meet the cost of necessary imports of food and raw materials, and that, although for the moment the world may, because of universal shortage, be a sellers' market, it will not stay so, and within a very few years British exports will have to be sold on keenly competitive terms.

In effect, the change in Great Britain's international economic position has made the trade unions, willy nilly, partners in promoting industrial efficiency, because, unless they do help to promote it, their hopes of better conditions, or even of keeping what they have now, are bound to be disappointed. This makes them partners, whether their partnership be with the Government, as it is in the industries that are being transferred to public ownership, or with private, profit-seeking employers, in the much more numerous industries that are being left in private hands.

The second of these partnerships is, of course, a most uneasy one; and there are many who persist in denying its existence. It is not and cannot be a partnership of friends; for the interests of the parties, in respect of their industrial relations, remain as opposed as ever. But it is none the less a partnership, because both parties must, for sheer survival, aim at delivering the goods at prices which the purchasers can afford to pay, and because both parties are afraid of the consequences of an uncontrolled inflation, such as would be set going if the trade unions were to insist on using their bargaining power to the full.

Certain consequences of this changed situation are already becoming apparent: others, there is still a deep reluctance to face, not only among employers, but also on the trade union side. It is obvious that, with labour scarce in most occupations, and skilled labour very scarce indeed, employers, even if trade unions hold back from making demands proportionate to their bargaining power, have to mind their P's and Q's much more than ever before in their handling of individual workmen, and especially of those whose skill is a highly valuable asset to the firm. An increase in the politeness of "master" to "man" follows as a matter of course; and foremen, as well as employers, have to mend their manners. With this goes a change in works' "discipline"; and one hears many laments that, under the new conditions, "discipline" is utterly breaking down. Obviously this is not true, or the results would have shown markedly in production; but it is true that the discipline of the factory has to become much more nearly an *agreed* discipline, accepted as reasonable by both parties, and cannot be, as much as before, an *imposed* discipline, enforced by the perpetual threat of the sack. There is much more "joint consultation" in the factories and workshops, because there has to be—in fact, because without it discipline would break down.

This change in factory relations, which is bound to be permanent if this Government succeeds in living up to its promise to maintain full employment, is of the deepest significance for the future of the trade unions. In conjunction with the realised impracticability of getting higher real wages and improved conditions except as an accompaniment to larger output and increased efficiency, it means that the centre of effective trade union action is shifting. It is shifting from the national and district machinery of collective negotiation between employers' associations and trade unions into the factories and workshops, and is giving an immensely greater importance to the leaders of workshop opinion, whether they are formally designated as "shop stewards" or members of "shop committees" or not.

What this means for the trade unions is that if they wish to retain an effective control over their members—and they can do this only by keeping closely in touch with what their members want—they must base their organisation much more than in the past on the workshops, and must give shop stewards and works representatives a much more influential recognised status in the trade union machine. Many trade union leaders are reluctant to accept this necessity, both because they are used to conditions which put most of the power and responsibility into their own hands, and called for only a passive support from the main body of the members, and, still more, because they are afraid that, if the centre of trade union gravity is shifted to the workshops, it will be a good deal easier for Communists to expand their influence.

I am not denying that this fear may have substance; but what if it has? If the men and women in the workshops choose a considerable number of Communists to represent them, it does not follow that they are Communists, but it does, I think, follow that the Communists have so far shown themselves more alive than most other trade unionists to the requirements of the changed situation. This has been at least in part because the official leadership of the trade unions has been slow in recognising the importance of workshop organisation, and in encouraging the membership as a whole to develop it to the full.

Of course, it follows from this shift of emphasis to the workshop that the right basis for trade union organisation, at any rate over a large part of the field, is by industry and not by craft, or at the least is not by crafts spreading right across industrial divisions and preventing the achievement of solidarity in the industries affected. There may be cases in which the best form of organisation is a close industrial federation linking together a number of district craft unions within a single industry—e.g., printing, or cotton, or perhaps building. But it simply will not do to have the less skilled workers in an industry organised quite separately from the skilled workers, or to have unions based on crafts which straddle across a large number of industries and have no real co-ordination with the unions representing the rest of the workers in the industries to which they extend. I am not suggesting that British trade unionism can, or should, be linked up so as to conform strictly to a single pattern; but, like Dr. Barou, I am convinced that large structural changes are urgently needed, and that they must take the direction of (a) more organisation by industry, and less by crafts, and (b) more power and recognition inside the trade unions of shop stewards and works committees as

viii

negotiating bodies about matters of concern to the workers in each individual shop or establishment.

Changes of this kind are no less needed in industries which are being transferred to public ownership than elsewhere. In privately owned industries still conducted for profit, it is highly undesirable for the trade unions to accept any joint responsibility with the employers, save to the extent to which they are acting under the auspices of the State and the State also shares the responsibility and indeed has the final voice. What was wrong with the Whitley Councils set up after the First World War was that they were meant to induce the trade unions and the employers to become partners, not in carrying out plans approved by the State, but under the conditions of uncontrolled profit-making enterprise. The new plan based on the technique of the Working Parties is essentially different, because the bodies which it is proposed to set up are to include nominees of the State, as watch-dogs of the public interest, and because the intention is to ensure that the policy of the industries affected shall fit in with the requirements of the Government's economic plans. On such bodies, the representatives of the trade unions and of the Government should be able to pull together; and the power vested in the Government can be used to secure the employers' conformity with the public interests. I say "can be" and not "will be"; for neither I nor anyone else can yet know how the experiment will work out. All that can be said at this stage is that it is not doomed to failure from the start, as "Whitleyism" was.

In publicly owned industries and services, the problem is rather different; for here it is a question of devising ways and means for the workers to be taken into real and cordial partnership with the Public Boards and Corporations to which the responsibility for management is being entrusted under the various Acts. I am convinced of this: the National Coal Board, the Transport Commission, and the rest of the new nominated public agencies will not succeed unless they do create this spirit of partnership, not merely with the trade unions as national or regional bodies, but with the actual workers in every pit, station, port or works that is brought within the ambit of public enterprise. This too will call for a reconsideration of trade union methods and techniques, and for a new relation between the trade unions as national bodies and the local and works machinery through which their members co-operate in the Boards' and Commissions' efforts to get the industries concerned into a condition of thorough efficiency.

I have touched on only a very few points among the many which struck me forcibly when I read the manuscript of Dr. Barou's book. More, I have no space to touch on: I can only commend it cordially to everyone who wants to understand how British trade unionism is situated to-day, and in what direction it is moving under the influence of the radically altered conditions with which it has now to deal.

G. D. H. COLE

February, 1947

stimulates investigation into these fields where the feel and poverty of information are vitally handicapping the development of the trade union movement.

The last years of the War in London were not the best for scientific research. The work had to be done mainly in time of it overflown war-work and other emergency duties. I am therefore deeply indebted to numerous institutions and friends, who helped me in my work. My thanks are due especially to the Research Departments of the T.U.C. and of the British Soviet...

AUTHOR'S FOREWORD

THE rôle of trade unions in society was never potentially greater than to-day, and what the British trade unions do now will be significant not for Britain alone, but for the other peoples of the world. That belief is a main reason for this work.

I have been concerned, both practically and theoretically, with trade unionism over a long period. My active participation in trade union organisation began in 1913 in Russia, and in the difficult period following the October Revolution and the German occupation of the Ukraine, I became one of the General Secretaries of the Trades Union Congress in the Ukraine.

I have been observing for over thirty years the aims and methods, the strength and weaknesses of the trade union movement in this country, in the U.S.A. and in other lands, and have followed closely the growth of the Soviet trade union movement—the only such movement in the world to operate in a planned and nationalised economy.

Since those early days I have been deeply interested in the theoretical study of the trade union movement—of its organisation and methods—as I firmly believe that it is impossible to build and operate a system of planned and organised socialist economy in a democratic State without a functional industrial organisation resting on a trade union and co-operative democracy.

I expected the political victory of Labour in this country after the end of the Second World War and believed, as I still believe, that the British trade union movement will face under the Labour Government its most difficult and arduous time. I consider, therefore, that it is essential for the Labour movement to know as much as possible about its organisation and work.

The book lays no claim to treat every aspect of the subject, but it shows clearly that a much wider investigation is badly and urgently needed. Part of its purpose will be served if it

xi

stimulates investigation into these fields where the lack and paucity of information are vitally handicapping the development of the trade union movement.

The last years of the War in London were not the best for scientific research. The work had to be done mainly in time left over from war-work and other emergency duties. I am therefore deeply indebted to numerous institutions and friends, who helped me with material and information, and especially to the Research Departments of the T.U.C. and of the Fabian Society, and to the Labour Research Department and the Registrar General of Friendly Societies for their assistance.

I want to thank Mr. G. D. H. Cole for his general advice and suggestions, and especially for writing the Preface.

I am greatly indebted to Mr. B. Rahmer for collecting data and calculating statistical tables, and to him and Mr. Henry Owen for assistance in collecting and summarising a good deal of the material.

I am greatly indebted to Mr. L. Small, who brought an experience of value to every stage of the book, and especially in helping to shape its final form.

I want to thank Mr. G. Brown, M.P., Mr. A. Flanders, Mr. J. Gray, Mr. Jim Griffith, M.P., Miss M. Heinemann, Mr. J. Jacobs, Mr. A. Kalmanovsky, Mrs. Y. Kapp, Mr. J. Lander, Mr. J. C. Little, Miss E. McCullogh, Mr. Ian Mikardo, M.P., Mr. Ellis Smith, M.P., Mr. G. D. N. Worswick, Mr. G. Woodcock and Mr. M. Zwalf for helpful advice, criticism and suggestions.

The book could not have been written or completed without the untiring help of my wife.

N. BAROU

October, 1946

xii

CONTENTS

INTRODUCTION

I

Many years have passed since the Webbs published their classic works[1] on British trade unionism. These brought out the strength and weakness in the organisation of the workers of that day and the way socialist ideas were finding expression in the activities of trade union, Co-operative and Labour organisations. With the exception, however, of G. D. H. Cole's three works, "The World of Labour", published in 1913, "An Introduction To Trade Unionism", 1918, re-issued, with new matter, as "Organised Labour" in 1924, and "British Trade Unionism To-day" in 1939, no serious attempts have been made to produce an up-to-date survey of the whole trade union movement in this country, though a good deal of useful information has been published on various special aspects.

Such a survey is badly needed to-day more than ever before. The British trade union movement is facing the post-war world under a Labour Government, itself pledged to introduce fundamental social and economic changes and authorised by the nation to do so.

It must not be forgotten that Labour's victory is due to a considerable extent to the support of the trade unions and their organisation. This organisation has expanded, and became more active during the war, when the Labour Party's local machinery had considerably contracted and in parts even disappeared. This lesson of the war days should not be easily forgotten, and the personnel and great experience of the unions should be fully employed in the economic and industrial peace drive.

The victory in the parliamentary elections of July 1945 opened, for the British Labour movement, therefore, quite a new era. For, the long struggles it had waged in the political and the industrial fields, both for social justice and for recog-

---

[1] The Webbs themselves recognised how necessary it was to have their work continued and brought up to date. As early as in 1932 Mr. Sidney Webb suggested that I should do it under his supervision. Circumstances prevented my accepting this generous proposal, and only much later was I able to undertake the present study—unfortunately without that invaluable guidance Mr. Webb could have given.

nition of the place due to organised labour in the life and the government of the country, have at last been crowned with signal success. The scale and nature of that success make it incumbent on the whole movement to take stock of its resources and quickly to adapt them, wherever required, to the new tasks and opportunities.

The early period of struggle was both long and grim. The failure of the first (minority) Labour Government and the defeat suffered in the General Strike of 1926 caused deep discouragement. The restrictive legislation introduced by the Trade Disputes and Trade Unions Act of 1927 crippled the political activity of the unions. It intensified in the British workers, from that time right up to the early years of the war, an inferiority complex that affected alike their personal outlook and their capacity for corporate action. Whatever ground there may have been before for that lack of confidence, it ought to have vanished for good in the unequivocal and unique mandate Labour received from the nation in the last election.

It is well at the same time to remember that the democratic urge from which that Labour victory came was not confined to Britain. Democracy, in the sense of the individual liberty that social democracy engenders, was as surely the driving force of the millions of men and women of the United Nations who fought in the Second World War as it was the purpose of the men and women who, towards the end of that war, gave British Labour its parliamentary majority. What Labour achieves in this term of office will have repercussions throughout the whole world. The main battle for the success or failure of international democratic Socialism will be fought in this country and by our generation. That truth adds point and urgency to the central theme of this book—namely the need to reorganise the British trade union movement on the lines of a fuller industrial democracy.

International trade union activities will not be dealt with here, neither will the attitude of the British unions to international trade union problems, nor the part they, in fact, did play in re-establishing the new international trade union organisation. If these matters are left out here it is not because their importance is under-estimated, but because they call for special study. Such a study would have to investigate the part which trade unions can play in an internationally planned or co-ordinated economy in which new methods and machinery of international co-operation would replace power-politics, im-

2

perialism and colonial exploitation. Further, in the fight for such a new order the rôle of trade unions nationally and internationally would have to be carefully defined.

To do that will not be easy, largely because of the lack in trade union circles of sufficient positive experience in the international field. For, up till now, trade unions, whether of the left or of the right, have generally been satisfied with rather ineffective general political declarations against war, against exploitation, against imperialism, against fascism, generally *against* something. If they did anything positive or constructive in the international field it was mainly when formulating programmes and demands for the I.L.O. or some international conferences. But to-day the special rôle played in post-war international relations by the "Great" Powers, the revived quest and establishment of "spheres of interest" and the rebirth of power politics on an unprecedented scale, will not make easier the functioning of an effective international trade union organisation.

In what follows we will limit ourselves, therefore, to the situation in Britain, believing that in solving effectively their domestic problems British trade unions will be materially helping towards the formulation of a workable international programme.

The urgent task of the unions is therefore to see more clearly their proper place in the framework of a Labour Britain. They must ask themselves some obvious fundamental questions: how far have their methods proved effective? how efficient are their machinery and organisations? in what way does trade union democracy express itself to-day? And, finally, in the light of the answers, has the trade union movement, with its present structure and organisation, the power required to play its full part in the transition from a monopolistic capitalist society to the planned and organised economy of a socialist Britain?

To contribute towards answering these questions, we will here examine specially what resources the movement has at its disposal and what adjustments in these, if any, should be made in order to secure the best results for the people of Britain in the crucial years ahead.

II

Among Labour's rich resources must be counted, as this book endeavours to show, its huge membership—the millions of

3

trade unionists, co-operators, members of the Labour Party and affiliated organisations; their spirit of solidarity in the common cause, shown whenever distress afflicts any one section of the movement; the hosts of voluntary workers willing to devote their limited leisure to strengthening the movement; and the mutual aid, educational facilities and other services freely offered to members. High, too, among its assets for the tasks ahead is the vast experience that its membership has gained in the fields of legislation, organisation, administration and local government; in production, distribution, catering and co-operative activities; as well as in educational, recreational, welfare, public relations and many other key services.

That Labour has these tremendous assets not even its critics or opponents can deny. But unfortunately it is hard to prove that they are used in a way which gets the best practical results in the economic, political and social fields. Even the statistical information available does not readily reveal the exact strength and distribution of the members, the quality of their organisation and the measure of their interest in daily activities.

An outstanding weakness of the Labour movement, in a matter in which its very composition would enable it to be very strong, is the lack of anything like the fruitful co-ordination which is possible between its three great branches—the trade unions, the Co-operative organisations and the Labour Party. The majority of those who voted Labour in the July 1945 elections belong to one or all of these three—to the trade unions in their capacity of wage-earners, to the Labour Party as citizens exercising their political responsibilities, and to the Co-operative Societies as consumers, distributors or producers of essential commodities. The fact that there is nevertheless so little effective co-ordination or co-operation between them in matters of vital common concern is surely as surprising as it is unjustifiable. It is true that in the National Council of Labour, machinery for this purpose exists, and that the Council's constitution explicitly empowers it "(a) to consider all questions affecting the Labour and Co-operative Movements as a whole and (b) to endeavour to secure a common policy and joint action, whether by legislation or otherwise, in all questions affecting the workers as producers, consumers and citizens".

That is exactly what is really wanted and what, if put into practice now, could facilitate the socialising efforts of the Government while increasing, through regular joint activities, the deliberate voluntary cohesion and integration of the whole movement. But, largely, perhaps because of the attitude of some or all of its three components, the Council is unable, as at present organised and equipped, to get anything like the results possible out of that "common policy and joint action" proclaimed in its very constitution. Therefore, the National Council of Labour is one of the first agencies whose position and possibilities should be thoroughly re-examined and made effective without delay.

The whole movement should be brought to realise that Parliament is unable of itself to balance effectively the complicated industrial relations and problems of modern industrial society—it can only prescribe at what levels and along what general lines it should proceed. Parliament must be supported and supplemented by the activities of those functional democratic organisations, of which the trade unions and the Co-operatives are alike the most important, the most responsible and the most ripe for collaboration. *The whole of the Labour movement outside Parliament* must, therefore, so adjust its own organisation as to be able to live up to the great challenge inherent in its having a majority *inside Parliament.*

III

To restrict as narrowly as does the trade union movement the scope of its systematic research into the most essential facts of trade union activities and organisation reflects a popular though misguided attitude to the study of social and political problems. Persistence in that unscientific and unbusiness-like attitude to-day, after the political victory, can have calamitous national effects. Political slogans and programmes, and even winning on the strength of these a term of parliamentary office, are not enough: to inform, maintain and strengthen an electorate that will ensure Labour being entrusted with office again, both better organisation and political education of the people are required; provided they are organised on lines better adapted to the structure of modern industry and trade, trade unions can, by their very existence and the daily experiences in the workshop, educate their members and give them a more practical grasp of democracy, and therewith more confidence in it, than can any other form of adult education. It is only as functional democracy that modern democracy can survive, and functional democracy finds, or can find, its highest expression in industrial trade union organisation.

Further on it will be shown that in the very effort to achieve

5

the power and speed required to defend the workers' interests in a capitalist society, trade union organisation in this country has been developing along two different lines: on the one hand we find over-growth and over-centralisation in some of the great national unions, and on the other insufficient cohesion and authority in the factory, in local and even national trade union organisation.

The danger of over-growth and over-centralisation—which is probably inevitable in the case of the huge General Unions covering each over a million of workers, dispersed in dozens of industries—has made it very difficult to maintain democratic management and close contact between the mass of members and the leaders; it is unavoidable, under those conditions, that a rift between them frequently occurs.

The powers delegated to the central executive organs are so great that the ordinary rank-and-file members of great powerful unions feel of little or no account individually in moulding the decisions taken in their name. It seems timely, therefore, to ask whether trade union machinery cannot make it easier for the ordinary, scattered members to know the facts on which their agents and leaders have to take decisions, to form their personal opinions on the facts, and feel that they really influence the decisions taken. For, certainly, wherever the information on which one is supposed to form a personal opinion is not easily come by, or where it is felt that such ordinary opinions, though formed, carry little or no weight with the national leadership, ordinary members must inevitably lose both interest in their unions and even any deep sense of comradeship with fellow-members.

It is often, of course, a vicious circle, but it too often happens that, owing to this impotence felt by the average member, local branches are left in the hands of a small group of members, with the result that general interest slackens and indifference leading to inaction spreads.

Apart, however, from cases of over-centralisation, it is also true that the system of education and the conditions of the daily life of wage- and salary-earners leave them little time as a rule to give sustained thought to fundamental problems: how their industry or trade might be more democratically run, how their own trade unions frame general policy and whether through the T.U.C. or otherwise it is being carried out. Much less, therefore, can they give thought to the part which the trade union movement as a whole might play in the transition from a dominantly capitalist economy to a socialist Britain. Yet, if more information about these matters or other forms of encouragement were offered to the ordinary worker, the discussion of just such problems could be fostered throughout the movement industrial, political and co-operative. In that way the fight for a new planned non-capitalist Britain would become part of a more deliberate action that would be more stimulating mentally and morally to the individual worker and his group.

In that situation it becomes a main task of leadership to find out the ways that will enable rank-and-file members both to be and to feel actively associated in all major decisions.

Further, even apart from action inside any given union, and because of the contradictions inherent in the present structure, trade union organisation on other levels—inside the factory, in the local Trades Councils, and even in the Trades Union Congress—is not sufficiently integrated or co-ordinated to secure the necessary unity of action and willing discipline.

The national unions are formed mainly[1] on the basis of local branches, the members of which live in the area covered by the branch. This traditional geographical principle of organisation is not sufficient for present-day industrial conditions, and requires urgent adjustment on more functional lines. The main centre of regular interest for any member of a union is his workshop, and the conditions found there are of the greatest importance to himself and his mates, who may themselves belong severally to half a dozen or more different unions. The natural desire of the worker is, however, to unite with the men and women working in the same place and under the same conditions, and from this natural desire springs the shopsteward movement. This movement was essentially an attempt to overcome the difficulties due to the fact that members of so many different unions found themselves side by side in the same workshop or factory. Some co-ordination or unification of action became necessary. The effective response to this most important need of joint action would be the development of an effective trade union machinery in and around the place of employment, the establishment of effective district organisation and the growth of industrial trade unionism in general.

At still another level—that of local or area organisation—the

---

[1] Though a considerable number of unions has branches formed in the place of employment or based on trade groups (like Transport and General Workers Union).

position is hardly more satisfactory than the one inside the factory. Here, too, the desire for joint action felt by members of different unions who work in the same town or area is met to some extent by forming Trades Councils. The purpose of these is to bring together the branches of different unions existing independently within a locality and to introduce some co-ordination, though they do not usually deal with industrial matters. This would presuppose and require resources, both material and in personnel, as well as in authority, which the Trades Councils very often lack.

Finally, at the highest national level of organisation, the same weakness through lack of cohesion is evident. Within the T.U.C. the member unions are very loosely knit together. Because the unions have in the past been jealous of their independence and autonomy, the T.U.C. lacks in many fields the authority to take binding decisions and the confidence that its constituent bodies will carry them out.

IV

These are the principal shortcomings and anomalies—largely the result of historical developments—which militate against optimum industrial effort and against effective trade union co-operation with the Labour Government in preparing the policies to which it is committed and in having them effectively carried out. Adjustments to rectify weaknesses—some integration and co-ordination, some stream-lining of trade union organisation—could make an enormous contribution to the success of a socialist Britain and therewith to the advance of Socialism elsewhere.

Yet, the facts necessary to get a clear picture of the movement to-day, of the position and powers of the unions and of their activities and aims, are comparatively little studied. In particular, a very limited number of trade union publications give such elementary facts as the proportion of individual members who take part in local branch meetings, or how far such meetings give rank-and-file members any real opportunity to discuss the questions on which national leaders will vote, either in meetings where the union's own policy is determined or in the T.U. Congress itself. Nor is it any secret that only a small percentage of members ever attend and that the average member's knowledge of what his own union or the T.U.C. is doing is far from what is needed if the unions are themselves to be effective working democracies.

8

Study of the position and prospects of British trade unionism is, therefore, an important and urgent task for the Labour movement as a whole, and more especially for its research students and organisations. No less important is the widest dissemination of the results in popular though accurate form.

It must nevertheless be realised that trade union research is no easy matter, since original data are scarce and what exist are not easily accessible. No research organisation on anything like an appropriate scale has yet been established by the unions: until quite recently they did not take enough interest in systematic fact-finding themselves, and they can hardly be said to have encouraged outsiders working in the field. Further, in many trade union statistics published at present no mention at all is made of various quite important aspects of their work; and such statistical information as is issued by the Labour movement, found for the most part in the Annual Reports of the Trades Union Congress or individual unions and of the Labour Party, covers only a very limited ground.

The sources of most of the summary information about the trade union movement are the publications of the Ministry of Labour and of the Registrar General of Friendly Societies. This information is useful in computing average figures for various branches of trade union activity, and is used in the chapters which follow. The value of average figures must not, however, be over-estimated, and they must not be allowed to conceal certain important special features.

That the information available is neither adequate nor easy to get was fully realised when the writer started this study of trade unionism, and the result so far is a mere outline of some of the main problems confronting the British movement. Its chief aim is to show that strong forces quite outside the unions have so changed the very facts and problems the unions have now to handle that the old forms of union organisation need to be re-examined, and in many ways overhauled or transformed. They must be revised, that is to say, if the trade union movement is to remain democratic in the sense that its policies are understood, deliberately accepted and willingly, even cheerfully, supported by the masses of the workers in Britain's forward march to Socialism. Some such revision or transformation is required if its due contribution to planned economy is to come from the mass of the people upwards and to become really what they can feel and see to be their own economic creation. Thus, wage- and salary-earners and the farming community will all alike participate, through their trade unions and co-operatives, first in the everyday planning of the economic schemes which Parliament must approve and, when that is done, take each his or her due part in their execution. It is the author's hope that among the ideas and concrete suggestions here presented some will serve as a contribution, however modest, to the revision called for by Labour's new opportunities.

PART ONE

STRUCTURE, ORGANISATION AND DENSITY

CHAPTER I

TYPES

(A) ORIGIN

TRYING TO get a full and clear picture of trade unionism in Britain to-day is somewhat like visiting an ancient city full of architecture of different periods and styles. The buildings reflect the social needs, the materials available and the ways of bringing them together that were proper to their several periods. So it is with the bewildering variety in the types of trade union now surviving here. In both cases the historical approach helps to an understanding alike of the surviving types and the latest styles and of the processes of change leading up to the present situation. Further, important changes are seen to be still going on, whether those within the movement are aware of it or not.

But, unlike architectural works, trade unions are not made of dead stone. They are composed of men and women united for the purpose of maintaining or improving the conditions of their working lives. As such they have come into contact and into conflict with other interests and established social customs which sometimes decreed that their very right to associate for that purpose be forbidden by law. As the emphasis of this study will be principally upon the present situation and trends and upon new conditions that must influence future developments, this introductory section will give only so much of the past as seems essential to understanding the present. It will sketch the general background, the conditions in which different types of associations grew, and indicate such general trends as are evident to-day. A second chapter will recall briefly the impact of the law on the unions.

One thing which makes it especially hard to see the British trade union movement as an organic whole is the fact that during its long development it grew in depth and width and strength through incorporating, one after another, unions which had come into being independently, were of different types, and often embodied contradictory principles. Some were the result of economic conditions which later developments have long since left behind. It would indeed be a miracle, considering how profound have been the economic and political upheavals of the twentieth century, if at least some of the existing features of trade union structure were not already very much out of date.

The associations of working men, in which trade unionism began in this country, go back several centuries. They started among the better-paid skilled artisans, who would meet in the local trade club and whose main concern was to protect their own members by eliminating competition through restricting the inflow of trained workers. This they did by means of friendly negotiations with the employers or petitions to the authorities. They were little concerned at the lot of the women and children around them working for a pittance in sweated industries. Thus they are hardly to be considered conscious protagonists in a class struggle, yet they did represent a first step in the direction of organised trade unionism. As such they came to be treated by their "masters" with suspicion or apprehension that became hostility and deepened with the advance of the Industrial Revolution. The local trade club was about as far as British trade unionism had advanced by 1800, particularly in the London area.

Over wider areas outside the capital the main examples of workers' associations, which sometimes even included lower-grade workers in their membership, were in the woollen industry. Its workers wanted some form of combination more effective than the trade club, mainly because they were afraid of being displaced by the new machines. Though the local trade club hardly survives in the economic conditions of to-day, yet purely local organisations still play quite an important part in trade unionism—the woollen industry providing the best example. This seems due partly to the fact that spinning, weaving and allied trades, which were among the first capitalist industries of this country, have long ceased to be, technically speaking, among the most advanced branches of the country's economic life, and partly because textile workers are often still living in communities that have little contact with one another. The fact explains much parochialism in their present trade union affairs.

12

During the first half of the nineteenth century the trade union movement grew in strength, but was prevented from becoming a real force, owing mainly to the hostility of Governments. The nineteenth century had been ushered in by the Combination Acts of 1799 and 1800, which created not so much new offences as readier methods of punishment by summary jurisdiction, whereas under the common law cases had to be taken to a High Court. Even after the repeal of the Combination Acts in 1824 intimidation of industrial workers did not cease. Of the many early victims in the unequal fight for the trade union cause most notable were the Tolpuddle Martyrs of 1834. Nevertheless, in the semi-legal guise of friendly societies some local trade clubs of craftsmen managed to survive, and associations of all sorts sprang up spontaneously, especially among factory workers and miners, in protest against the brutality of the working conditions imposed in those early days of capitalism.

In his "Condition of the Working Classes in England in 1844" (London, 1926, pp. 215–16), Frederick Engels described British trade unionism in the years following the repeal of the Combination Acts. The passage quoted below [1] refers, it will

---

[1] "In all branches of industry Trades Unions were formed with the outspoken intention of protecting the single working-man against the tyranny and neglect of the bourgeoisie. Their objects were to deal, en masse, as a power, with the employers; to regulate the rate of wages according to the profit of the latter, to raise it when opportunity offered, and to keep it uniform in each trade throughout the country. Hence they tried to settle with the capitalists a scale of wages to be universally adhered to, and ordered out on strike the employees of such individuals as refused to accept the scale. They aimed further to keep up the demand for labour by limiting the number of apprentices, and so to keep wages high; to counteract, as far as possible, the indirect wages reductions which the manufacturers brought about by means of new tools and machinery; and finally, to assist unemployed working-men financially. This they do either directly or by means of a card to legitimate the bearer as a 'society man', and with which the working-man wanders from place to place, supported by his fellow-workers, and instructed as to the best opportunity for finding employment. This is tramping, and the wanderer is a tramp. To attain these ends, a President and Secretary are engaged at a salary (since it is to be expected that no manufacturer will employ such persons), and a committee collects the weekly contributions and watches over their expenditure for the purposes of the association. When it proved possible and advantageous, the various trades of single districts united in a federation and held delegate conventions at set times. The attempt has been made in single cases to unite the workers of one branch over all England in one great Union; and several times (in 1830 for the first time) to form one universal trade association for the whole United Kingdom, with a separate organisation for each Trade."

13

be noted, to various attempts made to unite workers in industry throughout the country in one great union and to form one universal trade association for the whole United Kingdom, with a separate organisation for each trade.

The history and structure of British trade unionism in the twentieth century would have been a wholly different matter had things developed directly from those trades federations of the early nineteenth century, several of which were already developing features of what is now called industrial unionism. Obstruction came, however, not from the State alone: it came, too, from the employers, who were in a far stronger position than their "hands", and could in all but skilled crafts employ women and children, and engendered the bitter, brutal class struggle that characterised the early stages of industrial capitalism and drove the workers to establish their unions. But the national federations, as Engels points out, "never held together long, and were seldom realised even for the moment", and, on the whole, "the history of Unions is a long series of defeats of the working-men, interrupted by a few isolated victories". In the years of defeat, nevertheless, political propaganda, whether of early Socialism, of the Anti-Corn Law League or, much more important, of the Chartists, found willing ears among the working people, disillusioned by the results of efforts made in the industrial field alone. These facts and the beginnings, in this period, of Consumers' Co-operation show that the workers were feeling their way towards new forms of social organisation, calculated to mitigate their suffering at the hands of those who controlled the nation's economic life.

In quite new circumstances and under different forms trade unionism was to be revived later on. The latter half of the 1840's marked a turning-point in British economic and social history. The repeal of the Corn Laws, the ending of the dangerous economic crisis of 1847 and the political defeat of Chartism—all these marked the beginnings of "the Golden Age of Free Trade". Food and raw materials could now be imported at low prices; some of the "superfluous hands" emigrated from England and Ireland to the United States; and the capitalists at home adopted a far more liberal and conciliatory attitude than in the preceding period. Independent political action by the workers was dormant or sporadic until the 1860's with their considerable political activity and the great awakening in the 1880's.

14

Owing to the fact that it was the specialised craft workers, particularly in London, who first grasped the new possibilities inherent in the new Age of Liberalism, the new trade unions were for the most part craft unions—but assumed forms that became very much more effective than the primitive trade clubs of earlier days. In 1851, with the formation of the Amalgamated Society of Engineers, a new type of trade union came into existence which other groups of craftsmen imitated and which was rightly called "new model" unionism. From the early sixties onwards it became the typical form of organisation not only for engineers, but also for carpenters and joiners, iron-founders, bricklayers, and boot-and-shoe workers. In the metropolitan area their organisations were especially strong, and inaugurated the powerful London Trades Council. Indeed, a new powerful political force came into being in the more influential leaders of the craft unions of the "New Model" type who formed the so-called "Junta".

The aim of "New Model" was to secure the most effective organisation attainable within the narrow limits of pure craft unionism. It tried to bring together all the skilled workers within one craft, or group of crafts, of every kind and grade—for example engineers, carpenters and so forth. Secondly, its organisation was national and centralised, whereas the earlier craft unions had been, if not purely local, at the best loose federations of local unions. The central executives took complete control over the individual branches, strike action had to be sanctioned by the national bodies and the funds were kept in a national pool. Clearly, the nature of their membership and this "pooling" of authority and funds combined to endow those executives with financial and other powers, far beyond anything ever dreamed of by earlier trade union organisers.

The "Junta" and the "New Model" unions did not despise either strikes or political action, at least not in principle. They did, however, discourage strike action by their branches, and inclined to prefer peaceful means of settlement. A good deal of their funds they devoted to friendly benefits, such as unemployment or sick pay. Similarly, though the "Junta" leaders deliberately joined the First International Workers' Association, they as decidedly departed from its policy after the French workers proclaimed the Paris Commune. In home politics they led the struggle for the legal recognition of trade unionism which resulted in the passing of the Trade Union Act of 1875, but even in this struggle they hesitated for a long time before

15

joining hands with the miners and other unions in the North of England; they could not bear being suspected of "ungentlemanly" connections.

Throughout the second half of the nineteenth century the "New Model" unions operated almost exclusively in trades where there was a vastly increasing demand for skilled labour; and the opportunity thus created for themselves they used very cleverly. So far as their immediate aims went, they were undoubtedly highly successful and the artisans they represented enjoyed for decades wages and a standard of living comparatively high in themselves, and in glaring contrast with that of the mass of women and youths and other unskilled labourers unprotected and exploited in the sweated industries. Thus, owing in great measure to the "New Model" the skilled artisans of certain trades formed a privileged minority—a kind of workers' aristocracy—throughout the second half of the last century.

The attempted leadership of British trade unionism by the Junta did not, however, go entirely unchallenged. In the sixties and early seventies they had strong rivals among the miners and other industrial workers in the North. The miners' organisations were from the beginning far less exclusive; in the several local fields they tended to include those engaged in any type of work in the mine. On the whole they were much more militant than the London unions, and often called on their members to strike. Miners were the first two representatives of the British workers in the House of Commons. It was, too, the Miners Union that took the initiative to have the T.U.C. set up. Their lead was followed very reluctantly by the Junta. But one weakness of the miners, which continued until recently, was that their several district organisations developed along quite different lines. Geographically the coalfields of England, Scotland and Wales are separate, and it therefore took time to establish close connections between the regional union organisations of the miners. It was only in 1888, after many valiant attempts at national organisation by the pioneers had proved abortive, that the Miners Federation of Great Britain was at last established. Even so, this "federation" was a very loose body compared with the national unions of other skilled workers.

It was much the same with the textile workers. While regularly keeping up their unions, they still suffered from their old lack of centralisation; the iron and steel workers' organisations, too, were comparatively weak. Then during the boom around 1870 came a movement to strengthen trade union organisation among the less skilled trades. By combining with such movements the miners effected some sort of temporary counter-weight to the Junta. But the long period of economic slump of the late seventies and eighties, with its high volume of unemployment among all but the most highly skilled groups of industrial workers, nipped these developments in the bud. The beginnings of a new trade unionism that had been spreading among the many branches of unskilled labour did not yet have the strength to withstand that depression. Nevertheless, the skilled cotton-workers and the north-east coast miners acted mainly with the "New Model" unions. In these years of adversity for the others the unions of the "New Model" type became the unchallenged masters of the movement.

Notwithstanding the hopes deferred and the postponements, it has become clear that the "under-dogs" of the working class were by no means unorganisable. The socialist propaganda that revived in the 1880's was no barren political ideology, but one which, towards the end of that decade, stirred the dockers and gas-workers and match-girls of London to strike for better conditions of life. Their standard of living was so obviously below what it could be that their wrath became an elemental and irresistible force as soon as improving conditions made strike action feasible. And, as always when the time is ripe, the movement found its brave, clear-headed leaders in its own ranks. Men like Tom Mann, Ben Tillett, John Burns and others became the champions of something quite new in the country's industrial history—it was a mass movement in favour of a trade union based mainly on the unskilled workers. The fact that most of them lived in London made the movement the more politically important, and robbed the Junta of many of the advantages they had enjoyed in their earlier rivalries with the miners and other organised workers. The new movement of unskilled workers enrolled in "General" unions were rightly described as "New Unionism". This "New Unionism", conspicuously militant, put less stress on benefits and much more on independent working-class political action.

As against the exclusiveness of the craft unions, the strength of "New Unionism" lay in the width of its appeal and the number of its adherents. The London dockers, who so successfully struck in 1889, naturally decided to become a permanent association, and accepted in their organisation all types of qualified workers, whether inside or outside the docks. New unions of the "general workers" type grew up during the next generation, and therewith a constant tendency for the new unions themselves to combine. When it was feasible to combine within one union workers of every kind and grade, from all industries, why was it necessary, they asked, to have separate unions at all? Was it not enough to have *one* big union, including all the workers in the country? Mergers between different unions have been a special feature of recent trade union history, and though this has not created the *one* big union, we have seen come into being *two* giant national unions, each a good deal centralised in structure, one based mainly on transport and the other on municipal workers, but both surpassing in membership other unions and including, indeed, workers from almost every industry.

In the circumstances whoever grows impatient at the general pace of trade union development may well reflect that although the Junta was all-powerful in years still within the memory of surviving veterans, there are to-day among the strongest pillars of the Labour movement two general workers' unions. Historically, the creation of unions of the general workers' type was probably the only possible step forward from a state of affairs where craft unionism had grown too strong. It is therefore with full understanding of what the champions of "New Unions" and the leaders of the general workers' unions have achieved that we ask whether the structure of these unions enables them to cope with the economic and political conditions that are upon us to-day, as fully and quickly as is required.

While asking that question, we must also recognise that even for the development of the craft unions themselves "New Unionism" was a revolutionary fact. First of all it presented the craft unions with a greater incentive to unite their efforts and to form strong national unions that would include many types of craftsmen, instead of just the original localised and specialised craft unions; in other words, the tendency towards what had formerly been called the "New Model" was once again strengthened, since otherwise craft unions would have become quite unimportant compared with the new forces. Secondly, the union leaders could no longer be indifferent to the lot of the unskilled and semi-skilled grades working inside their own industries; they were obliged at the very least to take into

18

account organisations set up by their less privileged colleagues, and to decide from time to time on possibilities of co-ordination. This became all the more necessary, since the economic and technical developments of the twentieth century, with their over-mechanisation, led to permanent encroachments upon the special status of the craftsmen in different industries. In their own interests they often had to join forces with the unskilled and semi-skilled workers, even while the fact of their being organised in separate unions made effective co-ordination sometimes very hard. Now it is those craftsmen themselves who have to pay dearly for the former exclusiveness of their organisation.

On the other hand, some of the industries which had developed strong craft unions long before the "New Unionism" appeared, are now for that very reason developing in the direction of industrial general unions. That is the case particularly of the Amalgamated Engineering Union and the Electrical Trades Union; though they are still essentially unions of craftsmen, they are also organising workers of every kind within their industries. The National Union of Boot and Shoe Operatives also comprises every type of worker in the trade.

The same trend is assuming different forms in other trades, where we find that special unions have been created for the less skilled grades while all unions in the group are combined in a single federation; the most significant example is the printing trade.

In the case of industries where many types of workers, skilled and less skilled, were already included in the unions at the time of the Junta's predominance, some have developed still farther in the direction of a national industrial union. Of this development the most important examples are the Iron and Steel Trades Confederation and, above all, the new National Union of Mineworkers.

Finally, in quite a number of industries, where trade unionism became a force only after "New Unionism", the organisations were absorbed neither by the huge general workers' unions nor by other outside bodies. That applies particularly to industries or trades which are dominated by the State or public bodies and where the phenomenon of occupational unionism has come into existence—Civil Service, public employees, co-operative workers, and also on the whole the railways. In the same category are the clothing trades, sea transport and agriculture.

It is true, therefore, as the foregoing examples suggest, that the British trade union movement has in some cases been developing in the direction of industrial organisation, as distinct from craft or general workers' organisation; it is no less true that even those unions which have travelled farthest along that road have hardly started to provide for the organisation of their own professional, clerical, scientific and similar workers. A striking exception to that rule is found, however, in the Printing and Kindred Trades Federation, whose unions include many groups of professional workers. Generally speaking, up till the war of 1914–18 the "white-collar" employees were practically outside the movement. Now these are tending more and more to come inside the trade union movement. Yet most of their organisations developed into what might be called "professional unions"—and in essentials remain identical with craft unionism.

(B) CLASSIFICATION

The foregoing chronological summary has shown developments in British trade unionism from its beginnings in the local trade clubs down to modern embodiments of something like industrial unionism. Recapitulating, we can now get a more systematic appreciation of its principal types—the craft union, the general union and the few semi-industrial unions which have grown up in special industries, such as mining, printing, textiles, engineering and transport.

(a) *Craft Unions.*

The craft union is the simplest form of trade unionism; it is usually formed of workers with the same craft, training and specialisation, no matter in what industry or trade they happen to be employed. Members of craft unions have usually served a long specialised apprenticeship.

Sometimes they limit membership to people working on a special material. The Amalgamated Society of Woodworkers, for example, enrols cabinet-makers, carpenters, joiners and others. A more complicated type, like the Weavers Amalgamation, embraces a number of different but interconnected groups of skilled workers in the same industry, such as weavers, winders and warpers; on the other hand, the Electrical Trades Union covers workers in a whole multitude of industries.

Craft unions, pioneers of trade unionism, had to fight hard against powerful enemies, and the movement is deeply in-

20

debted to them for their courage, devotion and even vision. But they must now adjust their organisation to the new industrial environment.

During the last two generations craft unions had to face on the one hand the vastly increased use of semi skilled or unskilled labour, even in work of high precision, and on the other hand the very rapid growth of employers' organisations. Their policy of excluding the less skilled workers has been thus undermined by fundamental changes not only in industrial processes due, to technological advance, but also in industrial organisation. The wide use of machinery, combined with technical planning inside each unit, has made it easy for a mechanically minded worker to change over, not merely from one craft to another, but even from one industry to another.

With these developments taking place, craft unionism gradually lost its place as the leading and sole form of unionism, and the way was cleared for the growth of more modern types, catering in "general" workers unions for unskilled labour and women.

Nevertheless, craft unionism, to use Cole's words, "dies hard". It always emerges at an early state of capitalist development, and it long retains its grip even under new and changed conditions. The need for special protection is felt by the craftsman so long as his craft is not radically threatened by technical or organisational changes. But it is clear by now that craft unions must find their legitimate place inside wider industrial unions or federations and become special sections of such bodies. Only in some such way will they be able to protect their own member craftsmen and to ensure their participation either in the control of industry or in a democratic planning organisation.

(b) *General Unions.*

When the few pioneers started working to get unskilled labour organised, the conditions of employment were terrible and men had to work "in many cases 18 hours at a stretch" (Clynes). The semi-skilled workers felt themselves often more at home in general unions than in craft unions, for in the latter, if and when they were admitted, they were treated as junior partners, and effective control remained in the hands of the craftsmen.

Starting with the organisation of unskilled and semi-skilled workers, the general unions gradually extended their efforts to trades requiring more craftsmanship and skill, though in many cases too small in potential membership for an individual specialist union. Those trades usually lack any regular system of apprenticeship, which is the commonest basis of a craft union.

At the same time, general unions enrol unskilled labour, too, in industries which already have their own effective unions, as in the case of labourers in the Building and in the Iron and Steel industry. They have also made some progress in industries with insufficiently effective specialised trade union organisation, like the Food, Confectionery and Chemical trades.

It is characteristic of the "general" unions that the national agreements they negotiate cover chiefly minimum rates for unskilled workers. Matters affecting skilled workers are negotiated by those unions not on a national, but on a factory basis, and such arrangements may often militate against the "new skill" workers, such new skill being developed in new industries —chemical, plastics, etc.

It is characteristic of the general unions' membership that, alongside a large body of workers engaged in some special industry or service, the remainder come from a multitude of trades. Thus, it is estimated that in the whole membership of the Transport and General Workers Union before the war only about half were transport workers, and in the case of the National Union of General and Municipal Workers only about a quarter were employed in municipal enterprise. The rest were spread over dozens of industries and trades.[1]

There is one fundamental difference between the way the general unions and the craft unions approach their problems of organisation. The general unions aim at becoming all-embracing organisations, accepting as a new member practically any wage- and salary-earner, whatever the place or the character of his work, or whatever his industrial qualifications may be. In principle, there is nothing to prevent a general union from developing into an all-embracing national union

[1] The composition of the membership of the Transport and General Workers Union in 1944 was as follows: Transport Workers—Passenger 169,007, Road Haulage 99,480, Docks 85,991, Waterways 9,320, or a total of 363,798; Metal, Engineering and Chemical 264,810; General Workers 256,563; Government Workers 79,386; Power Workers 45,761; Building 34,992; Clerical, etc., 20,746.

and including in its ranks all the wage- and salary-earners of a whole country. Indeed, some people advocate just such an organisation. One fundamental disadvantage of such an organisation is that it leaves so little close contact, personal or organisational, between the sections, committees and offices at the head of the union and the individual members. A worker in, say, a chemical concern or in a catering establishment will probably hesitate to acknowledge the leadership of the national committee of his union if it consists primarily of representatives of dockers, busmen and other workers having little in common with his particular kind of work. The general unions have, of course, divisions corresponding to different grades and types of workers, but even the representatives of the subordinate sections are often considered as representatives of the national union committee rather than as representatives of the men in the section.

(c) *Industrial Unions.*

Finally, the third and most up-to-date type of trade unionism is the industrial union, which organises wage- and salary-earners belonging to a single industry or to a group of related industries or services. The chief characteristic of industrial unions is their willingness to admit into membership anybody employed in the industry, regardless of differences of craft or skill, grade, calling or position. Another characteristic is that industrial unions usually organise their branches on the basis of the member's actual place of work, and not on the basis of his place of residence, though some large sections in the general unions apply the same principle to their branch organisation (busmen, dockers, etc.).

Even though there is in this country hardly any union that combines all the characteristic features of an industrial union, there are certainly signs of a trend towards industrial unionism. The newly formed National Union of Mineworkers,[1] successor of the former Mineworkers Federation, comes very near to that type, except that it does not cater for the industry's clerical workers; and few of these are organised in any union at all. Some other industries (especially the printing and building trades) are built on what might be called semi-industrial lines: most of the workers belong to craft or occupational unions, which are linked up in an industrial federation —a sort of half-way house to full industrial unionism.

[1] See Appendix I, pp. 237–39.

23

The Amalgamated Engineering Union is now open alike to craftsmen, unskilled workers and to technicians; it tends therefore to become a union for workers in the engineering industry, while catering at the same time for many craftsmen in others.

"Employment union" is the term sometimes used for a particular branch of industrial unionism. It covers unions that admit wage- and salary-earners who work for certain categories of employers, operating as a rule under special charter, and including public enterprises, municipalities, railways and public utilities. In this country the National Union of Railwaymen is a case in point,[1] although most of its higher-grade workers belong to their own unions: clerical workers to the Railway Clerks Association, the footplate staffs to the Associated Society of Locomotive Engineers and Firemen and others to various craft unions.

A problem that arises for all "employment unions" is to find the clear and proper line of demarcation between themselves and unions that cater for workers in similar occupations under private employers. Also, some better method for "transfer" of members from one union to another is of importance, and will become more necessary still under conditions of full employment.

A union of this type is the National Union of Distributive and Allied Workers (now amalgamated with the Shop Assistants Union), which caters mainly for Co-operative employees; but demarcation from private employment is less urgent in that case, since the union does not exclude employees in private distributive trades. In theory, the union reserves the right to organise in its rank all Co-operative employees; in practice it has no objection to seeing many of these enrolled in craft unions.

The aim of industrial unions is much wider than that of craft unions and narrower than that of general unions. Industrial unions seek to cover all wage- and salary-earners in each single industry or trade and in each of its separate units. They try to ensure that in each unit (factory, store, post-office depot, office, hospital, etc.) every man and woman, from the manager to the night watchman, joins the union. Though their progress towards the enrolment of managerial personnel is slow, their membership is usually divided into three main

[1] It is interesting to note that it also organises the catering workers in railway hotels and restaurants.

24

sections—manual, clerical and managerial or technical. Each section looks after the special interests and working conditions of its own members, and a multitude of subsections takes good care of the craft interests of the membership.

One characteristic of industrial unions deserves special attention for its bearing on the problem of transition: the fact of admitting among their members managerial and technical personnel equips industrial unions, far better than any other type, for dealing with problems affecting the industry as a whole. They are, thus, in a better position for joint action with the employers' organisations, as well as for ensuring workers' participation in the management of their industry. For these reasons they are, too, the type of union best adapted to paving the way from a dominantly capitalist economy to an organised and planned industrial system.

The main objection to industrial unionism is the difficulty of delimitation between different industries. This was the main argument the T.U.C. advanced when they did not accept industrial unionism in their Report in 1927.

One has to admit that in capitalist economy the delimitation of industries is not easy. In certain basic industries, such as coal, transport, steel, the group of enterprises and workers to be included in the limits of an industrial union are fairly clearly indicated by the production process or service. On the other hand, in many other industries, especially new ones, the distinction is not so clear. In what industry should a press-steel plant producing prefabricated houses or car bodies fall—building, motor industry or engineering? Is nylon-making a chemical or a textile industry? The reply depends on what constitutes an industry—the process of production, the use made of the product or its destination.

On the other hand, those workers who, like the engineers, are in every industry and trade find it difficult to see how engineering can be treated as a special industry in regard to trade union organisation. The problem is complicated still farther owing to the existence of huge combines that unite under a single roof a multitude of industries built up on vertical lines.

The position will, however, change very considerably with the introduction of planned economy under a Labour Government with a socialist programme. A system of planned economy cannot be established without clear delimitation between industries, and Parliament will have to come to an agreed decision. The industrial trade union movement will have to adjust its organisation to such delimitation. It ought to result in the establishment of quite a large number of national unions, and their grouping will have to be much more detailed and numerous than that accepted by the Trades Union Congress for various purposes to-day.

The experience of the Soviet Union in this field is of special interest, as the introduction of planned economy resulted there in the establishment of about 180 trade unions, Federal and Republican, built on industrial lines.

It seems that a similar structure may develop in this country —a possibility for which the trade union movement ought to be preparing.

If the T.U.C. should decide to step up the reorganisation of the movement on industrial lines it would have to adopt a very flexible attitude when introducing such delimitation and establish special machinery of its own for dealing with any problems or difficulties which may arise. The nucleus of such machinery is already in existence for settling disputes between the unions and it could be developed for further action.

(d) *The New Conditions.*

The features peculiar to industrial unionism generally correspond to the essential changes which capitalist industrial organisation underwent during the twentieth century, and they go far to meet the demands which those changes are now rendering necessary in trade union organisation.

We should be clear as to what those demands are. In every branch of economic life, both national and international, new monopolistic tendencies prevail. Following upon concentration of industries into ever larger units, mighty associations of employers grew up rapidly, and the employers with whom trade unions have to deal are now strongly organised in each industry on a national, and often an international scale.

But it is not changes in economic structure or in technical processes alone that urgently call for a correspondingly radical reorganisation of the structure of trade unionism. There have been great social changes, too—one of the most significant being urbanisation. Over 50 per cent. of the population of this country now live in or around fourteen towns. In the U.S.A. about 25 per cent. of the population live in less than 100 towns, while in the period before the outbreak of the war, when statistics were still available, Germany and other industrial countries were rapidly developing in the same direction.

26

One important result of urbanisation is the great and growing proportion of workers who live so far from their place of work that they must make the long journey between home and work twice every working day. That very fact applying to so many wage- and salary-earners has undermined the old bonds of democratic organisation based on the "local" or residential principle: it imperatively demands a new functional approach from the point of view alike of workers' organisation and of modern industrial and political democracy. For all these reasons it is imperative to have alongside or instead of local branches special trade union bodies representing the trade union membership in the place of employment. Established in the vicinity of the place of work, such an organisation would become the backbone of modern trade unionism. The district organisation of the Amalgamated Engineering Union uniting the shop stewards from all factories in the district might serve as one of the prototypes of such an organisation.

Other factors exercising profound influence on trade unions and their policies are the new functions assumed by the modern State. The State can no longer remain a mere arbiter between capital and labour: it has begun to take a direct part in the organisation of the national economy. With the economic functions that it has had so rapidly to assume, a new form of capitalism has taken root in economic life.

In the industries in which the State became directly interested, the unions were confronted before the war and, more unescapably, during it, with a new problem—the productivity of labour and output. Under private enterprise they were not concerned with these questions, except in so far as they had to conclude agreements with the employers on the norms of output and the corresponding rates of pay. In State capitalist enterprise, working for the community as a whole, and especially in war, trade unions were assuming for the first time responsibility not only for the conditions of labour, but also for the results of the work and the productivity of the industrial unit.

Neither craft nor general unions—which imply the coexistence of many unions in each enterprise—are capable of tackling successfully this new problem, and in order to solve it industrial unions will become a necessity, at least in State-controlled industries.[1]

[1] It is interesting that such an experienced trade unionist as George Gibson writes in his foreword to Herbert Tracey's interesting book "Trade

27

Thus, the combined effect of these social, economic and political changes is to make imperative a change-over from craft and general unionism to unions organised on the basis of the industry, alike in separate enterprises and in industries as a whole. Such unions will be able not merely to defend the conditions of labour, but also to play their part in the organisation and conduct of industry. The changes in question make it essential that the trade unions become organisations inclusive of all the wage- and salary-earners in each industry, and that they abandon the old exclusiveness of craft unionism, or the all-embracing approach of the general unions.

For the same reasons, trade unions had to change their attitude to the State, switch over from defensive methods to active participation in the political and economic life of the nation, and consequently establish their right to representation in the economic institutions created by the State.

In the post-war period the power of the trade unions—especially under a Labour Government—to master the multitude of complicated political and economic problems confronting them will depend above all on the strength of the forces built up *within* the movement, on the effective organisation of their members, on their real understanding of the machinery of their own industry and the implications of planned economy in general.

(e) *Definition.*

In the light of that background and the growing responsibilities we may now make an attempt to define the term

Unions Fight For What?" (1940): "For myself, whilst I welcome every extension of workers' control in industry, I do not believe that it can be successfully applied until we have a considerable reorganisation of the Trade Union Movement. I consider such reorganisation a condition precedent to any effective system of workers' control. One may refer back to the Plumb Plan instanced by Tracey. The control of railway administration by Trade Unions, if separated from the interests of the ordinary citizen, could result in putting employees in such an industry in a privileged position as compared with the rest of industry. A corollary of successful workers' control must in my view be the reorganisation of Unions on a functional basis. That would not necessarily mean the disappearance of craft Unions as wage-fixing bodies. But it would mean for constructive, legislative, and administrative purposes either condominiums of Unions, or, what is more probable—the transfer of considerably greater powers than they now possess to the General Council of the Trades Union Congress; aye, and the scientific development of the group system of organisation and representation within the Congress."

"trade union". The classical definition as suggested by the Webbs is "a continuous association of wage-earners for the purpose of maintaining and improving the conditions of their working lives". This definition is already out of date, because the unions bring together not only "wage" but also "salary" or "fee" earners, and can be formed by any class of employed persons. Also they go farther than merely looking after the "working lives" of their members and "maintaining and improving the conditions", if these terms are meant to refer only to hours, wages and health conditions in the place of employment.

Mr. Shvernik, reporting to the Soviet trade unions on the British organisation, described a trade union as "an organisation, the chief aim of which is the regulation of mutual relations between the workers and employers". Even this is an incomplete definition, since it leaves out the relations between trade unions and the State—relations which are now assuming ever greater importance for the unions themselves.

The 1913 Act, in a minor addition to the Registration Clause, gave a third definition. It provided that unregistered unions might, for a small fee, ask the Registrar to certify that they were genuine trade unions—i.e., combinations whose principal objectives are "the regulation of the relations between workmen and masters or between workmen and workmen, or between masters and masters, or the imposing of restrictive conditions on the conduct of any trade or business, and also the provision of benefits to members".

The three definitions taken together cover the main functions of the unions in capitalist economy. The first emphasises the organisational task—the combined effort of members to protect their interests as wage- or salary-earners. The second concentrates on the relationship established between trade unions and individual employers or associations of employers, and stresses its twofold and complementary nature. The third emphasises the possibility of imposition of "restrictive conditions", and the provision of benefits.

The definition of present-day trade unionism would read somewhat as follows: "A trade union is a continuous voluntary association of wage-, salary- and fee-earners for the following purposes: (a) for maintaining and improving the conditions of their working lives through the regulation of their relations with employers and provision of services and benefits; (b) for the regulation of the relations of the two groups with the

29

State in matters of mutual concern; and (c) for the participation of wage- and salary-earners, as an organised group of producers, in the life of the nation."

CHAPTER II

THE STRUGGLE FOR TRADE UNION RIGHTS

THE PRESENT position of trade unionism in this country is a result of a prolonged social struggle—a struggle to secure for working men and women the right to combine in a corporate body and to act together in settling their relations with the employers and the State. This fight has been going on for nearly a century and a half, during which the economic, political and social life of this country, and indeed of the world, changed beyond anything that could be conceived in the early days. The ruling classes put many obstacles in the way of the growing trade union movement, and they gave ground very reluctantly and under the greatest pressure. Some idea of the bitter, unrelenting fight can be got by glancing through the legal history of British trade unionism. There are two characteristic features of the story: the gradual change from the use of force in the form of strikes and lock-outs by the two sides in industry to methods of negotiation and conciliation, and the gradual participation of the State in fixing and regulating many aspects of industrial relations.

(a) EARLY HISTORY

The right of the workers to combine, and to act in combination in their own interests, is one of the essential freedoms of modern civilisation. In any given country and period, in fact, the degree to which this freedom to combine has developed is a fair measure of the distance that country has advanced along the road to political freedom.

During the first decades of the struggle those rights of free association were denied to the workers of the world. Trade unionism in Britain, as in the rest of the world, had to fight against the hostility and prejudices of the ruling classes. Various legal obstacles were devised to hamper the efforts of the early trade unionists: more especially was any organised combination of workpeople held to be an act "in restraint of trade" and inimical to the divine existing order of

30

society, and therefore illegal. When, towards the end of the eighteenth century, the unions began to gain new power and significance, new Combination Acts were passed in 1799 and 1800, which, together with the provisions of the existing Common Law, rendered trade union activity illegal. These made any form of combination a statutory offence punishable by imprisonment.

It says much for the courage of the workers, and is eloquent of the appalling conditions of work which made even imprisonment a risk worth facing, that trade unionism continued underground. The Government and the Justices of the Peace—its willing tools—spent much of their time trying to ferret out the union leaders. They employed bribery, spies like Castles and Oliver, *agent-provocateurs*, every device, in trying to break the solidarity of the workers.

In 1824 a measure was passed repealing the Combination Acts and abolishing the prosecution of unionists for conspiracy—a short-lived gain, for it was in turn repealed in 1825. The Act of that year allowed combinations only for bargaining about wages and hours, but coupled with this was a provision making "molestation" and "obstruction" crimes. These words were interpreted so widely by the judges—the cry of "Baa, baa, black sheep" was once, for example, held to constitute molestation—that the effect of the 1825 Act was such that any strike rendered workers liable to prosecution. The unions had won mere legal recognition, but were denied real striking power. Moreover, there were other methods of punishment in the hands of the State. The "Tolpuddle Martyrs", already mentioned here, were deported not for joining a trade union, but for "administering illegal oaths" in their inauguration ceremony for new members.

In 1855 the Friendly Societies Act gave the unions the means of securing some protection for their funds against defaulting officials, and in 1859 the Molestation of Workmen Act legalised peaceful picketing.

In 1869 the case of Hornby *v.* Close raised in an acute form the bogey of restraint of trade. That case decided that as unions were illegal because they were in restraint of trade, they could not take advantage of the provisions of the Friendly Societies Act, 1855. The considerable funds which had been accumulated under the conservative policy of the Junta were immediately jeopardised. This, and the grossly exaggerated "Sheffield outrages" of 1866–67, brought the whole position of

31

trade union rights to the fore. This time, however, the unions were in a better position. In 1867 there had been a substantial extension of the suffrage to large new sections of the working class. The Parliament of 1868 was the first to be elected with the participation of working men, and from then on Liberal and Conservative politicians had to reckon with the working-class vote. Trade unionists took advantage of their new power by bombarding M.P.s with demands for the revision of the Common Law relating to combinations and "conspiracy", and in 1871 Parliament passed its first and most fundamental Trade Union Act which legalised trade union organisation and action.

(b) LEGALISATION

According to this Act of 1871 no trade union member can be rendered liable to criminal prosecution for conspiracy or otherwise, and no union agreement can be rendered void or invalid merely because the purposes of the union "are in restraint of trade". The Act provides for optional registration of trade unions in the same way as of Friendly Societies. Registered unions must abide fairly by strict rules as regards constitution, accountancy and so forth, and may in certain circumstances be fined for breaking these rules. They are further permitted to hold property in the name of trustees, and to obtain summary convictions against fraudulent officials. In respect of business transactions and payment of taxes they have various other advantages over unregistered unions. Above all, registration affords members some proof that the union accepts standards analogous to those of a strictly run business. The great majority of unions are registered with the Chief Registrar of Friendly Societies.

Thus at last in 1871 were legalised all "peaceful" trade union activities such as ordinary negotiations with the employers regarding wages and labour conditions, and in particular their Friendly Society operations. The Liberal majority which passed the Act, however, wanted to prevent as far as possible any militant action by the unions. With this in mind they coupled the Trade Union Act with a new Criminal Law (Amendment) Act, 1871, which contained penal clauses against obstruction, intimidation, picketing and similar actions in a strike movement. It repealed the Act of 1859 and restored the 1825 position, save that its definitions of "molestation", "obstruction" and "intimidation" were even stricter than in that Act. The 1871 Act legalised financial transactions by

32

trade unions, rendered legal their Friendly Society and mutual benefits, but destroyed their industrial power by making the most peaceful forms of picketing virtually illegal. In face of the strong Labour opposition it aroused, that Act was short-lived, and was repealed as early as 1875—this time by a Conservative Government. The Conspiracy and Protection of Property Act, 1875, which replaced it, restored the position. It allowed peaceful picketing—only for giving and obtaining information, it is true, and not for purposes of persuasion—and despite some obscure wording, was on the whole satisfactory from the trade union point of view. Some minor amendments to the Trade Union Act of 1871, advantageous to the unions, were also enacted, and for the remainder of the nineteenth century trade union activities were no longer hampered by law.

(c) THE NEW CHALLENGE

A much more serious menace to the legality of trade unionism appeared in 1901 with the judgment pronounced in the Taff Vale Case.[1] The facts were these: members and officials of the Amalgamated Society of Railway Servants took steps in support of railwaymen during a strike to prevent blacklegs, hired by the Taff Vale Railway Company, from replacing them. An action brought against the union for an injunction and damages succeeded on the grounds *inter alia* that picketing by the union's members was unlawful and that the union was responsible for the wrongful act of its members and officials.

The decision was based on the revival of the old doctrine of conspiracy. This maintained that, whilst a harmful act by one person against another might not be illegal, a similar act by a number of people acting in concert was an unlawful conspiracy in respect of which damages could be claimed. This Common Law doctrine had often been used against the actual leaders of a strike. By the Taff Vale decision it was extended to include the union concerned, it put the strikers virtually in the position of the union's agents and the union in the position of principal in an unlawful conspiracy. The judgment, which clearly showed the limits set in law on the right of "peaceful picketing", and which imposed new and heavy responsibilities on the unions (damages and costs borne by the union in this case were about £50,000), was rightly considered by the whole trade union movement as a great menace and a step backwards

[1] Taff Vale Railway Company *v.* Amalgamated Society of Railway Servants (1901), A.C. 426.

from 1875. It spurred the trade union movement to mobilise its resources, and to resort to political action.

After several years of greatly hampered trade union activity, Labour opposition to the legal consequences of the Taff judgment at last succeeded. A new Trades Disputes Act of 1906 made it clear that "an act done in pursuance of an agreement or combination by two or more persons shall, if done in contemplation or furtherance of a trade dispute, not be actionable unless the act, if done without any such agreement or combination, would be actionable". Further, the Act explicitly removed the possibility of suing a trade union (or its officials or members) for any tort alleged to have been committed by or on behalf of the union. It laid it down, too, that a man should no longer be liable to punishment merely because his action in a trade dispute induced other persons to break a contract of employment, or interfered with their trade, business, etc. Finally, the practice of picketing, if peacefully carried out, was legalised by this Act not only for purposes of information, but also for purposes of persuasion.

Thus, in 1906 trade unionism won a complete victory in the legal field. By the enactments of the 1870's workers could combine for the purpose of collective bargaining, and the 1906 Act removed the last doubt that they might use ordinary strike practices to gain their objectives.

(d) Trade Unions and Politics

In the meantime the trade unions decided to enter politics independently of the existing parties, and began to divert part of their funds and energies to supporting Labour candidates. They distributed literature, organised meetings and took various steps to further the political education of the workers. The legality of such activities was not at first questioned. In 1909, however, through the action of a trade union official named Osborne, a decision of the Courts invalidated the right of trade unions to use their funds for political ends. The purpose of the Osborne judgment was to starve the political Labour movement, which did all it could to have the decision altered. It was only in 1913, however, that legislation to modify its consequences was embodied in a new Act of Parliament; even so, the new Act was not a clear-cut victory for Labour, but a compromise with its opponents.

The 1913 Act permitted trade unions to have other aims than the primary one of safeguarding the immediate interests of their members. At the same time certain limitations were established with regard to political activities, such as financial support for Parliamentary candidates, distribution of literature, etc. It was first of all laid down that unions might undertake such activities (and spend money on them) only when a majority of the members, voting in a ballot under the supervision of the Registrar, were in favour. Secondly, even if these political activities had the support of a majority, they might not be financed out of the unions' general funds, but separate political funds had to be formed for the purpose. Moreover, any members objecting to these political activities might "contract out" and appeal to the Registrar, if they felt that they were not being accorded the full rights of members in everything not directly connected with the control and administration of the political fund.

In 1917, by a further amendment to the Trade Union Acts of the 1870's, it was laid down that amalgamations of unions could become valid if endorsed by simple majorities of the members concerned. Until this date specified majorities had been required, and the new provision facilitated the progressive and healthy historic trend towards unification of the movement.

Thus, though trade unionism was at first hampered by legal restrictions of one kind or another, as it developed in power these were gradually cast off. During the great labour unrest about the end of the last war the unions were practically free to engage in all those activities which were legal for ordinary citizens and other organisations. Only exceptionally were certain political activities forbidden, but even so the compromise reached in the Act of 1913 was more or less acceptable to the Labour movement. When, however, the unions, thus protected by law, began after the First World War to take large-scale action in the interests of the workers, there was the inevitable reactionary outcry for new anti-trade union laws. The zenith of Labour activities in the inter-war period was reached in the General Strike of 1926, and after its defeat the Conservative Government of the day submitted to Parliament a new and crippling anti-labour bill, which was enacted in 1927.

(e) THE TRADE DISPUTES AND TRADE UNIONS ACT, 1927

The Trade Disputes and Trade Unions Act of 1927 weakened the position of Labour in at least four vital respects:

1. The New Act made illegal any strike or lock-out calculated to coerce the Government either directly or by inflicting hardships upon the community, and whose objects were not entirely restricted to the furtherance of the interests of those within their own particular trade or industry. Offenders were liable to heavy penalties under this Act, and any member who refused to take part in a trade dispute declared unlawful by this Act could not be deprived of his rights by his trade union.

2. The question of picketing was reconsidered in the Act. Persons were liable to punishment if by their picketing they "cause in the mind of a person a reasonable apprehension of injury to him or to any member of his family, etc.". The term "injury" was specified to include any injury with regard to property, business or employment. Picketing homes was made illegal.

3. Under the 1913 Act political funds were lawful, subject to the rights of members to "contract out"—*i.e.*, stipulate that they did not wish to contribute to the political fund. By the 1927 Act the system of "contracting in" was substituted, whereby members had to declare expressly their willingness to pay the political contribution.

4. Finally a particularly heavy blow fell on the trade unions catering for Civil Servants and public employees. Civil Servants were forbidden to belong to a union whose activities extended beyond the sphere of the service itself. The Civil Service unions were therefore compelled, against the wishes of their individual members, to sever all connections with the T.U.C. Public Authorities were forbidden to make any conditions as to whether their employees should belong to a union or not; nor were they allowed to make similar stipulations with regard to the employees of firms with whom they dealt.

In 1946 the Labour Government repealed the Trade Disputes and Trade Unions Act of 1927, and the position is now back to where it was prior to the passing of that vindictive piece of class legislation. It is no more clear now, however, whether a general strike is legal than it was before 1927. The Government confined itself to a plain repeal of the 1927 Act and did not seek, by fresh legislation, to strengthen the rights of the unions.

Some lawyers argue that a general strike is sanctioned by the 1906 Act as any other strike—that the difference in size does not affect the principle. Against this it is also argued that a general strike is essentially different in principle from an ordinary strike: its object—exerting political influence on the Government by industrial pressure—is different from an ordinary strike in furtherance of an industrial dispute. For this reason, it is argued that such a strike cannot plead the protection of the 1906 Act because its whole object is illegal. An attempt to intimidate the Government even by one man would be illegal; *a fortiori* it is so when carried out by a number in combination. Refusal to work owing to a genuine trade dispute, on the other hand, is not illegal if by one man alone and, hence, by reason of the 1906 Act, is not an illegal conspiracy merely because it is carried on by a number. This is not the place to settle that dispute. The legal history of trade unions, however, shows how uncertain the position still is.

The General Strike had a further consequence—it accelerated a tendency which was already becoming noticeable—namely, the increased emphasis which both unions and employers were putting on industrial negotiations as the first step and holding the strike or the lock-out for use only in the last resort. The Mond–Turner Conferences initiated the process, which reached its logical conclusion in the Conditions of Employment and National Arbitration Order, 1940. This, as a war measure, gave, among other powers, legal force to the decisions of the National Arbitration Tribunal, and made them binding on all employers, whether or not they were affiliated to the particular employers' federation concerned in the dispute. It provided that, where the established "Union–Employer" negotiating machinery had failed, resort must be had to the National Arbitration Tribunal, the successor of the 1919 Industrial Courts Act, but with far wider powers. Finally, it prohibited resorting to the strike or lock-out until all other expedients had failed and, even then, not until three weeks notice had been given to the opposite party and to the Minister of Labour. In short, it gave statutory sanction to negotiated agreements, severely restricted the right to strike and strengthened the normal negotiating machinery by making compulsory the submission of disputes to the National Arbitration Tribunal. In its essentials this order is being carried on in peace-time, and may well become part of the permanent law. The wheel of history will have turned full circle, from statutory banning of trade unions to their full recognition by the State.

37

CHAPTER III

NATIONAL ORGANISATION

ONE OF the most significant facts about trade unionism to-day is the marked differences remaining between the various bodies it comprises. This striking lack of similarity, besides reflecting the very different conditions obtaining in the various industries in this country, discloses an amount of overlapping between unions that is a matter of much more serious import. The growing unification of modern industrial and technical conditions makes it imperative that this lack of uniformity and of co-ordination should be eliminated.

Trade unions are organised on vertical as well as horizontal lines: whereas the vertical organisation of national unions embraces trade union branches throughout the country, the horizontal or local organisation covers the branches of different trade unions in a given locality, district or region.

Let us look first at the vertical organisation—the national unions, and their central organisation, the Trades Union Congress, through which inter-union co-ordination is mostly exercised.

(a) NATIONAL UNIONS

The great divergence we have already observed is clearly reflected in the multiplicity of types of trade union organisation. "In one works alone" (to quote the report on Great Britain of the Soviet Trade Union delegation of 1942) "there can be not one but several trade unions. In some concerns there are as many as 30 or 40 unions. That is because British Trade Unions are not organised on an industrial but on a craft basis. Together with the powerful trade unions such as those of the engineers, transport workers and unskilled workers, which have a very large number of members, a factory may also have members from such trade unions as the pattern makers, electricians, and so on, which have literally only one or two members in each place."

A great danger of overlapping and of lack of co-ordination exists, mainly due to the fact that the different unions, such as the Amalgamated Engineering Union and the Transport and General Workers Union, recruit members on different principles. But this danger is further enhanced through the fact that hundreds of "lilliputian" unions, which cater mainly for specialised groups of workers, are also in existence. The number of these unions, and their chaotic influence on the whole structure of trade unionism, are still important though the number of workers in them is small. In 1943 unions of membership under 5,000 numbered 829, and, among them, those of under 1,000 members each numbered 648 out of the total of 972 registered unions. That is to say the first group of unions with its 594,000 workers represented 7·4 per cent. and the second, with 148,000 members, less than 2 per cent. of the total organised in trade unions. Even among the unions affiliated to the T.U.C. these small organisations form a majority. They are particularly numerous in engineering, building and the metal-working industries.

There is a certain tendency towards amalgamation of both big and small unions, though the process of eliminating the very small unions by amalgamation is rather slow. (See Appendix III on Amalgamations, pp. 240–42.) The tendency towards concentration of the membership in the largest unions is much stronger; after the war of 1914–18 the movement towards concentration proceeded rapidly, and this process gathered pace during the Second World War, the majority of members (64 per cent.) belonging in 1945 to fifteen largest unions only. Grouping the trade unions according to the size of their membership in 1938 and 1945, we arrive at the following distribution :—

Size of unions.		Numbers of unions.		Membership.	
		No.	%.	(1,000's.)	%.
Under 5,000	1945	637	83·3	500	6·4
	1938	881	86·1	595	9·9
5,001–25,000	1945	85	11·1	910	11·7
	1938	101	9·8	1,068	17·6
25,001–100,000	1945	28	3·6	1,415	18·1
	1938	27	2·7	1,427	23·5
100,001 and over	1945	15	2·0	4,978	63·8
	1938	12	1·2	2,964	49·0

When dealing with membership of the movement the question of the turnover of members is of great interest and importance. Unfortunately there is very little information on the subject. The figures we were able to secure about the

39

membership of the Amalgamated Engineering Union for the year 1944 are illuminating; it must not be forgotten, however, that conditions in 1944 were largely abnormal, and no guide to peace conditions.

Total membership at 1.1.1944	908,893	100%
Members recruited during the year 1944 . . .	170,653	19%
Total	1,079,546	119%
Members lost during the year [1]	181,038	20%
Total Membership at 1.1.1945 . .	898,508	99%

[1] Of those about 4,000 owing to death.

These figures show a high turnover, which must have a considerable influence on the activities of the organisation. The problem deserves urgent investigation and reflection.

Leaving out of account the right of nearly all unions to expel members for anti-union activities, the greatest single cause of members leaving their unions is their falling into arrears with contributions. Every union's book of rules sets out provisions for writing-off members who are in arrears (lapses) and the terms of their subsequent re-admission. Here are a few examples showing how these rules, which vary with different unions, are framed.

In the Transport and General Workers Union a member ceases to be a financial member if he is more than six weeks in arrears. In the Electrical Trades Union a full benefit member who is £1 10s. 4d. in arrears is liable to be expelled. In the National Union of Railwaymen arrears of thirteen weeks put the member out of benefit, but he immediately comes into benefit again when the arrears are paid; sixteen weeks arrears causes him to remain out of benefit for three months after the arrears are paid; twenty-six weeks arrears will lead to expulsion unless the member can show that the position is due to domestic hardship or the negligence of the branch officials in not receiving his payments.

Similar types of sliding scales of penalties appear in many rules. In the National Union of Distributive and Allied Workers, for example, any arrears disentitle the member to benefit, but up to four weeks he is restored to benefit on payment of arrears; five to thirteen weeks arrears lead to a four-week penalty even after payment of arrears; thirteen weeks
40

arrears render the member liable to expulsion if the E.C. of the union so decide, and in any event results in thirteen weeks loss of benefit even after arrears have been paid. The National Amalgamated Furnishing Trade Association has an even more complicated scale, and a member is expelled, unless he produces a very good reason, after eighteen weeks arrears, and will only be re-admitted on payment of all arrears, all dues he would have paid had he remained a member, and a 6s. fine. British Iron, Steel and Kindred Trades Confederation members lapse after twenty-six weeks arrears and have to pay double the entry fee on re-admission. The Amalgamated Union of Building Trade Workers expels on twenty-six weeks arrears, and will only re-admit if the arrears on expulsion were less than fifty-two weeks, and then only on payment of all arrears and on production of a doctor's certificate as to the members own or his wife's ill-health; the re-admitted member has to face a twenty-six week period out of benefit. The Amalgamated Engineering Union puts a member out of benefit as soon as he gets into arrears and excludes the member on eighteen weeks arrears.

These are typical provisions relating to the exclusion of members for getting into arrears—by far the most important cause of lapsed membership. Many unions make detailed provisions for giving warning to members in arrears. It thus appears that lapses and re-admission depend on—

1. The efficiency of the union's dues-collecting machinery.
2. The provisions for warning members of their indebtedness.
3. The length of arrears which are permitted prior to exclusion; the longer this period is, other things being equal, the fewer the lapses.
4. The severity of the penalties on rejoining.

The figures given for the Amalgamated Engineering Union show a high rate of suspensions of membership, and we believe that other unions show even higher figures. But the figures should be interpreted in the light of what has been said above. They do not represent necessarily a turnover of membership, as would be the case if so many had permanently left the union and so many joined as new members. The majority of such "turnover" will be members lapsing and then rejoining in the same year. There are no figures published to enable one to say what proportion of the turnover is due to this cause or what is

41

due to permanent departure from the union on the one hand and to fresh entrants on the other.

The question which naturally arises is how the numerous national unions, seeking essentially the same ends, co-ordinate their membership enrolment? How do they avoid competition and rivalries? Such things, admittedly, cannot be entirely avoided, but they are largely the result of lack of consistency in organisational structure; generally, craft unions maintain the right to cater for craftsmen in whatever industry they may be working, whereas the other unions want to organise all workers, irrespective of their occupational status or skill. Open conflict between some unions is one undesirable result of chaotic trade union organisation in some industries, and, unfortunately, not the only one. Even the official Interim Report[1] leaves no doubt that faulty machinery is often the reason for ineffective industrial action.

The Report acknowledges that conflicts do occur, and that inter-union competition exists and cannot be ignored—for example, "notwithstanding the developments which have taken place, either by the Congress proposals for the avoidance of disputes, informal Union consultations, formal joint working arrangements, amalgamation, and the development of Federations, it is clear that the liability of inter-Union competition has still to be faced. . . . Joint working arrangements and understandings alleviated difficulties at many points, but the conflict is a lasting source of trouble, as complaints received by the T.U.C. show." That being so, it will be interesting to see what steps the unions have taken to achieve inter-union co-ordination, for which, of course, the Trades Union Congress is the most important instrument.

(b) TRADES UNION CONGRESS

The Trades Union Congress goes back as far as 1864, but had no permanent machinery until 1868. Its purpose was not to centralise the trade union movement in this country, but to co-ordinate it. That is effected through three main organs— the Annual Congress, the General Council and the General Secretary. To the Annual Congress all affiliated organisations may send delegates in the proportion of one to every 5,000 members (or fraction thereof).

The General Council consists of thirty-two representatives

[1] "Interim Report of Trade Union Structure and closer unity", see T.U.C. Report, 1944, p. 348.

42

of the seventeen trade union groups.[1] It conducts the business of the T.U.C. between meetings of the Annual Congress. From its members it constitutes six industrial Group Committees.

The General Secretary is the main executive official of the T.U.C.

The contribution of affiliated organisations to the T.U.C. is at the rate of 3*d*. per annum for every full member.[2]

According to its Rules and Standing Orders, the objects of the T.U.C. are:—

(*a*) To do anything to promote the interests of all or any of its affiliated organisations or anything beneficial to the interests of past and present individual members of such organisations;

(*b*) Generally to improve the economic or social conditions of workers in all parts of the world and to render them assistance whether or not such workers are employed or have ceased to be employed;

(*c*) To affiliate with or to subscribe to or to assist any other organisation having objects similar to those of the Congress.

(*d*) To assist in the complete organisation of all workers eligible for membership of its affiliated organisations and "subject as hereinafter set forth in these Rules" to settle disputes between the members of such organisations and their employers or between such organisations and their members or between the organisations themselves.

The Rules also provide that, in pursuance of these objects, the T.U.C. shall endeavour to further legislation to nationalise

---

[1] See Appendix II, p. 239. Since the repeal of the 1927 Trade Disputes and Trade Unions Act the eighteenth group—that of Civil Servants—is re-established.

[2] T.U.C. Rules and Standing Orders, Rule 3 (as amended), reads:

"Each affiliated organisation shall pay the undermentioned fees, based upon the full numerical strength of the society—probationary, free or otherwise:—

(*a*) "An affiliation fee of 3*d*. per member per annum, to be paid quarterly at the rate of ¾*d*. per member for each quarter of the year.

(*b*) "Such annual contribution towards the expenses of the World Federation of Trade Unions as may be determined by the General Council, but which shall not exceed £4 per thousand members."

The unions have therefore to contribute annually £12 10*s*., excluding international fees, or up to £16 10*s*., including the international fees, per 1,000 members.

land, mines, minerals and the railways, and to extend State and municipal enterprise, including the provision by them of social necessities and services. Among other objectives are adequate workers' participation in the control and management of public services and industries; a legal maximum working week of forty-four hours and minimum wages for all industries and occupations; training and other facilities for unemployed workers; adequate housing and educational facilities; compensation for all forms of industrial accident and disease; and State pensions for widows, children and all persons over the age of sixty.

The General Council is further supposed to watch industrial movements, co-ordinate industrial action and, where necessary, initiate labour legislation; to promote common action by the organised workers on general questions; and to carry out propaganda. It is also the duty of the Council to represent the British trade union movement in the international field.

Thus, its own Rules and Standing Orders confer upon the T.U.C. duties and functions of the highest importance. The large body of progressive unionists which desires a re-organisation of the Congress as a General Staff of trade unionism finds the fullest justification in many of these provisions. The Council, if it were able not only to promote common action and to co-ordinate it, but also exercise more authority based on discipline, would really be serving in the industrial struggle as a General Staff of the organised workers.

But aims and purposes laid down in a constitution are one thing, and the possibility of carrying them out is another. Unfortunately the very Rules and Standing Orders that set out these important aims starve the General Council of the means of carrying them out. So far none of the affiliated unions has sacrified any of its autonomy, and the T.U.C. still remains essentially a loose federation of independent bodies.

Apart from the limits set to its formal powers, the composition and method of election to the General Council exercise great influence on its authority.

Classified roughly according to industry, the unions affiliated to the T.U.C. are divided into seventeen groups, each of which is entitled to one or more members on the General Council. The basis of representation of these groups, although first laid down in the Standing Orders passed in 1920, remains, in very different conditions, still the same to-day. In addition, women members are entitled to two seats on the General Council irrespective of industry. Below are shown the seats apportioned to each group, its membership in 1925 (earlier figures are not strictly comparable), and also an assessment, arrived at by calculations[1] set out below, of the number of seats to which each group would be entitled in each of the two years on a strictly membership basis.

Group.	No. of seats allowed by Standing Orders and remaining in operation, in the General Council.	1925.		1945.[3]	
		Member-ship.	Seats to which the groups would be entitled on basis of member-ship.	Member-ship.	Seats to which the groups would be entitled on basis of member-ship.
Mining and Quarries .	3	840,543	5	638,094	2–3
Railways . . .	3	454,924	3	561,903	2
Transport other than Railways	3	397,126	2–3	1,130,183	4–5
Shipbuilding . . .	1	122,850	1	131,472	1
Engineering . . .	3	394,051	2–3	1,215,728	4–5
Iron and Steel[2] . .	2	153,932	1	169,272	1
Building, Woodworking, Furnishing .	2	349,658	2	444,651	2
Printing and Paper .	1	167,665	1	189,428	1
Clothing . . .	1	90,428	1	138,326	1
Cotton	2	234,864	2	143,205	1
Textiles other than Cotton	1	152,307	1	92,877	1
Leather, Boot and Shoe .	1	86,868	1	107,104	1
Glass, Pottery, Food, Drink, Tobacco, Brush-making distribution	1	186,534	1	493,270	2
Agriculture . . .	1	30,000	1	104,400	1
Public Employees .	1	150,627	1	185,511	1
Non-manual Workers .	1	62,845	1	163,283	1
General Workers . .	3	475,760	3	666,947	2–3
Women . . .	2	—	—	—	—
	32	4,350,982	32	6,575,654	32

[2] Iron and Steel includes minor metal trades, which have become partly merged in the General Workers Unions.
[3] Figures for 1944 published in 1945.

It will be seen that in 1925 the actual allocation led to under-representation of the miners and over-representation of iron and steel workers. In 1945, having regard to the changes in

[1] The estimated figures for representative apportionment are arrived at by taking the average number of members per seat on the General Council, allowing one seat as of right to each of the small groups and then excluding them from the calculation, and apportioning the remaining seats among the remaining (larger) groups.

relative economic importance not reflected in changes in the composition of the General Council, there was under-representation of transport (other than railways), engineering and distribution, and over-representation of iron and steel, railways and cotton.

There is another interesting feature about the election of the General Council. Each group is entitled to a fixed number of members, and the unions which are members of each group put forward their nominations; the election of the members for any particular group is, however, not confined to the members of the group concerned; every union is allowed to vote for each of the General Council members. This fact emphasises the importance of the biggest unions in deciding the representation in the General Council, not only for the group of which it is a member, but for all other groups as well, merely because of its great voting strength in Congress. A good deal of political lobbying goes on, and the representatives of some unions, although of predominant strength in their own group, may yet be out-voted at the election. Thus might be explained, for example, the presence of a representative of the Quarryman's Union, North Wales, with only 8,000 members, which is affiliated to the Transport and General Workers Union, as one of the three representatives of the mining group.

Though affiliated unions are supposed to keep the General Council informed about trade disputes, there is no compulsion to do so, and if they do not the Council is not supposed to intervene. True, when a dispute looks like becoming serious the Council may call in the union representatives and "tender its considered opinion and advice"; but even in such a case the union concerned is not bound to accept it. There is another provision in the Rules which tends to make unions pay more heed to the opinion or advice of the T.U.C.:

"Where, despite the efforts of the Council, the policy of the employers enforces a stoppage of work by strike or lock-out, the Council shall forthwith take steps to organise on behalf of the organisation or organisations concerned all such moral and material support as the circumstances of the dispute may appear to justify".

Further, the General Council may on request also act as umpire in disputes between two affiliated organisations, whether these disputes relate to general questions or to a demarcation of work. In the last resort the Annual Congress has power to disaffiliate any organisation whose conduct is detrimental to the Council's interest or policy. This provision also applies, in particular, to organisations which refuse to obey the awards of the Disputes Committee of the General Council.

The Scottish trade unions and the Scottish branches of the British unions have formed a special organisation—the Scottish Trades Union Congress—which is organised on similar lines to the T.U.C., except that it admits as member organisations local Trades Councils, in addition to the trade unions. Industrial Scotland has always been an important field of trade unionism, and the Scottish Congress now represents over 600,000 union members. The vast majority of these are members of Scottish branches of all-British trade unions, which cover the whole of Britain, and affiliated also to the British T.U.C. in London. In addition, there are a number of local unions, especially in the textiles, building and printing trades, and among the bakers. Technically speaking, the Scottish and the all-British T.U.C.s are quite independent bodies, but the dual membership has created many links between the two organisations, and the influence of the Scottish T.U.C. has grown in recent years.

The position in the Irish trade union movement is more complicated: it is not easy to understand Irish trade unionism without knowing something of Irish politics, which is too wide a problem to go into here. Here we shall not attempt to analyse motives or causes, but to give a factual account of the position.

Until 1943 the Irish T.U.C. held the dominant position in the Irish Labour movement. It was organised like the British T.U.C., and some of its affiliated unions drew their members from Ulster, as well as from Eire and British-based unions.

A split occurred in 1943, when anti-British feeling was at its height, and a rival organisation was set up, called the Congress of Irish Unions. The alleged cause of the split was the Communist "domination" of the Irish T.U.C.—an allegation for which it is impossible to find any justification. The Congress of Irish Unions is, in fact, nationalistic, Catholic and anti-British. Its members total 75,000–80,000, almost entirely in Eire. The biggest member in it is the Irish Transport and General Workers Union.

The Irish T.U.C. has 120,000 members—80,000 in Eire, the rest in Ulster. Affiliated to it are a number of British-based unions, including the Amalgamated Engineering Union,

47

Painters, Plumbers, National Union of Railwaymen, Railway Clerks, Association of Amalgamated Society of Woodworkers, Boot and Shoe Operatives and the Transport and General Workers Union.

The Government's attitude has varied. In 1943 the general impression was that it was not averse to the split and supported the Congress of Irish Unions—an attitude arising naturally from the political set-up at that date. There was talk at that time of Government legislation to ban the operation of British-based unions in Eire altogether, but this attitude changed. This was largely due to improved relations between Britain and Eire, and partly to the Government finding that the split and the ensuing inter-union squabbles interfered with production. The Government are now acting as mediators, and there is no suggestion at the moment of anti-British union measures.

(c) Trades Union Congress Affiliations

The distribution of members as between unions which are and those which are not affiliated to the T.U.C. deserves examination from the point of view of the size of the unions and the industries concerned.

T.U.C. and Ministry of Labour statistics show that at the end of 1938 there were 1,384,000 members of non-affiliated unions (23 per cent. of the total); this figure increased to 1,446,000 by the end of 1943 (an increase of less than 5 per cent.) and about 18 per cent. of all trade union members belonged to unions that are not affiliated to the Trades Union Congress, so that the degree of affiliation shows improvement compared with 1938.

The Trades Union Congress regularly publishes information about the industrial distribution of its membership. As shown in Appendix II,[1] the engineering industry had, in 1943, the largest membership of all: 1,215,147 (18 per cent.); next in order came the transport unions with 1,191,457 (18 per cent.); general workers with 732,744 (11 per cent.); mining with 627,944 (9 per cent.); and railways with 560,835 (8½ per cent.). The above five groups were responsible for 4,328,127, or 65 per cent. of the membership.

The General Council of the T.U.C. summed up in the "Interim Report" of 1944 (p. 349) the position of the affiliated unions in these words: "Except in the teaching profession and

<hr>

[1] See Appendix II, p. 239.

in local government, Congress caters for every Union of importance".

Another very important exception, of course, was the whole field of Government Service: the unions admitting Civil Servants were excluded from affiliation to the T.U.C., but by the Trade Disputes and Trade Unions Act of 1927, now repealed, and not of their own free will.[1] Further, some important professional organisations which might be considered to be rather on the edge of trade unionism are not affiliated.

It is possible to compare in a rough way the industrial distribution of the affiliated and the non-affiliated union membership before the war; any more detailed analysis is hardly worth while, since the respective statistics are compiled by two different bodies, and on slightly different bases. The fact emerges, however, that out of a total of 1,384,000 members of non-affiliated unions in December 1938,[2] only 280,000 belonged to any of the manufacturing industries, or to agriculture, mining, building, public utilities, etc., and of this comparatively small number about half came from the textile industries, where small local unions still prevail. All the rest of the "non-affiliated" members—that is, 1,184,000— belonged to the remaining spheres of economic activity—*i.e.*, to central and local government and the professions (particularly the teaching profession), or to commerce, finance and entertainment. Among the unions catering mainly for manual workers affiliation is, therefore, nearly 100 per cent.

The table on page 50, which is based on the T.U.C. Report of 1944, shows the composition of the affiliated unions (at the end of 1943) according to membership.

It becomes obvious, if we compare the composition of the affiliated unions with the table on page 39, which refers to *all* unions (whether affiliated to the T.U.C. or not),[3] that most of the non-affiliated unions are small. The average membership of the 972 unions included in the Ministry of

[1] The Staff side of the National Whitley Council for all Civil Service in 1937 numbered 290,000, Post-Office 175,000, Civil Service Confederation 125,000, National Union of Teachers 154,000, National Federation of Professional Workers 145,300.

[2] A good many of these unions were either in the Scottish T.U.C. or in the General Federation of Trade Unions.

[3] Various divergences in the methods of classification make it impossible to carry the comparison between the two sets of statistics very far. For instance, the Mineworkers Federation appeared as a unit for the purposes of the T.U.C. statistics, though their different regional organisations were separately registered as trade unions.

No. of members.	No. of unions.	Total membership.	Percentage of total no. of all unions.	Percentage of total membership of all unions.
Under 5,000 . . .	99	160,000	52·2	2·4
5,000 to under 25,000 .	51	537,000	26·8	8·1
25,000 to under 100,000.	31	1,630,000	16·3	24·6
100,000 and over . .	9	4,315,000	4·7	64·9
Total . . .	190	6,642,000	100·0	100·0

Labour statistics appears to have been only about 8,000. It would appear that out of the total of 1,446,000 members of non-affiliated unions (in 1943), no fewer than 433,000 were spread over forty unions with between 5,000 and 25,000 members, and an almost equal number belonged to a large number of small unions, each with membership of less than 5,000.

Account must be also taken of the fact that trade union registration is based on the legal definition of "trade union", which has a far wider interpretation than that of the T.U.C. Among the unions included in the Ministry of Labour statistics are quite a number which the T.U.C. would reject, or has already rejected—on the grounds, for instance, that they are not genuine organisations of workpeople, or because they cannot be trusted to observe trade union principles, standards of fair play, etc.[1]

The question of Civil Service unions apart, membership of the T.U.C. may still grow through the affiliation of several unions catering for teachers and local government employees, and also by winning over some of the smaller unions in the textile industries and elsewhere. But the possibilities of such development are limited, and the main hope for further growth

[1] Sir Walter Citrine, speaking at the Blackpool Conference of the T.U.C. in October 1944, said: "The mere fact of a union being registered within the terms of the Trade Union Acts was no evidence whatever of its *bona fides*. Every trade unionist knows that there were employers' organisations professing to work in the sole interest of the employers, acting as their agents in negotiations with trade unions, who in fact were registered under the Trade Union Acts as trade unions. Consequently, the fact of registration was not regarded—and had never been regarded—by the Trades Union Congress as the test of *bona fides*" ("Annual Report", p. 18).

lies in a prospective increase in the membership of the unions already affiliated to the T.U.C.

(d) AMALGAMATIONS

Since the beginning of the present century the number of trade unions has decreased from 1,302 to 972 (1943). Some of the unions have amalgamated, others went into liquidation. The great national unions have benefited considerably through amalgamations, absorbing smaller unions and growing in size and importance.[1] The movement for amalgamation "may be divided into two types—official movements, in which the Executive Councils and other governing bodies of various unions meet for the purpose of achieving closer union of forces; and unofficial, of rank and file movement, in which the rank and file members of different unions meet for the purpose of propaganda on the subject of amalgamation and of stirring the official bodies to act more promptly and decisively".[2]

There were always many difficulties in the way of amalgamation—legal, financial and difficulties connected with the officials and personnel of the unions.

The legal difficulties have been eased by the Trade Union (Amalgamation) Act of 1917, though the position is still far from satisfactory: the law still requires that 50 per cent. of the members shall vote and that the proposal for amalgamation should secure a 20 per cent. majority of those voting. It is difficult to understand why these special conditions should be necessary, and why the decision should not be left to a simple majority.

The urge for amalgamation came as a rule from the membership, but the most successful amalgamations came about when there was support from the union's leaders. On the other hand, "rank and file movement in the direction of amalgamation have almost always been", as shown by Cole, "of an Industrial Unionist character—that is to say, they have desired to bring about amalgamation into one union of all workers employed in a particular industrial group".

[1] The General and Transport Workers Union was formed by amalgamation of eighteen unions in 1921. During the following twenty-five years another thirty-three unions were amalgamated to it: four in 1923, one in 1924, one in 1925, three in 1926, one in 1928, two in 1930, four in 1933, two in 1934, one in 1935, one in 1936, three in 1937, two in 1938, two in 1939, three in 1940, one in 1942, one in 1944, and one in 1946.
[2] G. D. H. Cole, "An Introduction to Trade Unionism", p. 46. Labour Research Department, London, 1918.

As Cole rightly emphasised, the movement towards amalgamation "has shown considerable signs of change during the years 1917–1920, as a result of the growth of the shop stewards movement, which diverted the 'amalgamationist' energy into new channels".[1]

During the last sixteen years[2] we could trace five larger amalgamations, resulting in the formation of the National Union of Tailors and Garment Workers (1931), the National Union of Dyers, Bleachers and Textile Workers (1937), National Union of Clerical and Administrative Workers (1941), the National Union of Mineworkers (1945), and the amalgamation of the National Union of Distributive and Allied Workers and the National Union of Shop Assistants, Warehousemen and Clerks (1946).

(e) INTER-UNION CO-ORDINATION

The unions have agreed on a number of "main principles" for such co-ordination and on other measures, such as recognition of cards, advisory councils, federations and joint working committees. We will deal with each of these separately.

Certain "main principles" in what is to be considered as "good trade union practice" were accepted by the Congress at Hull in 1924, and again, in an extended and clarified form, by the 1929 Congress at Bridlington. Those principles[3] are as follows:—

"(A) Unions should consider the possibility of joint working agreements (with unions with whom they are in frequent contact) in regard to: (1) Spheres of influence, (2) Recognition of cards, (3) Machinery for composing difficulties, (4) Conditions of transfer of members.

"(B) No member of another union should be accepted without inquiry from that union.

"(C) No member of another union should be accepted where inquiry shows that the member is (1) under discipline, (2) engaged in a trade dispute, (3) in arrears with contributions.

"(D) No union should commence organising activities at any establishment or undertaking in respect of any grade or grades of worker in which another union has the majority

---

[1] G. D. H. Cole, "An Introduction to Trade Unionism", p. 49.
[2] See Appendix III, pp. 240–2.
[3] See "Interim Report", pp. 367–68.

of workers employed and negotiates wages and conditions, unless by arrangement with that union.

"(E) Each union should include in its membership form questions on the lines of the T.U.C. Model Form in regard to past or present membership of another union."

These "principles" are admirable as far as they go, but their working depends completely on the separate arrangements of 190 unions, with greatly varying organisation structure and ideas, and in practice it is almost impossible for the T.U.C. to enforce them.

1. *Recognition of Cards*

An important step was taken by the General Council in July 1940, when a strong appeal was made to the executives of individual unions to agree to the principle of the general recognition of cards. Even after lengthy deliberations the unions have not decided on any general scheme, but 106 unions have agreed to a mutual recognition of cards, and twelve unions are acting similarly with a special threepenny trade contribution. At present about two-thirds of all affiliated unions would seem to have more or less accepted the principle of recognising the membership cards of other unions, though among those who still refuse are some of those "primarily concerned". The General Council is resolved to maintain and extend this principle.

2. *Advisory Councils*

A number of advisory councils and other joint bodies were set up between 1924 and 1941 to facilitate consultation between unions in a certain industry, or concerning common problems. These, it is interesting to note, though differing from one another on many points, have on their governing bodies representatives of the interested unions and of the T.U.C. itself. The advisory councils may therefore be considered as organs for closer co-operation not only between the unions concerned but also between them and the T.U.C. The "Interim Report" envisaged the extension of this form of co-operation at the end of the war. The first bodies formed (in 1924) were the National Women's Advisory Council and a similar body for non-manual workers which is now named "Non-Manual Workers' Advisory Council". The National Advisory Council for the Nursing Profession and the Local

53

Government Advisory Committee were set up in 1937, the Insurance Unions Joint Consultative Committee in 1940 and the National Advisory Committee for the Engineering and Shipbuilding Industries in 1941. There exists also a Joint Committee for the Tobacco Industry, "but from reports received there is some difficulty in dealing with matters expeditiously" ("Interim Report", p. 346). The General Council's efforts to create similar bodies were unsuccessful in the case of the railway service and the mining industry.

3. *Federations*

Concentration and co-ordination of trade union effort have been greatly assisted by the formation of federations. This form of grouping enabled several unions belonging to the same industrial or service group to act as a single body in trade matters concerning the industry, and especially in the most important of them—wage policy. Federations tend to deal with matters like wage negotiations, prevention of disputes, both of an industrial nature and demarcation disputes between the affiliated unions, usually leaving the affiliated unions to deal with recruitment, dues collection and propaganda.

The "Interim Report" says that "a Federation is in effect a loose form of Industrial Unionism, and is an example of where the Industrial, Craft or the General Workers Unions, who are concerned in any industry, may get together to pursue jointly the problems affecting the industry with which they are all concerned".

To say that "a federation is in effect a loose form of industrial unionism" is probably an exaggeration, but the admission indicates how real is the tendency towards industrial unionism, and at the same time how limited are the means by which trade unions are trying to meet these new needs.

The federation, according to the Report, is a "half-way house" on the road to full amalgamation, and "usually does a tremendous amount of good work in presenting a common point of view in negotiations with employers and also in assisting to avoid inter-union competition and overlapping".[1]

The functions and the composition of federations vary widely. A federation, therefore, should not necessarily be regarded as a half-way house to full amalgamation, any more than a cartel can necessarily be regarded as a step towards full trustification, although in both cases it often works that way.

[1] "Interim Report", p. 357.

Some of the organisations united in the federations have, however, amalgamated since the end of the First World War. At the end of 1917 there were in Great Britain and Northern Ireland as many as 182 trade union federations, with a membership of over six millions. By the end of 1943, out of a total of 972 unions, 500 were still affiliated to one or more trade union federations in the United Kingdom in respect of either all or part of their membership. The total number of such federations had, however, come down to fifty-six; and their total net federated membership (*i.e.*, after elimination of double reckonings) was 2,559,000.[1] An example of a federation which has quite recently developed into an industrial union is the former Mineworkers Federation, representing an affiliated membership of slightly over 600,000, which has now become the National Union of Mineworkers of Great Britain. This federation differed considerably from other federations[2] because of the geographical character of its units.

As a rule federations are not in any way linked up with the T.U.C. itself; indeed, they themselves include many unions not affiliated to the Congress. Typical of these are the printing and paper industries, where most of the old-established unions are organisations of craftsmen and not all affiliated to the T.U.C. They are all, however, members of the Printing and Kindred Trades Federation, which directs most of the industrial policy of the unions concerned.

There is no recognised classification of federations, and we believe that one can be devised in accordance with (*a*) their functions, (*b*) scope and (*c*) type of membership.

Looking at them that way, we would find (*a*) that according

[1] It is not possible in every case to give figures of the membership of the federations considered because they are not all confined to the specialised unions in the industry in question, but include representatives of those general unions which have members in the industries concerned. It would be quite misleading to add in the total membership of such unions in every case—*e.g.*, to add the entire membership of the Transport and General Workers Union into the National Federation of Building Trade Operatives merely because, by reason of their recruitment of a relatively few building workers, it is represented on the Council of that federation. Some of the general unions do not publish a detailed analysis of their membership, and therefore the membership of the industrial unions concerned is given and the general unions also involved are named, but their membership is not included in the total.

[2] The problems which had to be faced in the formation of the new National Union of Mineworkers of Great Britain are described in some detail in Appendix I. The blastfurnacemen were in the same position until they amalgamated.

to their functions some of the federations, especially in their early stages, serve only as consultative and co-ordinating agencies, while others are active and policy-making bodies. (*b*) According to the composition of membership there are three types of federation: (1) full—embracing all the potential unions, (2) partial—embracing a considerable number of the unions and (3) embryonic—embracing only a few. Finally, (*c*) according to *the type of membership* there are two groups: federations composed of *collective* members (national and local unions) only, and federations which also admit directly *individual* members—*i.e.*, the National Federation of Building Trade Operatives.

I. The most important federations are those which formulate policy and take action and, by enrolling all or nearly all potential members, operate as full federations. This type is best represented (*a*) by the Confederation of Shipbuilding and Engineering Unions, (*b*) by the National Federation of Building Trade Operatives,[1] (*c*) by the Printing and Kindred Trades Federation, and (*d*) by the National Joint Council of the Railway Unions. The following pages give some idea of the main features and composition of those federations.

(*a*) The largest and one of the most advanced federations is the Confederation of Shipbuilding and Engineering Unions, embracing the shipbuilding and all but a few of the engineering unions. In 1943 it had affiliated to it thirty-five unions with some 500,000 members. The only important ones outside the Confederation were the Amalgamated Engineering Union and the Amalgamated Union of Foundry Workers. In 1941 the National Engineering Joint Trades Movement was formed; this was a

[1] The National Federation of Building Trade Operatives has direct members in places so small as not to warrant the setting up of a branch of one of the affiliated unions. Where this is the case building workers of all types, grades and trades join as *direct members* of the Federation itself, but this direct membership accounts for only a very small proportion of the total members affiliated.

Even more striking has been the part played by the Printing and Kindred Trades Federation in the recruiting of members. Wherever a particular locality is found to be badly organised the member unions second their organisers to the Federation for the time being. The Federation itself then organises the drive for union membership, signs on the non-unionists and allocates the new members to the appropriate unions. When the area concerned has been thus cleaned up the organisers go back to their respective unions. The same methods are followed in dealing with a "black" shop—*i.e.*, one in which none of the workers belongs to a union. In that case the Federation itself approaches the employer as the spokesman for all its affiliated unions.

consultative body on which were represented the Confederation, the Amalgamated Engineering Union, and the Amalgamated Union of Foundry Workers. Its object was to present to the employers a common programme on wages and conditions. This joint consultation proved of the utmost value, unity in action increased and by 1944 both the Amalgamated Engineering Union and the Amalgamated Union of Foundry Workers established very close relations with the Confederation.[1] It now caters for the whole of the shipbuilding and engineering unions, with a total membership of over 1,300,000. The Confederation has conducted all negotiations on wages and conditions for its affiliated unions, and will continue to do so through its District Committees and Executive Council, and at its quarterly and annual meetings. Relations between the shop stewards of the various affiliated unions in the workshops have always been close and cordial. This was of great importance during the war, notably in the recruiting of women, where there might have been a serious risk of inter-union conflicts. The consolidation of the Confederation in 1944 is, with the formation of the single Mineworkers Union, the most important event of the last ten years inside the trade union movement.

(b) The National Federation of Building Trade Operatives, formed in 1918, is perhaps the best organised in the Labour movement. Affiliated to it are all the industrial unions concerned with building, with a total membership of 444,651 in 1945, and the Transport and General Workers Union, which enlist unskilled building labourers (see footnote to p. 22). The Federation is the negotiating body for the building industry, and meets the corresponding body for the employers on a Joint Industrial Council, which is highly organised nationally, in areas and regionally. Through these bodies wages and conditions are negotiated, and all trade disputes are referred to the Council.

(c) The Printing and Kindred Trades is a very strong federation of all the fourteen unions affiliated to the T.U.C., as well as the Map and Chart Engravers and the Pattern Card Makers, which are not affiliated to the T.U.C. The membership of these two unions is not known accurately, but is small; the other fourteen total 189,428 members. The Federation lays down lines of demarcation between the various trades, deals with inter-union disputes and decides all questions of general

[1] A ballot for an affiliation of the Amalgamated Engineering Union took place in August 1946 and the great majority voted for.

policy connected with the industry. It is also the negotiating body for the industry in all questions of general principle, and since the war it has been the Federation, and not the constituent unions, that has conducted wage negotiations.

It is noteworthy that the direct Federation influence extends right down to the shops themselves. Each trade in any shop has its own chapel under its "Father" or "Mother", but, in addition, in most of the larger shops an "Imperial Father" is to be found, representing the Federation as such.

(d) National Joint Council of the Railway Unions. Three unions cater for all railwaymen except those employed in the railway shops. These are the National Union of Railwaymen, the Railway Clerks Association and the Associated Society of Locomotive Engineers and Firemen, with total membership of 591,903. Efforts made by the T.U.C. to secure amalgamation between these unions have been unsuccessful, and there was considerable inter-union rivalry. In 1943, when the National Arbitration Tribunal rejected wage claims submitted by each of the three unions separately, the National Joint Council was set up to co-ordinate their industrial activities. The success of the joint wage claim submitted by the three unions gave the new organisation a splendid start. This was followed, as part of the unions' efforts to avoid inter-union rivalry, by a decision at the end of 1943 to promote joint activity on a district, branch, yard and depot basis; as a result, joint meetings were held of the local branches of the three unions, and led to the establishment in a number of cases of Local Joint Committees, which were able to solve local problems by united action. In some cases Joint Line Committees have been set up. The decision of the unions for the interchange of fraternal delegates at their annual conferences in 1944 and 1945 is an outward and visible sign of the progress in joint working and in removing mutual suspicions since, and largely because of, the formation of the Joint Council. The possibility of amalgamation of the three unions is immeasurably nearer now than in 1943, and if the formation of the National Joint Council brings this about, future Labour historians may well regard it as being one of the most important events in the history of the Labour movement.

II. The second type—the partial federation—is represented by (a) the Iron and Steel Confederation and (b) the Cotton Federation.

(a) The British Iron and Steel Trades Confederation, formed in 1917, is the largest union in the industry with 78,902 members. Its structure is federal, and other unions may by its rules still join by affiliation short of full amalgamation. Despite this, the Confederation does not act in a federal manner, since it in fact consists of several unions which are fully amalgamated, and any new individual member joins the Confederation directly. The machinery is there, however, for any other union to join forces with it without having to sink its identity. The only other big union in the industry is the National Union of Blastfurnacemen, with 18,958 members, and the working arrangements between the two bodies are so close in practice as almost to amount to federation.

(b) In the cotton industries the position is even more complicated. Here there are 150 self-administered, autonomous local and district associations. They are all (with two very small exceptions) members of one or other of six federations. Those federations, commonly called "amalgamations", are not conflicting, being each on an occupational basis and confined to certain sections of the trade; each "amalgamation" is responsible for negotiating wages and conditions, but each of the federated unions retains a wide measure of autonomy. The six federations are:

Amalgamated Association of Beamers, Twisters and Drawers	3,552 members
Amalgamated Association of Card, Blowing and Ring Room Operatives	38,575 ,,
General Union of Associations of Loom Overlookers	5,050 ,,
Amalgamated Association of Operative Cotton Spinners and Twiners	16,672 ,,
Amalgamated Textile Warehousemen . .	5,620 ,,
Amalgamated Weavers Association . . .	72,497 ,,

141,966

These amalgamations work in concert for certain purposes. They are all members of the United Textile Factory Workers Association (total members 143,205), which, although it has primarily political purposes, has nevertheless been able to co-ordinate to a certain extent general policy in the industrial sphere.

On industrial matters each federation negotiates directly with the employers, but the Northern Counties Textile Trades Federation performs certain co-ordinating industrial functions. This Federation includes some of the above "amalgamations" and two other small unions, totalling 87,958 members in all. Two other unions—the Card and Room Operatives and the

Spinners—have a Joint Working Committee for industrial purposes.

III. The third type is represented by a variety of organisations of different character operating in the field of (*a*) tobacco, (*b*) textiles, (*c*) insurance, and of (*d*) some of the professions.

(*a*) All the unions catering for tobacco-workers are represented on the Tobacco Wages Council. During the war they formed a War Emergency Committee for the industry. This is a federation in embryo, as its task is to conduct wage negotiations with certain employers for wages, terms and conditions higher than those of the Wages Council itself. On this committee are represented three unions catering for tobacco workers (with a total membership of 20,715), and also the National Union of Distributive and Allied Workers, the National Union of General and Municipal Workers and the Transport and General Workers Union.

(*b*) The National Association of Unions in the Textile Trade (other than cotton) is a loose form of federation which deals mainly with the negotiation of national agreements and acts corporately in convening representatives of the associated unions to register decisions. Its unions comprise 54,000 members, the biggest by far being the National Union of Dyers, Bleachers and Textile Workers, with 35,000 members. There are twenty more unions, all small, and for the most part purely local, attached to the Association. Only eleven out of the total of twenty-one unions concerned are affiliated to the T.U.C.

(*c*) The Insurance Unions Joint Consultative Committee is also a federation in a quite embryonic stage. It was formed in 1940 to act as a medium for consultation between the unions affiliated to the T.U.C. and for the co-ordination of policy. The three insurance unions involved total 45,183 members, and the National Union of Distributive and Allied Workers and the Transport and General Workers Union are also represented.

There is also the Insurance Workers Congress, in which are associated a number of unions of unknown membership not affiliated to the T.U.C.; the biggest affiliated insurance union —the National Federation of Insurance Workers, with 27,156 members—is associated with the Insurance Workers Congress.

The Insurance Workers Congress is trying to get the independent unions either to affiliate with it or else to join the T.U.C. and hence come within the Joint Consultative Committee; that policy encounters difficulties largely because of complaints against some of the unions concerned made by unions affiliated to the T.U.C. The position is, therefore, that there are two federations of bodies catering for the industry with the biggest union common to each, but that is as far as things have gone.

(d) The Federations of the professional groups are represented by such organisations as:

1. The Non-Manual Workers Advisory Council. This Council, set up in 1930, is a very loose consultative body hardly worthy of the title of a federation. Its aim is to bring into consultation all the unions catering for non-manual and commercial workers: forty-one unions and the National Federation of Professional Workers are represented on the Council.

2. The National Advisory Council for the Nursing Profession. This body also has not yet the status of a federation. Its object is to allow for consultations on general policy and on demarcation problems by the six unions catering for nurses. The three special unions involved total 41,011 members and the Transport and General Workers Union, the General and Municipal Workers and the National Union of Public Employees are also concerned. This Council and the Non-Manual Workers Advisory Council are mainly advising the General Council of the T.U.C. on policy concerning their trades, and not acting together on industrial matters.

3. The Federation of Theatre Unions. This was only recently formed, and is a loose form of organisation concentrating on preventing inter-union disputes and on the recruiting of members into one or other of the affiliated unions. This industry is notoriously badly organised. The member unions conduct their own negotiations on wages and conditions. Total membership of the three unions involved is 34,718.

4. The Film Industries Employees Council. Exactly the same remarks apply as to the Federation of Theatre Unions. Since the constituent unions are not even bound by the decisions of the Council, it is acting in a purely consultative capacity. The unions affiliated (which to some extent overlap with those in the Theatre Unions) total 33,975 members.

An organisation of a somewhat different type is the General Federation of Trade Unions. This body had been set up by the T.U.C. itself as long ago as 1899, and it was originally intended that it should play an important part as a sort of mutual strike insurance organisation of trade unions. Since,

61

however, most of the larger unions are not affiliated, its present importance is small.

4. Joint Arrangements

There are, finally, a great number of arrangements between individual unions which, while not quite amounting to a permanent federation, make for closer contact between them and help to settle matters concerning specific problems and their mutual relationship. The General Council promised an extensive survey of these diverse joint working arrangements in its "Final Report", the "Preliminary Report" giving only a few examples.

There are, for instance, agreements between unions about their respective "spheres of influence"—that is to say, the firms or occupations each may cover: some war-time arrangements between different unions allow members of one union to work during the emergency in firms controlled by another. Other such agreements between unions concern the employment of women. The two general workers unions have appointed a joint committee to go into all differences arising between them, and in 1943 the three railway unions set up a national joint committee to secure the utmost possible unity on all matters of common concern in which agreement is desirable.

There are other agreements that go farther than ordinary joint working arrangements, though they are neither exactly federations nor amalgamations. Such agreements have been made between the Transport and General Workers Union on the one hand, and the North Wales Quarrymen's Union and the National Union of Enginemen, Firemen, Mechanics and Electrical Workers on the other. These two latter unions, while retaining their identity and domestic autonomy, yet have an arrangement with the Transport and General Workers Union for the payment of members' contributions in respect of benefits and service.

CHAPTER IV

LOCAL ORGANISATION

(a) LINKS

IN LOCAL TRADE union organisation there are four links—factory, local, district and area. The workers of a large factory usually belong to a number of unions: in engineering it is sometimes the case that dozens of unions have members in a large factory. There is, however, not much co-ordination among them on the spot, except in factories where there are shop stewards, who serve as the representatives of the members of the unions and even of the unorganised workers for the whole factory or part of it, a "shop". The standing of the shop stewards and their functions vary greatly from union to union.

The main link in trade union organisation is the local branch, which is connected vertically with the national union, often through district committees. The local branches are formed either round the workers' place of residence or round the place of employment. Some unions have district committees embracing the activities of their membership in the district, and some have divisional committees covering larger areas.

Local branches of national unions are in many places united in area bodies—Trades Councils—serving as the horizontal link.

All these organisation links are handled in an amazing variety of ways in the rules of the different unions, and we have analysed those rules to see how they treat the problems of local organisation.

We have investigated the rules of forty-three national unions. These include all unions—forty in number,[1] with a membership of 25,000 and more in 1943—which were affiliated to the T.U.C., as well as three important Civil Service unions.[2]

(b) SHOP STEWARDS

In this country there were shop stewards in many factories long before the "shop steward movement" of the First World War brought them into the limelight. Even then they were by no means confined to engineering and kindred industries, where their activities were most widespread and noteworthy. In some industries, of course—such as tailoring and all sorts of woodworking—they are mainly concerned with those minor trade union functions which, by the nature of things, are better carried through in the shop than in the local branch.[3]

[1] See Appendix IV, pp. 243–44.
[2] Civil Service Clerical Association; Union of Post Office Workers; and the Post Office Engineering Union.
[3] Mining is the only industry in this country where the law provides for

There is a crying need for the joint representation of the workers at shop level to be fulfilled by shop stewards, especially in those industries in which the local branches of the unions are not formed on the "place-of-employment" principle.[1]

According to the rules of the unions shop stewards may act in three main spheres: firstly they may have to ensure that general trade conditions, as established by local custom and trade union agreements, do actually exist in the shop. With this duty goes the right to inspect periodically the trade union tickets of the workers, and to ensure, if possible, that there is 100 per cent. trade unionism.

The second function is to represent the workers of the shop, at least in minor affairs, in dealings with foremen and management. Any disagreement is, moreover, taken up by the union officials.

Thirdly, the shop stewards quite often collect union dues. Shop stewards are, thus, for one purpose or another, recognised in the Rules of a large number of unions: there are ten unions[2] whose Rules say that stewards *shall* be appointed except in special circumstances, such as the local membership being too small. In seven other unions[3] shop stewards *may* be appointed.

The remaining unions included in the present study do not provide in their Rules for shop stewards. Nine of these unions,

---

an elected representative of the workers in each unit of employment—in this case, the pit. The checkweighman, whose primary function is to check the weight of coal brought up to the surface, also acts as the representative of the workers in co-operation with the pit lodge of the union; the checkweighman is, however, not a shop steward.

[1] In the printing industry, where the place of employment *is* closely linked with the union "chapel", the "father" of the chapel takes on most of the duties of a shop steward.

[2] Amalgamated Engineering Union; Electrical Trades Union; National Union of Boot and Shoe Operatives; Boilermakers and Iron and Steel Shipbuilders Society; Iron and Steel Trades Confederation; Amalgamated Union of Foundry Workers; Plumbers, Glaziers and Domestic Engineers Union; Association of Engineering and Shipbuilding Draughtsmen; National Society of Brass and Metal Mechanics; National Union of Vehicle Builders.

The official title of the steward is "shop secretary" in the Rules of the Vehicle Builders, "Corresponding Member of the Office Committee"—Draughtsmen, "shop president"—Boot and Shoe Operatives, "works representative"—Iron, Steel and Kindred Trades Confederation, but these are differences in name only.

[3] Amalgamated Society of Woodworkers; Transport and General Workers Union; National Union of Tailors and Garment Workers; Ship Constructors and Shipwrights Association; National Union of Sheet Metal Workers and Braziers; National Amalgamated Furnishing Trade Association; and National Amalgamated Union of Shop Assistants, Warehousemen and Clerks.

however, are based on local organisations formed in one way or another according to the "place-of-employment" principle, so that some sort of organic connection between the union and the local workshops does exist.[1] There still remain fifteen unions[2] where neither shop stewards nor the "place-of-employment" principle are provided for.

The main industry where shop stewards play, or have played, an important part is the engineering industry. In the Amalgamated Engineering Union, the Electrical Trades Union and the Plumbers Union, all of which require the appointment of shop stewards, their range of duties is wide. They have to watch trade conditions and periodically inspect members' tickets, while at the same time representing the workers with the management. The Woodworkers Rules accord the same rights and duties, but do not demand election of shop stewards in each working unit. The Foundry Workers, Vehicle Builders and Ship Constructors provide their shop stewards with the right to watch trade conditions—the first two unions also authorise them to collect dues. The Draughtsmen and the Iron, Steel and Kindred Trades Confederation have shop stewards who are authorised to represent the workers, and in the former union also to watch trade conditions. Officially the Boilermakers give their stewards only the right to collect dues, but the fact that they make provisions to apply in the event of a steward being victimised suggests that the steward's actual functions are a good deal wider.

Wherever outside the metal, engineering, printing and wood trades shop stewards do exist they are for the most part just collectors of union dues.[3] The same is true of some of the minor

[1] National Union of Railwaymen; Associated Society of Locomotive Engineers and Firemen; Fire Brigades Union; the three Civil Service unions and the three printing unions (with the "chapel" organisation) included in this survey.

[2] National Union of General and Municipal Workers; National Union of Public Employees; National Union of Dyers, Bleachers, and Textile Workers; Amalgamated Association of Card, Blowing and Ring Room Operatives; National Union of Agricultural Workers; National Union of Distributive and Allied Workers; Amalgamated Union of Building Trade Workers (Great Britain and Ireland); Amalgamated Weavers Association; Bank Officers Guild; Clerical and Administrative Workers Union; Amalgamated Union of Seamen; National Federation of Insurance Workers; Railway Clerks Association; National Union of Enginemen, Firemen, Mechanics and Electrical Workers; Amalgamated Union of Operative Bakers, Confectioners, etc.

[3] National Union of Boot and Shoe Operatives; Transport and General Workers Union; National Union of Tailors and Garment Workers.

metal and engineering unions. In the case of the Shop Assistants the Rules do not define the function of shop stewards.

Co-operation with stewards of other unions has been introduced in the engineering trades, and is evidently regarded as important; it is especially mentioned among the duties of shop stewards in the Electrical Trades Union. In such unions as the Amalgamated Engineering Union, Plumbers or Woodworkers, where there are many local shop, yard or job stewards, special local spokesmen of the stewards may be elected.

Shop committees may be appointed to assist the shop stewards of the Amalgamated Engineering Union, the Boot and Shoe Operatives and the Plumbers Union in their general work. This is also largely true of the Draughtsmen, Ship Constructors and Vehicle Builders. The Rules of the Foundry Workers also provide for shop committees whose functions are to supervise trade conditions and trade union agreements in the shop (evidently in co-operation with the shop steward), and to sanction any agreement on payment by results or piecework. These shop committees are evidently not authorised to assist the steward in his other functions—*i.e.*, in representing the workers before the management; in that matter shop stewards are supposed to co-operate more closely with the higher union authorities.

Finally, the Tailors and Garment Workers Union, which authorises stewards only to collect dues, gives the shop committees much wider functions—namely, (*a*) to conduct general organisation, (*b*) to further workers' control in industry and (*c*) to supervise trade conditions and practices.

Shop committees are not provided for at all in the Rules of other unions covered by this investigation.

It is no coincidence that the more important functions of the shop stewards were developed during the two world wars—considerable ground being lost in the period between—and that in both wars the development was mainly concentrated in the munition and shipbuilding and in engineering industries. Prejudiced observers used to attribute the "shop steward movement" of 1914–1918 to "demagogic" influence. To quote G. D. H. Cole's[1] apt description "the words 'shop steward' came, in the mouths of many people, to signify a very high degree of wickedness and perversity. It was the shop stewards who were preventing Great Britain from winning the war, who

[1] "Workshop Organisation"; published in 1923 as part of the Carnegie "Economic and Social History of the World War".

were wantonly stirring up strikes, who were in league with Germany to prevent the prompt delivery of munitions which were urgently required at the front, and who, though they were themselves an insignificant minority of the workers, most of whom were 'sound at heart', were, so it was thought, somehow successful in leading their innocent fellow-workers by the nose."

G. D. H. Cole tried after the 1914–1918 war to get the picture into true perspective and to show that the shop-steward movement was, in fact, the spontaneous result of certain economic and social tendencies; and the fact that the Second World War once again stimulated the same movement within the same industries can be taken as a vindication of his claim. This renewal of an identical movement under similar conditions a quarter of a century later is more striking in that the Labour movement was even more deeply concerned in the Second World War to help the war effort. How widely the rôle of the shop stewards is now recognised by the employers and workers alike can be seen from the agreement between the trade unions having members employed within the engineering industries and the Engineering and Allied Trades Employers Federation. The main functions of the shop stewards can be summarised as follows:

(a) to recruit members and to stimulate among the workers interest in trade unions;

(b) to raise with employers questions arising in the course of employment with the object of settling within the workshops such grievances as may legitimately arise in regard to working conditions, wages, etc.;

(c) to take the necessary steps in insuring the observance of existing agreements and operating new agreements concluded between the union and Employers' Federation, or awards made by arbitration institutions.

In addition to those three normal functions of shop stewards, general instructions were issued by the Executive Committee of the Amalgamated Engineering Union to the District Committees, requiring them to report such cases as came to their notice of mismanagement and inefficiency, and the shop stewards were to embody such information in their quarterly reports to the District Committees.

In the development of the shop stewards' movement that last task became much more significant during the Second World War. In theory most of the actual work it involves has been

67

done by the workers' side of the Joint Production Committees (which are described in Chapter XIV), but it is, of course, also true that in actual fact the workers' delegates to these committees are very frequently, though not necessarily, shop stewards: they work best when the two practically coincide.

The engineering industries and, from 1939 to 1945, more particularly the aircraft factories, were expanding very rapidly, and one of the problems that had to be decided by workers' representatives "on the spot" was how far it was compatible with the workers' interests to accept dilution by unskilled or other workers. Following their employment, the newly admitted workers had to be got into the unions, and a system of trade union representatives who worked for 100 per cent. membership became more necessary than ever before. It also became more difficult, because the war brought into the munitions, aircraft, shops and shipyards many workers who had to travel long distances every day from their place of residence to work. As the main engineering unions are based on branches located for the most part in the members' place of residence, the consequent difficulties tended to increase during the war, and could be best bridged over by having shop stewards. Generally speaking and in spite of some reassuring signs within the Amalgamated Engineering Union and other unions concerned, it is still correct to say that trade union organisation lags far behind such recent developments in the engineering industries. In many medium-size shops a great multitude of craft, general and semi-industrial unions have members. Small wonder that the swift expansion during the war years generated a deep and strong urge for modernisation of the workers' organisation on the workshop level itself.

Thus, the industries in which the shop stewards' movement had made outstanding progress are those that were expanding, more especially engineering, shipbuilding and aircraft. The movement established itself firmly in the engineering industry because that industry expanded rapidly, because expansion was uneven (so that many wage negotiations could be best conducted on the "shop" level), and finally because payment was often by piecework and the worker had a personal interest in increasing his output and payment by "result": in such "piecework" bargaining the shop stewards played a very important part. Their being on the spot and making negotiation possible on the shop or factory level often helped to localise disputes and to obviate strikes that would otherwise have spread.

Shop stewards have two sets of tasks: to represent the collective interests of the workers and their unions in regard to conditions and remuneration, and to represent the interests of the individual worker by increasing the productivity of labour and the scope of production and simultaneously his or her remuneration. In war conditions the management was deeply interested in the increase of production, and so it will be in peace-time in nationalised industries.

Some unions have tried hard to restrict the shop stewards to one enterprise or shop, and refused to recognise their right to act as a body on any wider regional or on the national scale. Other unions, and especially the Amalgamated Engineering Union, went a long way to improve their shop stewards' organisation. They organised quarterly district meetings of their shop steward representatives, formed special schools for them and gave them representation on district trade union committees. The shop stewards serve in the Amalgamated Engineering Union as the link between the branches and the membership in the district organisation—a method which deserves special study and encouragement.

Was the Amalgamated Engineering Union justified in adopting such an expansionist attitude? To answer that question one must understand that the shop stewards' movement really arose as a means of overcoming the disadvantages of the multiplicity of unions in any given industrial enterprise in the absence of industrial unionism. They became the part of the machinery of labour in industry that was best able to speak for all the workers employed in a given workshop, even though all or most of these workers might belong to several unions. The shop stewards are not union officials specialising in trade union work, but direct representatives of the workers on the spot; at the same time they are trade unionists themselves, and speak as workers of the factory and trade unionists.

(c) LOCAL BRANCHES

Considering that the local branches are so essential a part of trade union organisation, it seems strange that there is no definite information about the total number of them. It would, of course, not be easy to publish a trade union map of the country, since the number as well as the distribution of branches keep on changing all the time.

As far as we were able to find out in 1945 there were four unions with over 2,000 branches each—the Transport and

General Workers Union, with 4,136; the National Union of Agricultural Workers, with 2,466 (in 1944); the Amalgamated Engineering Union, with 2,229, and the National Union of General and Municipal Workers with 2,200. Four other unions had over 1,000 branches each—the National Union of Railwaymen, 1,605; the National Union of Distributive and Allied Workers, 1,401; the National Federation of Insurance Workers, 1,398; the Amalgamated Society of Woodworkers, 1,276.

Information about thirty-eight leading registered unions shows that their branches numbered in 1945 about 23,300 (see Appendix V, pp. 244–45). It seems probable, therefore, that there are between 50,000 and 60,000 trade union branches in the country.

It is interesting to note that the number of trade union branches is probably twelve to fifteen times larger than the total number of other local labour organisations, including the Labour Party, with its 3,200 divisional and local parties and about 1,000 co-operative societies.

Definite guidance as to the principles on which trade union branches should be formed is given in the official rules of only a minority of the unions investigated. There are only three[1] unions whose Rules say that branches shall, in general, take in members according to their place of residence. Of these three, the National Union of Seamen, however, has also an "escape" clause according to which a member may choose to join a branch in a place different from his usual place of residence. There are eight unions whose Rules provide that members should, as a matter of course, be organised in branches located at their places of work.[2]

One union[3] has the provision that *apprentices* shall be organised in the branches situated where they are employed.

The other unions use both methods together, though only two of them[4] mention specifically in their Rules that local branches may be based on either industry, service or locality. The mineworkers are usually organised in pit lodges which

[1] National Union of Boot and Shoe Operatives; National Society of Brass and Metal Mechanics; National Union of Seamen.

[2] National Union of Railwaymen; Associated Society of Locomotive Engineers and Firemen; National Union of Tailors and Garment Workers; Civil Service Clerical Association; Fire Brigades Union; Electrical Trades Union; Union of Post Office Workers; Post Office Engineering Union.

[3] National Society of Painters.

[4] National Society of Operative Printers and Assistants; and the Clerical and Administrative Workers Union.

70

are formed on the "place-of-employment" principle. Similarly, all unions belonging to the "printing" group, even though their branches may be constituted according to the members' residences, are in fact based on "chapels" in the workshops. The busmen's branches of the Transport and General Workers Union are also organised round the places of employment.

The "place-of-employment" principle, which, as a rule, tends to strengthen the local organisation—though it may have certain disadvantages that should not be overlooked, prevails in a number of industries, particularly in mining, printing, tailoring, in railway transport and among busmen; in electrical trades (at least for the skilled men organised in the Electrical Trades Union), as well as in the Civil Service and fire brigades.

There are a few unions—e.g., the Agricultural Workers', the miners', and most of the weavers' unions—where the place of employment is practically identical with the place of residence, so that for them the problem hardly arises. There are, of course, cases, such as the Union of Seamen, where organisation on "place-of-employment" lines may be impracticable. Nevertheless, the majority of unions have members organised in branches at their place of residence, a situation calling for re-examination.

Available information about the composition of branches and their functioning is very scanty. A recent publication by Political and Economic Planning (P.E.P.)[1] makes a useful attempt to summarise some of the known facts. It frankly admits that "the material to be analysed has many gaps, for the trade unions in many cases do not keep, or do not disclose, a detailed record of their activities. For an objective analysis quantitative data are preferable to impressions and judgments, but in the present state of knowledge complete quantitative data is not obtainable."[2]

The number of branches is given by P.E.P. in a table[3] covering thirty-two national unions with a total of 12,526 branches, with a membership over 2,600,000. The sizes of the branches differ very considerably between different localities and different unions. Only nineteen (out of thirty-three) unions give in-

[1] *Planning*, No. 249, May 10, 1946.
[2] *Ibid.*, p. 3.
[3] *Ibid.*, p. 14. With four exceptions all the figures cover the years between 1937 and 1941 exclusive.

formation about the size of their branches. In some unions many members are in branches with a membership of 1,000 and more: the National Union of Boot and Shoe Operatives have 88 per cent. (in 1938) in such large branches, the National Union of Dyers, Bleachers and Textile Workers 52 per cent. (in 1936), the National Union of Distributive and Allied Workers 38 per cent. (1937) and the Typographical Association 28 per cent. (1939).

Ten unions of the group analysed have about a fifth of their members in branches numbering between 500 and 1,000 members. Other unions have a great proportion of members in branches between 200 and 500 strong, among them the Amalgamated Engineering Union 62 per cent. (1941); Boilermakers and Iron and Steel Shipbuilding Society 61 per cent. (1939); Iron and Steel Trade Confederation 53 per cent. (1938); Electrical Trades Union 48 per cent. (1939); National Union of Vehicle Builders 46 per cent. (1939); Ship Constructors and Shipwrights Association 42 per cent. (1935); National Association of Operative Plasterers 41 per cent. (1937); National Union of Railwaymen 41 per cent. (1940), and the National Amalgamated Furnishing Trade Association 36 per cent. (1939). The Amalgamated Union of Foundry Workers (1939), The Transport and General Workers Union (power section) and the Amalgamated Society of Woodworkers 35 per cent.

In thirteen of the eighteen unions that give information about the sizes of their branches a third of the members and more belong to the smaller branches with anything up to 100 or 200 members.

The natural conclusion is: branches vary in size from a handful to many thousands of members. The average size in the medium-sized craft unions is round about 100 and in the smaller craft unions less than 100.[1] Semi-industrial unions tend to have a relatively high proportion of large branches, partly because the industry for which they cater usually has its main concentration in certain localities.[2]

The branch is the centre of any participation by the

---

[1] Of the thirty-two unions investigated, one has an average membership per branch of over 1,000; one over 500; four between 300 and 500; four between 200 and 300; fourteen between 100 and 200 and eight less than 100.

[2] We understand that the Amalgamated Engineering Union has been for many years contemplating the setting up of large (up to 5,000 members) branches with a full-time paid secretary, but the cost of such an organisation has been prohibitive and has not been followed up.

mass of ordinary members in the activities of the union. As a rule it has a lot of elected voluntary officials, such as a president, vice-president, secretary, treasurer, auditors, referee, sick stewards, check steward, money steward, doorkeeper, committee-men and trustees. In some unions, such as the Amalgamated Society of Woodworkers, for which detailed information is available,[1] a branch may have from fifteen to twenty officials. These officials form the backbone of the branch and its activities; the secretary usually receives a very modest remuneration for his work (a secretary of a branch of the Association of Scientific Workers with 250 members, for example, gets £23 a year) and sometimes members of committee are paid travelling expenses on a very modest scale; such payments show clearly how essentially voluntary are the activities of the branch secretary and of the officials.

It is mainly through the branch that trade union democracy finds its chief and natural expression. It is shown in the attendance at meetings, in voting and in ballots for the election of national officials, as well as in the resolutions adopted dealing either with local or national trade union matters or with more general problems.

Unfortunately the attendance at branch meetings is very low. Sometimes, indeed, members will come to the meeting only to pay their dues, and go away before the business of the meeting proper begins. From the contents of the three tables showing the votes cast by members the authors of the P.E.P. summary[2] came to the following conclusions:

"The proportion of members turning up to branch meetings is on an average low. There is a tendency for a nucleus, largely consisting of officials, to turn up regularly. Many Unions have special quarterly branch meetings, and rank and file may be fined for not attending these, unless they present their excuses; similar ad hoc meetings may be called on particular issues of importance to the Unions, and it is often at these special meetings that voting is taken, whether for election of officers, or, for example, on the ratification of a national agreement. A higher proportion of the membership takes part in the meetings where a vote is taken, than in the regular routine meetings, but even so in the majority of branches and the majority of unions only a fraction of the membership participates."

[1] *Planning*, p. 6.   [2] *Ibid.*, p. 7.

73

Analysing the figures, the authors emphasise "in general the larger the branch, the smaller is the proportion of its membership which takes part in the voting". On the other hand, in some unions, such as the printers' union, "voting is done through the shop organisation, or chapel, and the size of the branch is immaterial. These unions register a very high poll, when votes are taken, and this result is to be expected whenever voting is through the shop rather than the branch. In some of the general unions, stewards get members to register their votes as they go round the shop collecting dues. This also produces a relatively high poll, but the result may be somewhat artificial unless the vote is taken at a proper meeting following discussion."[1]

The P.E.P. has been able to obtain the percentage of the membership voting on various issues for sixteen unions:[2] percentages vary from 2 per cent. to 30 per cent., "but are mainly between 15 per cent. and 25 per cent.". The general unions where votes are collected in a different way appear to muster a poll of about 50 per cent. on most occasions. The printers' unions, where voting is taken in the chapels, which are based on place of work, show very high polls. Thus, in the London Society of Compositors, of twenty-three votes taken on separate occasions, in 1930, 1935 and 1939, the lowest poll was 56 per cent., the highest 86 per cent. and average 70 per cent.

Two factors influence the percentage poll: the number of branches which do not vote (usually small branches) and the lower proportion of voting in large branches, so that unions with large branches show a smaller average percentage poll. According to the authors of the Report, "on the rather scanty evidence it would appear that the average poll has not varied much over the past 25 years", and "this fits in with other evidence that the second-level (branch level, N.B.) membership is relatively unaffected by fluctuations in the total membership. It is natural that the minority which takes the trouble to vote at branch meetings should also be the most persistent in retaining union membership. In a similar way, the great war-time increase in the membership of many unions has not been followed up by a proportional increase in the percentage poll."[3]

The figures for the Amalgamated Engineering Union show for the years 1856–86 a proportion of 18 per cent. voting members, and voting on the national agreement in February 1922,

[1] *Planning*, p. 7.   [2] *Ibid.*, p. 8, also Appendix II.   [3] *Ibid.*, p. 9.

34 per cent., 1924, 12 per cent., 1926, 19 per cent., 1934, 22 per cent., 1939, 11 per cent., 1943, 8 per cent.

The evidence on the influence of the size of the branch on the percentage poll is not conclusive, but the available figures (for seven unions) show that in branches of medium size the percentage of the poll is one and a half times that of the very large branches.[1] Even in a union like Boot and Shoe Operatives the voting in large branches (with 5,000 to 8,000 members) is only 14 per cent.

Clearly a thorough statistical investigation is urgently needed, if we want to learn more about local branches and the functioning of trade union democracy, as expressed by mass membership in the branches.

It is between the factory and the branch that the link in the trade union chain is the weakest. It must be remembered that a considerable proportion of the workers is employed in small and medium-size factories, and that in the local branch workers belonging to different types of factories and trades mix together. This offers them a greater variety of approach and outlook and compensates for the narrowness of "one" place of employment branch.

There remains a good deal of controversy between the two views in regard to the method and the optimum size of branch organisation. From the practical point of view it seems obvious that the establishment of the branch *in the* factory or in the locality of employment would greatly facilitate matters. The first would require certain readjustments, both technical and legal—the workers would have to get permission, for example, both to hold trade union meetings "on the premises", perhaps even during their working hours; and also for their representatives to collect membership subscriptions on the spot, etc.[2] But in present-day conditions in this country that should not prove too difficult to achieve.

The other school of thought, admitting the technical advantages, believes them greatly outweighed by the ideological disadvantages. They consider the local branch, with all its limitations, an excellent melting-pot, in which workers belonging to big and small factories mingle and develop the uniform progressive trade union attitude which is the greatest asset of the movement. It produces a membership which is not too engrossed in its own surroundings, nor so exclusively influenced by the conditions obtaining in one factory, that they are un-

[1] *Planning*, p. 10. [2] *Ibid.*, p. 10.

able to see the wider horizons of the industry or trade. People with considerable knowledge of the engineering industry insist categorically that in localities where many branches are composed of workers belonging to one very large factory, trade union work becomes very difficult and unstable and any conflict easily becomes disproportionate.

Branch organisation is one of the most important and pressing problems for the future of trade unionism, and everyone must make up his mind, however difficult it may be, about it. We believe that the trend of modern planned economy will lead to the formation of trade union branches in and around the places of employment. We admit the validity of the arguments of the defenders of local or geographical branches under ordinary capitalist conditions, but it is our contention that the introduction of planned economy must have a great influence in the opposite direction.

Under the new conditions the workers in each enterprise will have to get used to considering themselves as a unit, they will have to develop a new "we" psychology, instead of the individualist attitude of the past. Study of the factory organisation in the U.S.S.R.,[1] of the experiences of the Credit Unions in the U.S.A.[2] and of the collective settlements in Palestine[3] shows clearly the influence of an efficient "works" organisation on the workers' habits of mind, which are gradually changing from being very individualistic to a more social and co-operative attitude. The benefit of this change is so important, especially in the conditions of Labour Britain, that the disadvantages of a factory branch at the present time should not prevent its being introduced as part of industrial unionism.

Trade unions should intensify their educational and political work, developing an effective district union organisation for each industry, and by enlarging and improving the activities of Trade Councils. A factory union branch would not then feel itself isolated, but would function as a component of an alive vertical (National Union) and horizontal (Trade Council) organisation, deeply interested in the problems of the industry as a whole and in the problems of the district (locality or region) in which the factory is established.

It is essential that we should stop thinking in terms of the past, with all its difficulties and limitations, and take into con-

---

[1] See N. Barou's article on "Our Soviet Ally", 1943.
[2] See N. Barou's "Co-operative Banking", 1932.
[3] See H. Infield's " Co-operative Living in Palestine", 1946.

sideration the new conditions and possibilities, which the advent of the Labour Government and of the planned economy that will be the backbone of its programme and activities is opening before the unions.

(d) District Committees

The powers and functions of District Committees, and their relationship with the head office, the branches and the workshops, naturally vary considerably with various unions. They depend primarily, of course, on the degree of centralisation followed by each union, and the Constitution and authority of the branches.

The following account must not be read as covering every union. In some unions—normally those whose industry, and hence themselves, are geographically centralised in a small region—the need for District Committees does not arise. Where, as in the printing unions, the branch is identical with the workshop unit, they either do not need to exist or have fewer powers as the branch is correspondingly stronger and the need of workshop co-ordination correspondingly less. At the other end of the scale come industries—*e.g.*, iron and steel—where there are very few nationally negotiated wage agreements, and where the district has very great powers in that it becomes, for many workers, the sole negotiating body.

The following description of the powers and duties of District Committees can, however, be taken as giving a broad picture of the position in the majority of unions.

In general, the District Committee and its officials are the local agents of the Executive Committee, on the one hand, and the union's local headquarters and co-ordinators of local activity, on the other.

Particulars drawn from the Rules of various unions show that District Committees in the Amalgamated Engineering Union have, *inter alia*, the duty "to deal with and regulate rates of wages, hours of labour, terms of overtime, piecework and general conditions . . . to enter into negotiations with employers . . . they shall define systematic overtime in their district". In the Electrical Trades Union, the Amalgamated Union of Building Trade Workers and the Plumbers Union they have "power to deal with rates of wages, hours of labour and general conditions affecting the trade interests of members in their respective districts". In the National Amalgamated

77

Furnishing Trades Association the District Management Committee "shall be the recognised authority for negotiating with the local employers". The National Union of Distributive and Allied Workers describes essentially the same functions by saying that the duty of the District Committee is "to arrange programmes in connection with wages and conditions and to negotiate such programmes with the employers in the areas covered". With the National Union of Railwaymen the duties are naturally more limited; their powers "shall be consultative and propagandist, such as assisting branches in organising and holding meetings, and such other work as may be delegated to them by the Annual or Special General Meetings or Executive Committee". In the Amalgamated Society of Woodworkers District Committees are given specific power to control overtime, and "they shall undertake the general management of the movement". In the National Union of Sheet Metal Workers they have "power to deal with and regulate the district rates of wages, hours of labour, and general conditions of employment" and "to engage in aggressive disputes". In the Transport and General Workers Union the Area Committees' powers and duties include "the organisation of groups within the area, the co-ordination of the work of the various area trade groups and sections, the conduct of necessary propaganda, the administration of . . . general industrial movements, educational work, political administration, etc., the consideration of any dispute arising in the area . . . and disputes arising out of the non-payment of benefits".

The most important rôle of the District Committees—and this is almost universal—is that of a body negotiating with the local employers. It is their job to interpret national agreements in the light of particular local circumstances and peculiarities, and to negotiate fresh wage and other agreements—*i.e.*, the fixing of piece-work rates, etc. For example, the engineering trade has a national agreement laying down the wages to be paid to women who, during the war, were doing a man's job. The district officials will repeatedly be called in to apply that agreement to the position in a particular factory. Then again, a new process may be introduced locally which is not covered directly by a national agreement. It will be the district officials, normally in close collaboration with the shop stewards, who will then be called in to negotiate a new agreement. This sort of situation will constantly be arising where piecework payment is the basis of the wages system for the industry con-
78

cerned. Normally such agreements are subject to final approval by the union's Executive Committee.

The next general duty, common to most District Committees, is supervision of local branch activity. They are normally the link between the branches and head office. They deal with disputes which may arise between the branches and one of their members relating, say, to unfair conduct of the member concerned or payments of benefits. They act as arbitrators in such disputes. Sometimes they have considerable powers over branches, in the way of auditing of accounts, but this is by no means universal; more and more unions are closely centralising their actual administrative machinery in the hands of head office, and the districts are being increasingly left to the duties they are best fitted to perform—namely, local industrial activity and negotiation. It is almost universally laid down that the District Committee shall have no power over branch business and decisions as such.

Where shop stewards are a recognised part of the union machinery it is normally the district which co-ordinates and superintends their activities. As is pointed out elsewhere, the branch—as a unit—is normally divorced from the workshop. It is usually both too small to embrace all the workers in a particular factory—and thus look at the factory problems as a whole—and too diverse—because it includes members from several factories—to deal with workshop problems. It is the district that is the centre for the factory problems, not the branch. In the Amalgamated Engineering Union, for example, the Rules provide for direct representation of shop stewards on the District Committee on the basis of one shop steward for every 5,000 members or part thereof.

In these circumstances it is natural that the district forms an important part in the structure of collective bargaining.

In building and engineering—to give two of many possible examples—a site or workshop dispute goes straight to the district, because "trade union–employers" negotiation takes place at district level. If agreement is not possible there it goes either to area or divisional level, or, more frequently, to national level, for negotiation, and thence, if still no agreement is reached, it goes to arbitration.

In most trade unions the District Committee keeps an unemployment and black-firm register, and has power to control vacant book-offices in its area pending fresh appointments.

(e) TRADES COUNCILS

The Trades Councils and their federations are, alongside with the T.U.C. itself, the agencies for the promotion of joint activities and discussions between different unions in every locality or region. No all-embracing statistical reports have been published about these Councils during the last twenty years, and it is impossible to estimate what proportion of union membership is represented in them. The Ministry of Labour published annual statistics relating to these Councils until 1924, when there existed 476 individual Trades Councils, with 2,200,000 members, but to-day no comprehensive statistical accounts are being kept by either the Ministry of Labour or the T.U.C. It is believed that there was a slump in Trades Council organisation after 1926, and particularly in the early thirties, followed by a certain recovery in later years. G. D. H. Cole estimated the number of individual Trades Councils in 1938 at roughly 500; we believe, however, that their number increased during the war.

Trades Councils played a leading part in the formation of the T.U.C., but in 1895 they were excluded from the conferences. The official reason for this was that double representation of the membership must be avoided. In actual fact some of the Trades Councils were suspected because of their radicalism. In the meantime that attitude has been slightly modified; there exists to-day a Trades Councils Joint Consultative Committee (T.C.J.C.C.) under the auspices of the T.U.C., consisting of six T.U.C. representatives and six representatives of the Councils themselves. These latter are elected at the Annual Conferences of Trades Councils. There exist also a number of regional Federations of Trades Councils. The Annual Conference held at Leicester in May 1944 was attended by 249 delegates, representing 230 Trades Councils and nineteen Federations. One T.C.J.C.C. representative attends as a guest at the T.U.C. Conference.

The method of representation at the Trades Councils is by affiliation of local branches of each union; sometimes some branches within the area of the Council are affiliated and others are not. It often happens that important union branches are not affiliated to their Trades Councils, and the T.U.C. has now asked them to join up with their Trades Councils.

The General Council's Report to the T.U.C. Congress in Southport 1943, says:—[1]

"Difficulty is sometimes experienced by a Trades Council in securing the affiliation of a Union Branch in their locality, and the T.U.C., on being informed of the difficulty, have made direct approaches to the Head Office of the Union concerned asking them to use their good offices to persuade the branch to enter into affiliation. A circular was sent in May 1943 to all Unions informing them of the value which the T.U.C. places on the work of the Trades Councils, and suggesting that where necessary branches could be advised that affiliation fees might be paid on full membership."

It is evident that many union branches and a number of unions have not been very enthusiastic in their support of Trades Councils.

Only thirteen out of the Unions under our review[2] mentioned the Trades Councils in their Rules; and among those not making any reference to the Councils are such important unions as the Transport and General Workers Union, the National Union of Mineworkers, and the Amalgamated Engineering Union. Of the thirteen unions which refer to the Trades Councils, only two say that branches *shall* affiliate with a local Trades Council, if such a body exists: these two unions are the Boot and Shoe Operatives and the Tailors and Garment Workers. The affiliation of branches of the latter union are subject to the approval of the Executive Board. Both unions omit any reference to Trades Councils Federations.

The remaining eleven unions[3] state that their branches "may affiliate with a Trades Council". Five of these unions[4] make the same recommendation with regard to Trades Coun-

[1] See Report, Section 41.
[2] See Appendix IV, pp. 243–44.
[3] National Union of General and Municipal Workers; National Union of Railwaymen; Associated Society of Locomotive Engineers and Firemen; National Union of Distributive and Allied Workers; National Amalgamated Furnishing Trades Association; Plumbers, Glaziers, and Domestic Engineers Union; National Union of Public Employees; National Union of Enginemen, Firemen, Mechanics and Electrical Workers; National Union of Vehicle Builders; National Society of Operative Printers and Assistants; Fire Brigades Union.
[4] Associated Society of Locomotive Engineers and Firemen; National Union of Railwaymen; National Union of Distributive and Allied Workers; Plumbers, Glaziers, and Domestic Engineers Union; National Union of General and Municipal Workers.

cils Federations, though one[1] of them qualifies both recommendations with the clause that branches shall not affiliate with councils or federations whose policy is detrimental to that of the union.

Unions differ greatly in the method of financing the Trades Councils: affiliation fees are to be paid from central funds in the case of three unions,[2] from district funds by one union,[3] and from local funds by at least eight unions.[4]

The methods of financing Trades Councils vary very much throughout the country, and a recent Annual Conference of the Trades Councils asked the T.U.C. to ensure a unified national system. In any case, the contributions to the Councils are small, and not many of them are in a position to have a paid secretary.

The position of Trades Councils in the Labour and Trade Union movement is anomalous. They are not permitted to be members of the T.U.C., but "every scrap of moral influence which the (T.U.C.) General Council could give would be behind the movement to bring about the fullest affiliation to Trades Councils" (Sir Walter Citrine at 16th Annual Conference of Trades Councils, 1940); they are supposed to have no political connections, yet carry on a ceaseless activity of a quasi-political type; they are viewed with jealousy by some national trade unions, yet they spend much of their time recruiting members to such unions; they have no executive powers, yet very many of them display more local initiative and exercise more genuine executive ability than any other organisation of similar size in the Labour movement.

Much of this apparent contradiction is explained when their dual rôle is appreciated. They are at one and the same time a federation, or Parliament of the trade union branches within

[1] National Union of General and Municipal Workers.

[2] National Union of Boot and Shoe Operatives; National Union of Public Employees; National Union of Enginemen, Firemen, Mechanics and Electrical Workers.

[3] National Union of General and Municipal Workers.

[4] National Union of Tailors and Garment Workers; National Union of Railwaymen; Associated Society of Locomotive Engineers and Firemen; National Union of Distributive and Allied Workers; National Union of Vehicle Builders; Ship Constructors and Shipwrights Association; National Society of Operative Printers and Assistants; and Fire Brigade Union. (No financial provision is made in the Rules of the three remaining unions—viz. National Amalgamated Furnishing Trade Association; Plumbers, Glaziers and Domestic Engineers Union; and National Union of Firemen, Enginemen, etc. Fees are preferably levied from local funds.)

the area concerned and, in the great majority of cases, the recognised local agents of the T.U.C. for the carrying out locally of its general policy.

Naturally their activities vary greatly according to the varying eagerness and initiative within the local trade union movement.

Probably their primary rôle is to attempt to secure trade union recruiting within the area, by membership drives, by advice and assistance to newly formed branches, by organising factory gate meetings where unionism is weak, and by propaganda generally.

Of like inspiration is their agitation for the improvement of local working conditions. This takes many varying forms. Representations are commonly made to the local Council to get it to observe trade union rates and conditions with its own employees and to include fair-wages clauses in all contracts which it makes. Another almost universal activity before the war was raising funds and making propaganda in support of any local strikers. Most Trades Councils pay special attention to the wages and conditions of youths and apprentices, and women—some, but far too few, have special women's advisory committees—and the unemployed. During the bad years between the wars the Trades Councils did a great deal to fight for better conditions for the unemployed. Many of them were affiliated to the National Unemployed Workers Movement, and when discouraged on political grounds from continuing this association, either worked with it unofficially or organised the local unemployed themselves.

It is a short step from such activities to direct interest in local government affairs. Very many Trades Councils to-day have housing and education sub-committees, which either agitate against the local Councils for their slowness and reluctance to enforce permissive legislation, or co-operate actively with them in preparing plans, collecting information and helping to popularise its decisions. Many have prepared their own proposals for rebuilding their own town, and have had their plans very seriously considered and largely adopted by the local Councils. Plans for increased local amenities or agitation against increases in rents, for enforcing of rent control, for expediting bomb-damage repairs and for hastening re-housing, are common.

Action was commonly taken also with the local Councils and bus companies for better transport facilities, better amenities

83

on the transport services and more intelligent arrangement of transport schedules to fit in with local factory needs.

Naturally, Trades Councils were concerned with the location of industry. When, as part of the switch-over to peace, factories are closed, the local Council is invariably among the first to demand that new ones take their place, so as to keep industry in their town.

It may fairly be claimed that in no important form of local activity does a live Trades Council fail to play its useful part as the spokesman of the organised workers in its area. In that capacity it has the right, provided for in various Acts of Parliament, of nominating the workers' representatives on the numerous local committees that exist to act as quasi-judicial tribunals to administer the Acts concerned. For example, it nominates the workers' member of the Military Hardship Tribunals, Pensions Tribunals, Reinstatement Committees, Courts of Referees under the Unemployment Acts and similar bodies.

Apart from their continuous statutory activities a vital rôle is usually played by Trades Councils in time of crisis, or when it is important to mobilise the working-class solidarity throughout the country. Their record in the General Strike was outstanding. Without them the strike could never have developed as it did. The initiative, organising ability and courage of the working class displayed by workers straight from the bench and the mine were a wonderful encouragement to all who saw them.

Their sense of solidarity with the workers' cause in other lands was demonstrated by the Trades Councils' active participation in the emergency campaigns of later years on behalf of the people of China and Spain. Those qualities are still being displayed to-day, though in a less spectacular form, but the contribution which the Trades Councils as a whole, and particularly the more go-ahead ones, are making to the strength of the movement as a whole cannot be over-rated.

CHAPTER V

DEVELOPMENT AND DENSITY

(a) INTRODUCTION

THE TOTAL membership of the trade unions in Great Britain was about 8,117,000 at the end of 1943.[1] At the end of 1913 it

[1] The following table shows the growth of the total membership and its distribution between men and women during this century:—

stood at 4,135,000, and in 1938 at 6,053,000, while it reached its highest point at 8,348,000 in 1920.

In 1943 membership was nearly 307,000 (or 3·9 per cent.) greater than at the end of the previous year, but during 1944 and 1945 it has decreased by 374,000 (or 3·9 per cent.).

Women members, too, had increased both in number and in proportion to male membership: 1,870,000 women in 1943 represented over 23 per cent. of the total membership (going down to 20·4 per cent. in 1945). The increase of men and women members in the course of the present century was very uneven: the total number of trade union members increased nearly four times, over three times in the case of men, and twelve times in the case of women.

The contrast between the First and the Second World War periods is interesting in respect of the proportion of men and of women who joined the unions. During the five years of 1914–1919, which were wholly or in part war years, there were as many as 1,616,000 new male members, but only 772,000 new female members—that is, two men to every woman. During the comparable five-year period of the Second World War

Year.	No. of unions.	Membership total. (1,000's)	Men (1,000's).	Per-centage.	Women (1,000's).	Per-centage.
1900	1,323	2,022	1,868	92·4	154	7·6
1914	1,260	4,145	3,708	89·5	437	10·5
1915	1,229	4,359	3,868	88·7	491	11·3
1916	1,225	4,644	4,018	86·5	626	13·5
1917	1,241	5,498	4,620	84·0	878	16·0
1918	1,264	6,533	5,324	81·5	1,209	18·5
1920	1,384	8,348	7,024	84·1	1,324	15·9
1932	1,081	4,444	3,698	83·2	746	16·8
1939	1,012	6,244	5,264	84·4	980	15·6
1940	996	6,558	5,469	83·5	1,089	16·5
1941	988	7,109	5,729	80·6	1,380	19·4
1942	982	7,810	6,128	78·6	1,682	21·4
1943	977	8,117	6,235	76·8	1,882	23·2
1944	952	8,026	6,215	77·5	1,811	22·5
1945	765 [1]	7,803	6,206	79·6	1,597	20·4

[1] The reduction of the number of unions from 952 to 765 during 1945 is due partly to the amalgamation of the majority of the coal-mining unions into the National Union of Mineworkers, while a large proportion of the remainder was due to constitutional changes in a group of associated organisations in the Civil Service, as a result of which they ceased to function independently of the parent organisation (see the *Ministry of Labour Gazette*, November 1946, p. 314).

(1939–1943) the increase was 960,000 men and 897,000 women—men and women joining the unions in practically equal numbers.

(b) THE TRADE CYCLE

Over a long period the growth in membership of British trade unions has been remarkable, though the rate of increase during the last fifty years has by no means been steady. There were many ups and downs—periods of spectacular growth in membership followed occasionally by years in which it actually fell (see Appendix VI, pp. 245–46).

Such fluctuations were on the whole slightly less marked in the period before the 1914–1918 war than in the inter-war period, though they did occur before 1914. Between 1892 and 1913, for instance, the total membership of all British trade unions went up two and a half times; had the rate of growth been constant there would have been a regular annual increase of 4·7 per cent. In actual fact, however, there were as many as eight years during this period when numbers went down (though never by more than 2 per cent.). Total membership, on the other hand, rose as much as 22 per cent. between 1910 and 1911, and again by 21 per cent. between 1912 and 1913. For these annual fluctuations there are many causes, and only a careful year-by-year analysis could establish, for example, why the increase in 1898 was much less than in 1897 or 1899. Many quite accidental factors may play a decisive part in sending membership up or down, such as strikes, political events, membership drives and other propaganda campaigns. Nevertheless, as Appendix VI (pp. 245–46) shows, the ups and downs of trade unionism do follow closely the ups and downs of economic developments. A general upward trend in membership would always slow down in times of crisis and depression. The pre-1914 crises, however slight, were always discernible, and after each depression it took some time before membership began to rise again.

The main years of economic boom, at least before 1914, also meant a "boom" for the trade unions. This is hardly surprising, since employment is high at such times, wages are rising and the strategic position of the unions is at its strongest. Clearly, during a boom trade union membership inclines to rise almost automatically, whereas during a slump only a vigorous union policy can prevent a decline in membership.

Equivalent in some respects to the effect on trade unions of an economic boom are the conditions created by modern wars. A short initial period, during which the labour market becomes more or less disorganised, is followed by a period of marked decrease in unemployment and by a shortage of labour. Thus, whereas trade union membership in 1913 and 1914 increased only slightly, it mounted much more steeply during the latter years of the war, and again during the boom that immediately followed. Development during the Second World War was essentially the same.

The violent post-war crisis of the early twenties was very serious for the trade unions—far more severe than anything in the pre-1914 period. But in the inter-war years the most remarkable feature of all was the steady *decrease* in trade union membership during the ensuing economic revival. No doubt the defeat in the General Strike of 1926 was probably the greatest obstacle to trade union growth in the late twenties.

Yet another setback in trade union membership came with the crisis and depression of the early thirties; the loss in numbers was not so serious as in 1920–1921, but the world economic crisis occurred at a time when the unions were *already* stripped of most of their "unsafe" membership—that is, of those who join the unions in a boom and leave at the first setback.

The present high level of union membership was stimulated partly by the pre-war boom of the late thirties, but mainly by the tremendous increase in employment due to the war itself.

(c) Density before the War

By density of trade unionism is here meant the ratio of the number of workers who are actually members of trade unions to the number eligible for such membership. There is a good deal of information about the relative density of trade unionism as between men and women and among the workers of different industries in July 1939—*i.e.*, just before the outbreak of war.[1]

The population of Great Britain, excluding children below the age of fourteen, was estimated at about 37,414,800 in 1939, consisting of 17,745,200 men and 19,669,600 women. From this figure must be deducted about 14,499,200 persons

[1] The following data are taken from a paper on "The Industrial Distribution of the Population of Great Britain in July 1939", by H. Frankel, read before the Royal Statistical Society on May 29th, 1945. See also Appendix VII and VIII, pp. 247–49.

(including 12,763,900 women) who were "unoccupied" either because of old age (the group includes 2·1 million women and 1·1 million men over sixty-four years of age), or because they were housewives, students, invalids, pensioners, rentiers, etc.; an additional 250,000 men were in the Forces early in 1939.

The rest of the British adult population in 1939 fell into two main groups, whose numerical strength may be estimated as follows: approximately 21,200,000 (14,700,000 men and 6,500,000 women) were wage- and salary-earners; nearly three-quarters of this total (but a smaller proportion of the women) were manual workers; and approximately 1,300,000 persons (940,000 men and 360,000 women) were working "on their own account".

The total number of trade unionists at the end of 1939 was 6,244,000 (5,264,000 men and 980,000 women), so that the average density of trade unionists among all the 21,200,000 wage- and salary-earners who were available for membership was approximately 29 per cent.

These estimates of the density of trade union members would give a distorted picture if they were taken to represent the average proportion of trade unionists among the main groups of manual workers in British industry. For the figure of twenty-one million "workers" in Great Britain before the war included every highly paid employee and Civil Servant, as well as such "un-organisable" categories of workers as domestic servants. Only 15,400,000 workers were insured against unemployment in July 1939, and these included most, though not all, of those categories of workpeople who form the backbone of trade unionism in Great Britain. Thus, it is difficult to assess with any accuracy what percentage of the total number of workers in individual industries were members of their unions—or, in other words, what was the density of trade union membership in any given industry.

As we have already seen, many unions are not organised on an industrial basis, though some are, and in any case the basis of classification they adopt often varies with their organisation and do not correspond to the classifications used for the purposes of insurance or for the census. Moreover, unemployment insurance and census statistics are not in themselves ideal bases for estimating the size of employment in various industries in 1939, since the latest census statistics were then already nine years old, and unemployment insurance did not cover certain groups of wage- and salary-earners. In the absence of official data for our purpose we have made approximate estimates of trade union density over a number of different industries in 1939; the results will be found in a table in Appendix VIII, pp. 248–49. In the case of industries where the data did not permit exact calculation no percentage figures are given: and even those which are given are, at best, rough approximations. It may reasonably be claimed, however, that most of them are more than mere guesswork.[1]

It is in coal-mining and the railway services that by far the highest trade union density is found. Even at the outbreak of war more than 80 per cent. of the miners were members of their unions. The unions in the boot and shoe industries, the cotton industry and sea transport all contained more than 50 per cent. of the workers. Teachers were also in this category, though teachers' unions have so far remained outside the T.U.C. Among many of the road transport and dock and harbour workers, as well as among many workers in public utilities and in various branches of Government service, particularly in the Post Office, union membership was fairly high.

Next in density came two groups of industries which, while highly organised in certain branches, were comparatively weak in others, especially among the unskilled grades. In that category fell the printing and paper trades, engineering, metal and kindred industries. A similar state of affairs existed in the building and associated trades, where a fair proportion of the workers belonged to general workers' unions, and only 25 per cent. to the craft and industrial unions of the trade. The low density of trade unionism in "other textile industries" and "other clothing industries" (see Appendix VIII, pp. 248–49) is in strange contrast to the more or less parallel groups in the cotton industry on the one hand, and the boot and shoe trade on the other. Less surprising, in view of the obvious difficulties, is the low density in the spheres of entertainment and sport, commerce, distribution, banking and insurance and agriculture.

[1] The footnotes added to the Table in Appendix VIII should be studied before definite conclusions are drawn from the figures. Among minor statistical difficulties we mention that the membership figures for trade unions are diluted by members in Ireland and abroad, and by cases of double membership: furthermore, that insurance statistics refer to July, but trade union statistics to December. Add that a small number of professional and other persons who are not strictly "wage- and salary-earners" are trade union members.

D 2

Finally, some very important industries, such as chemicals, leather, food, bricks, and mining other than coal, have not yet developed any important trade unions of their own, or at least any of an importance commensurate with that of the industry itself. Only a small proportion of the workers in these trades are members of their own union, even though some are members of the General Workers or of minor unions of workers in specialised trades, such as tobacco, brushmaking, bakery, chemicals, etc. Among catering, domestic, laundry and similar workers trade unionism has gained so far little foothold.

The perennial backward state of organisation among women workers seems to be confirmed by the 1939 figures. These show the overall density among the 6,500,000 women workers as only about 15 per cent., as compared with a density of 36 per cent. among the 14,700,000 men workers. The difference in the average density as between men and women workers—although it has certainly diminished between 1939 and 1944—is still great.

We can see, however, from Appendix VIII (pp. 248–49) that in many of those trades where the proportion of women workers was high there was more uniformity in the density rates for men and women than the over-all figures would suggest. There was no appreciable difference in the ratio of men to women in the cotton industry, or among teachers, in the remaining textile and clothing trades, or in pottery and glass manufacture. In paper and printing, metal and engineering, the main strength of trade unionism was among the skilled grades; and the discrepancy between the density figures for males and females is largely because women are chiefly employed in the unskilled grades in these industries. In commerce, too, trade union organisation is confined mainly to those branches where more men than women are employed.

Although there is certainly scope for improvement in the trade union organisation of women in most trades, the main cause of their seeming lack of "organisability" is that comparatively few women are employed in the trades that are the main stronghold of trade unionism, especially coal-mining, railway and other transport services, certain branches of public utility services, engineering and the printing trades. On the other hand, there are great numbers of women employed in the catering trades, laundries, private households, the chemical industries, distribution and other branches in which trade unionism still has a long way to go. Where women *are* employed in large numbers in a strongly organised trade—as, for example, in the cotton industry—they do not lag appreciably behind the men in joining the appropriate unions, especially when they remain in employment after marriage, as they mostly do in the cotton industry.

(d) DENSITY DURING THE WAR

It is impossible, unfortunately, to say at all accurately what proportion of the workers in each category of employment was organised in trade unions during the war, but a short outline of the social composition of the population in this country after six years of war may help to give at least a rough idea of the present over-all density of trade unionism.

The White Paper on "Statistics Relating to the War Effort of the United Kingdom" (Cmd. 6564) gives some statistical data concerning British man-power in the age groups of working age, males between fourteen and sixty-four, and females between fourteen and fifty-nine. The population of 31,930,000 in these age groups in June 1944[1] consisted of 15,910,000 men and 16,020,000 women.

These people were, of course, divided between military and civilian occupations. In civilian occupations, which are obviously more important from the trade union point of view, we find that the total number of persons employed or directed to take up employment in industry, agriculture, commerce, or other civilian occupations, including Civil Defence, but excluding domestic service, was 17,545,000, consisting of 10,445,000 men and just over 7,100,000 women. Roughly 900,000 of these women were only in part-time employment, though no exact figure is available.

The strength of the armed forces was 4,969,000 (4,502,000 men and 467,000 members of the Women's Auxiliary Services). The remaining nine millions (about one million men and over eight million women), may be classified as "without occupation". The great majority of women had definite household duties, some being domestic servants outside their own homes, while the rest of the "persons without occupation" were students, invalids and so forth. The White Paper gives no clear

[1] The date gives the occupied population at its highest at the peak of the dilution of labour. Therefore the figures may be somewhat exaggerated when compared with peace-time conditions.

indication of the number of wage- and salary-earners, and the group from which trade union membership is mainly recruited.

Certainly, the great majority of the 17,600,000 people in civilian occupation were wage- and salary-earners; but in this total are included farmers, shopkeepers, industrialists, professional people and others working on their own account. Before the war, even excluding men over sixty-four and women over fifty-nine years of age, there were over one million persons "working on their own account" in Great Britain—a number considerably reduced by wartime developments. There must, nevertheless, be many men and women over sixty-four and fifty-nine respectively who took paid employment in 1944, and a smaller number of domestic workers, gainfully occupied during that year, were not included in the White Paper statistics. No satisfactory estimates are therefore possible, but it is probably true that the "over-age" wage- and salary-earners and domestic workers, taken together, almost equalled those "working on their own account" who are included in the Government White Paper statistics. British trade union membership[1] was 8,117,000 at the end of 1943. Therefore, it is fairly accurate to assume that the total number of wage- and salary-earners in Great Britain in June 1944 was practically identical with the number of these in civilian occupations, viz.—17,600,000.

Unfortunately we do not know how many of these trade union members were in the Forces and how many of the 8,117,000 were in civilian employment. For three different reasons the proportion of trade unionists among the 4,969,000 members of the armed forces is likely to be much smaller than among the 17,600,000 civilian wage- and salary-earners; firstly, because many trade unionists were in reserved occupations; secondly, because many persons who were not eligible for trade union membership (mainly middle-class people) were also in the Forces; and thirdly, because war-time recruitment for trade unions was, of course, confined to those in civilian occupations. Nevertheless, though an unknown factor, the number of trade unionists in the Forces is by no means small.

[1] This and the following figures of trade union members include, however, a number of Irish and foreign trade union members, while the population figures relate to Great Britain only. But the error resulting from this factor is in all cases small.

For the sake of argument, two extreme cases might be considered. Supposing, first, that the number of trade unionists—*i.e.*, about 8·1 million in June 1944—were distributed in equal proportions between the civilian workers in round numbers, seventeen million and the 4,969,000 soldiers, sailors and airmen, then the trade union density among all workers would amount to approximately 37 per cent. In the second case—*i.e.*, if the armed forces had no union members at all—the density among the civilian workers would have reached the high figure of about 48 per cent. The truth obviously lies somewhere in between, and it seems safe to say that the trade union density in June 1944 was above 40 per cent. of all civilian wage- and salary-earners.

CHAPTER VI

TASKS

TRADE UNIONS began as defensive organisations of workers against the hard conditions of employment imposed on them by their employers. For a long time they were concerned mainly with improving the pay and other conditions of their work, but gradually they were moved by deeper aspirations. The tasks they set themselves deserve detailed consideration, and will be examined in the chapters which follow. Before examining them in detail, however, it will be worth while making a brief survey of their general aims and of the new problems and conflicts which ensued.

(a) SECURITY OF EMPLOYMENT

Though the three main types of trade union, whose evolution we have already followed, faced similar tasks, each approached them in its own special way. This can be seen most clearly in the oldest and hardest problem of organised labour—that of achieving security of employment.

It is easy to understand why the unions should of all their activities concentrate on the fundamental two-fold task of ensuring regular employment for their members and preventing the employers from replacing them with surplus, unemployed, or casual labour. The very existence of the unions depended on the solution of this problem, for no

93

strike could ever succeed if the employer could replace the strikers with unorganised labour.

It is not in Britain alone, of course, that the efforts made to achieve security of employment had a great influence on the political development of the Labour movement. Some investigators consider that the influx of foreign workers into England and the United States of America, with its attendant dangers to native employment, strongly accentuated the national consciousness of the workers of these countries and retarded their developing class consciousness; this was one of the chief reasons why "the working-class movements of those two countries have not emerged from their trade-unionist framework".[1]

To achieve security of employment the craft unions tried hard to make their members indispensable in their own particular job, and used various methods to keep down the supply of craftsmen.[2]

The most important of these were making long-term apprenticeship an essential condition of employment and excluding women and young persons from trade union membership. Another was restricting the total output per unit of working time and yet another allowing craftsmen to work only at their own specialised jobs. Different unions adopted the methods best suited to their own type of labour.

It is not, of course, only for the craft unions that security of employment is of vital concern; it is no less so for the general and industrial unions. But the latter try to ensure it by the "closed-shop" principle. Catering for workers engaged in a multitude of industries, the general unions must, in their demand for a "closed shop", co-ordinate their action with a number of other unions serving the same industries and trades.

Industrial unions are in a different position: they seek to confront the employer or his association with a united force embracing both the manual and managerial, brain or technical workers of the industry.

The "closed-shop" policy is a child of the most violent

[1] B. Borochov, "The National Question and the Class Struggle", 1905 (in Russian), republished in English, Chicago, 1935, p. 36. We believe that Borochov exaggerated the influence of the influx of foreign workers in the Labour movement of this country, but he is certainly right as far as the U.S.A. are concerned.

[2] One of the methods adopted, and indeed still in practice, was the attempt of many unions to limit the number of apprentices to one for every three journeymen.

period of industrial conflict at times and in countries where capitalists used black-legs and armed force for strike-breaking and the workers refused to work side by side with men who refused to play their part in the unions' struggle for justice, by joining unions. But that policy contradicts the main principles of modern trade unionism, which claims that the union is a voluntary organisation, and objects to its members being forced into membership, either by legal prescription or by brute force.

The unions rightly insist that if some workers choose to remain outside the organisation they must accept in the factories the arrangements made between the unions and the employers. There is nothing arbitrary in that demand, for the unorganised workers have no right to expect a premium for their refusal to join the unions.

It is interesting that in Soviet Russia, after considerable discussion, the unions remained voluntary organisations, and that before the outbreak of the war about 16 per cent. of the Soviet wage- and salary-earners were non-union members.

It is evident that in a democratic State, where the freedom of the individual and of his association are protected by law, where the use of brute force in industrial conflicts is a punishable offence, and where a highly developed practice of conciliation and arbitration exists, there is not much need, and little justification, for the unions employing a "closed-shop" policy. The unions are right in aiming and working hard for a 100 per cent. membership—but they should be able to achieve it by proper organisation and education policy, co-ordinated with the other branches of the movement.

Clearly the problem of security of employment has undergone a great change in our generation: there should be less room in modern democratic industrial society, with a reasonable degree of social security, for the old restrictive practices of the craft unions, nor can "closed-shop" practices be justified for ever. The time is past when these could ensure security of employment and when the training of labour could be left to the mercy of individual employers, even in agreement with craft unions.

The problem of security of employment is, thus, transforming itself under our eyes into the problem of full employment, which cannot remain a task of separate groups of workers or employers. It is becoming generally one of the main objects of State economic policy, and was a vital part of the policy on which the electors returned the present British Labour Government to power.

(b) Collective Bargaining and Wages

The second great aim of trade unions has been to increase and safeguard wages through individual or collective agreements. The need to do so is due to the fact that even in a monopolist capitalist society the distribution of income is effected largely through the market-price mechanism, and human labour remains one of the main marketable commodities. The mechanism being there already, trade unions simply tried to improve it by collective bargaining and to swing it in favour of the wage- and salary-earners.

In collective agreements the conditions under which an individual member of a trade union sells his labour to employers have been the subject of discussion and consent with his fellow-workers in the appropriate trade union, and this collective bargaining has led to vast improvements in the wages and other conditions secured from employers.

The formation and the rapid growth of employers' associations and federations in each industry and nationally (Federation of British Industries), together with their agreement upon common policies regarding conditions of labour and employment, forced the trade unions to develop closer co-ordination and collaboration.

To reinforce their demands, trade unions have occasionally to revert to the method of the strike, withholding labour from the employers and from industry, especially at times when increased demand for it offered the workers an opportunity to improve their wages or other conditions. The use of the strike has, however, undergone great changes during the twentieth century, and these will be examined in a later chapter.

(c) Conditions of Work

As the unions grew in strength, so did the number of spheres in which collective agreements regulated conditions of work: they embraced the problems of shorter hours, improvement of hygiene in factories, introduction of safeguards against accidents, holidays with pay and others. The unions did not, however, seek better conditions only through direct negotiations with employers. They pressed hard, and often successfully, for State regulation of conditions, and that not only on the national level, but also internationally. The latter action was carried out from 1919 onwards through the International Labour Organisation.

During the present century State intervention in regulating and improving labour conditions has increased, especially with regard to health and safety. In this sphere, therefore, trade unions will inevitably rely in future as much on State action as on collective bargaining, and will take increasing initiative in advocating the necessary improvements by legislation and administrative action.

(d) LEGAL ASSISTANCE

Another field in which trade union action has grown is in rendering assistance to individual workers in any disputes they may have with employers, especially as regards wages, conditions of work, termination of contracts, etc. Even the most complete collective agreement is little more than a general framework—like a legal enactment leaving much room for different interpretations in individual cases. The individual worker is in a weaker position than his employer unless he has the assistance of a "poor man's lawyer" who can help him to formulate his claim, to advise him on the best way to put it forward, to write or talk to the employer on his behalf, and, if need be, to take his case up in a law court or before any other statutory tribunal. All these services are being provided for members by union officials or their legal representatives.

(e) SOCIAL SECURITY

Besides looking after their members whilst in employment, the unions had to face the problem of helping those who had lost their jobs through illness, accident, old age or other causes. This grave and many-sided problem had been tackled in this country by voluntary mutual and co-operative effort long before the State took any interest in social security.

Not all the needs of the wage-earner as such are covered by trade union activities. While these help to improve his working conditions and to get a better reward for his labour, the wage-earner has to spend what he earns on goods and services, and here lies the importance of the consumer's Co-operative movement. Together with the protection which trade unions afford the workers in their wage-earning capacity comes the further benefit afforded them as consumers through Co-operative Societies. In this country however, the consumers' Co-operative movement has concentrated mainly on the supply of goods,

97

leaving to the Friendly Societies such services as popular insurance.

The unions had therefore to set up and develop their own working-class mutual aid institutions, Friendly Societies, mutual loan clubs and other agencies for insurance and self-help. These developed as special branches of trade union organisation.

In its turn, the State has started to take increasing interest in social insurance and to assume direct responsibility for supporting men who were unable to work because of illness, accidents, old age or other causes. So long as private insurance companies and Friendly Societies remain channels for insurance services, the mutual aid branches of the unions will continue their work, and they will properly claim their share in the State's insurance operations; they already act as the recognised medium for operating the National Health Insurance services. The fact deserves notice that the benefit departments and societies established by the trade unions made little headway compared with other types of approved societies.[1]

In 1934 Sir Walter Citrine summarised the position as follows:

"It is not generally realised in the trade union and labour movement that only 9 per cent. of the insured population owe allegiance to trade union approved societies, although at least 20 per cent. are members of the trade unions on their industrial side, and that taking into account the members

[1] The relative strength of the various types of societies according to the last valuation was as follows:

CLASSIFICATION OF MEMBERSHIP BY TYPE OF SOCIETY.

Group.	No. of Valuation Membership (1,000's).		
	Men.	Women.	Total.
1. Friendly Societies with branches .	2,232	774	3,006
2. Friendly Societies without branches	3,467	1,670	5,137
3. Industrial Associations and Collecting Societies	5,120	3,344	8,464
4. Trade unions	1,184	289	1,473
5. Employers' Provided Funds . .	54	34	88
Total	12,057	6,111	18,168

of the families who are insured, as well as the trade unionists themselves, we should have a minimum membership of at least 30 per cent. of the insured population".[1]

Still more serious is the fact that the membership of the trade union approved societies decreased further, at least up to the outbreak of war, both absolutely and in proportion to the total insurable population. The last National Health Insurance valuation enumerates 18,168,000 members of societies of any kind, including only 1,437,000 members of trade union societies—that is, less than 8 per cent.—as compared with the 9 per cent. to which Sir Walter referred in 1934.

It is evident that trade union activities in this sphere must be transformed by the introduction of over-all social insurance, which will be one of the urgent tasks of the Labour Government.

(f) EDUCATION

Important needs of the workers in the field of education and in training of trade union personnel are hardly touched by the unions through the formation of recreational clubs and other methods; they are mainly met in a variety of educational facilities offered by the workers' adult education bodies. These activities, which could become invaluable assets to the political work and the effective strength of the unions, will be surveyed in a special chapter.

(g) POLITICAL TASKS

By the end of last century leaders of the trade union movement in this country had realised that any fundamental improvement in the conditions of the workers required the active support of Parliament. Through their political activities trade unions helped to create the Labour Party and have done much to educate the masses in the practical application of Labour democracy. Trade unions may well become one of the main instruments for a change from Capitalism to planned democratic Socialism if they equip themselves to act as a united and co-ordinated labour force. Their political activities will be dealt with in a special chapter.

To recapitulate, the main tasks of trade unions are at present these: (1) to secure employment for their members, (2) to safe-

[1] Sir Walter Citrine in introduction to a pamphlet: "Twelve Good Reasons Why All Trade Unionists Should be Members of Trade Union Approved Societies", published in 1934.

guard and increase remuneration and to improve working conditions through individual and collective agreements, (3) to be the medium of mutual aid, benefit and insurance services, (4) to improve the educational level and the professional standards of their members, and (5) to serve as a practical school for industrial labour democracy.

The foregoing picture suggests that is not easy to find any simple reason why a man or a woman joins a trade union; the motives here, as in most human acts, are mingled, but outstanding among them are surely these:

Workers join to get security of employment; to protect their wages and conditions; because the union is a club to which their friends "belong"; to get a general feeling of protection apart from the question of wages; in some cases as a disinterested sign of solidarity with the whole of the working classes; to qualify for a job in "closed shops"; for insurance and other benefits; in a moment of enthusiasm inspired by an eloquent organiser.[1]

Yet generally when a man joins his union he feels himself connected with a voluntary organisation, and does not take his obligations too seriously, especially as far as the national trade union body is concerned; the relationship which he does feel strongly is that with his mates in the place he works.

The trade unionist is more aware of his rights than of his obligations, which he accepts collectively through his national union. The unions might enable members to realise better the relation between their rights and duties. That is at present the most important task for the unions which would increase both the interest of the ordinary member in union affairs and their authority to act on his behalf.

[1] Compare P.E.P., *Planning*, No. 249, May 10th, 1946.

PART TWO

ACTIVITIES

CHAPTER VII

LABOUR DISPUTES

(a) INTRODUCTION

A SPECIAL chapter on labour disputes needs no apology in a book on trade unionism. Historically, trade unions and strikes are the twin offspring of the same industrial developments. Many unions came into being or revealed their possibilities in the course of an open labour conflict; on the other hand, many strikes were successful, or even possible, only because there existed in the trade union a strongly organised body of men. In the early nineteenth century some local trade clubs had already been established, it is true, for the express purpose of collective bargaining and for that purpose alone (see Chapter VIII). Such exceptions only confirm the general rule, however, that the main task of early trade unionism was to defend the interests of the workers and to do so, if necessary, in open battle.[1]

How essential an element in trade unionism is the power to strike has recently been demonstrated further, if indirectly, by the political technique of totalitarianism, particularly as practised in Hitlerite Germany. Even an undemocratic State apparatus can never quite suppress trade unionism, as long as the workers are not prevented from standing together in the factories in defence of their own interests, and thus maintaining latent possibilities of collective action. The death-blow to German trade unionism was completed only when the Nazis made it impossible for the workers to have recourse to the strike.

---

[1] It must not be overlooked that the cause of many strikes, especially before the First World War, was the fight for trade union recognition or sympathetic action. This meant that strikers were trying to get something not necessarily or primarily for themselves, but for the whole working class (see Appendix X), and the present smooth working of collective bargaining owes a good deal to this militant action.

The German Labour Front, largely because of its anti-strike attitude, was never a trade union.

It can, of course, be claimed that the strike weapon has been very sparingly used by British labour in recent years. Indeed, collective bargaining, arbitration and conciliation are largely designed to make unnecessary the loss and suffering that strikes and lock-outs bring. The developments of the last half-century —the period in which collective bargaining has played any important part in this country—will be considered briefly a little farther on, so as to bring out the extent to which disputes have really given way to collective bargaining during those fluctuating years. But even without any special historical survey it is pretty clear that labour disputes, especially those of any large scale, have been relatively rare since the General Strike of 1926. Of the strikes which did take place, during the second part of this period in particular, a high proportion was wholly without the official sanction of the unions.[1] This was especially true during the war, when the unions were very much concerned to abide by "peaceful" methods.

That in no way diminishes the importance of the strike weapon to the very existence of free trade unionism, however completely it is held in reserve in special circumstances. Trade union leaders very properly rejected any suggestion of renouncing the right to strike for the duration of the war, willing though they were to use it as sparingly as possible.

Trade unions have, of course, been doing their utmost to replace direct strike action by collective bargaining, but only on condition of retaining the right to strike as a last resort. That right is a condition of a union being able to bargain effectively.

Moreover, the strike weapon can become much more useful to the workers if their unions tend to rely too much on official negotiation and "peaceful" bargaining. It may easily happen that the more complicated and unwieldy the apparatus of the union, the less sensitive it will be to the wishes of its members, and the greater the danger of *unnecessary* compromises at the conference table. In such conditions an "unofficial" strike may often serve as a needed warning. "Unofficial" strikes are a sort of symptom of hidden disease, and it would be wise for trade union leadership to pay due heed to such symptoms of unrest and eliminate their causes by effective, timely action.

[1] See Appendix XVII, listing the important unofficial strikes in 1940–1946.

(b) STRATEGY

In the attitude of trade unions towards strikes there are two possible weaknesses. On the one hand, the weapon may be viewed romantically, as something to be used for its own sake in the class struggle; on the other, the more peaceful methods may mean only complacence in cases where much better results would come by so-called "direct action". If the one errs on the side of romanticism, then the other savours of fatalism and appeasement. To find the right middle course between these two approaches is the secret of what may be called strike strategy.

It is somewhat strange, considering how important the strike weapon is, that so little attention has been paid to the theory of stoppages and to the relation between trade union organisation and strike strategy; it should be obvious that success in strikes must depend largely on the strength of the organisation of the unions involved, just as, inversely, the bargaining power of the unions is in direct ratio to their ability to organise a successful strike. About actual strikes in the past a good deal has been written, but so far there has been very little theoretical study of trade disputes. A labour Clausewitz, able to treat this subject and analyse in sufficient detail the strategic and tactical conditions of successful striking, if with us, is still unpublished. For our immediate purposes, therefore, we must content ourselves with a brief survey of British strike movements of the last half-century, in the light of the statistics available. Fortunately, the Ministry of Labour and its predecessors have issued since 1890 a fairly detailed yearly summary of strikes and lock-outs in this country.

(c) STRIKE MOVEMENTS 1890–1945

As we will see in Chapter VIII, collective bargaining has long played an important part in certain industries where trade unionism was traditionally strong. Yet even in these, particularly in mining, the new method was by no means firmly enough established to make strikes unnecessary or rare. More significant still was the fact that towards the end of last century quite new strata of the British working class—many who had not yet been attached to the trade union movement—now joined up, and waged some fierce industrial fights.

The year 1889 had seen the London Dock Strike, a widespread stoppage in an industry with a majority of unskilled or

103

semi-skilled labourers mostly living in conditions of dire distress. That great strike, indeed, marks the end of a period; from that time onward trade unionism ceased in effect to be a monopoly of craftsmen; greater numbers of workpeople came within the influence of trade union organisation; general labour unions came into being and developed strength; the "New Unionism" was born.

From the point of view of strike action, the period following the birth of "New Unionism" may conveniently be divided into seven main sub-periods:—

(1) The first of these, roughly the 1890's, during which strike movements became widespread.

(2) On the contrary, they greatly diminished in the first six years of the twentieth century—1900–1905—largely owing to legal impediments following the "Taff Vale" judgment.

(3) The Trade Union Act of 1905, restoring the former legal conditions, a new wave of strikes marked the years 1905–1913.

(4) The First World War had a twofold effect. On the one hand, conditions of full employment enabled the workers to defend their interests through their unions; on the other hand, a genuine patriotic feeling militated against large-scale strikes, at least until 1917.

(5) With the aftermath of the war the workers' grievances brought a great recrudescence of strikes. 1918–1926 were the really "militant" years of the British working-class movement—the period of large-scale struggle for higher wages as well as more general changes in the industrial framework.

(6) For the whole period from 1927 to the outbreak of the Second World War (and later) there were few serious strikes. The main immediate causes were the failure of the General Strike of 1926, the aftermath of the Trade Union Act of 1927, the huge economic slumps during part of that period and the general feeling of tiredness following the eruptions of 1918–1926. At the same time the arrangements for collective bargaining which were almost completed during this period had a further steadying influence.

(7) During the Second World War essentially the same influences were at work as during the first, but the volume of strikes was less.

In successive periods during the half-century following 1890 the average yearly number of workers involved in strikes is as follows:—[1]

Average annual number during each period of : —

	Disputes.	Workers involved (1,000's).	Workers per dispute.	Working days lost per dispute by one worker.
1890–1899	818	303	370	34
1900–1905	472	155	329	18
1906–1913 [2]	714	455	637	18
1914–1917	727	511	704	10
1918–1926 [3]	859	1,354	1,580	28
1927–1938	534	305	571	10
1939–1943	1,240	402	324	10
1944–1945	2,238	678	305	5

[2] Without National Coal Dispute of 1912.
[3] Without General Strike of 1926.

A table so condensed permits misleading interpretations, for within each of these periods which vary from three to eleven years in duration there were great annual fluctuations in the volume of strikes. It may, however, serve for the study of certain general trends, while the fuller table in Appendix IX may be consulted for year-to-year fluctuations. In two cases—the years of the great nation-wide conflicts of 1912 and 1926—the figures were left out of the tables simply because their inclusion would have so influenced the averages as to distort their real value for purposes of comparison.

(d) NUMBER OF WORKERS CONCERNED

The actual number of workers involved seems a useful yard-stick for measuring and comparing the extent of strike action in different years or periods. In the eighteen-nineties the annual figures usually fluctuated between 200,000 and 400,000, though in the exceptional year, 1893, half a million workers were involved in strikes or lock-outs. The average annual figure of 303,000 throughout the nineties is probably much higher than in any comparable earlier period. Though that figure does not seem high by present standards, the enormous increase in the meantime of the total number of industrial workers has to be

[1] See Appendix IX, pp. 250–51.

remembered. The eighteen-nineties saw the beginnings of the really large-scale strike movements that became common much later.

The disastrous effects on the movement of an adverse political or judicial decision are reflected in the strike figures for the first five years of this century. At that time, of course, economic conditions did not particularly favour militant working-class action. Yet there is little doubt that the main reason for the drop in the average annual number of strikers to 155,000 (little more than half the average for the nineties) was the "Taff Vale" judgment, which made any kind of union support of strike activities very difficult indeed. In not one of these five years did the number of strikers reach the *average* for the eighteen-nineties, and in two of them it fell below 100,000—a low record never reached before or after in the whole period for which statistics are available.

From 1906 onwards there was a new wave of strikes. From that year until 1913 the average number of workers involved was 455,000 a year—three times that for the preceding period. Even this high average does not tell the whole story, for in the first three years strike actions were on a modest scale, increasing very steeply during the boom just before the outbreak of war. In 1911 the figure approached 1,000,000; in 1912—if we *include* the National Coal Dispute—nearly 1,500,000, as compared with two-thirds of a million in 1913.

At the outbreak of war in 1914 the number was at first much lower. For each of the years 1914 and 1915 it was just below 450,000, and for 1916 only 250,000. As the war went on trade union leaders began to lose much of their influence among certain sections of workers, particularly the shipbuilders and engineers, largely owing to the combined effects of the conscription laws in Britain, the Russian Revolution and the propaganda for a "negotiated peace". In a few short, but often successful, strikes the new shop stewards' movement assumed leadership. Strikes and lock-outs affected in 1917 872,000 workers—a higher figure than for any single previous year with the exception of 1911 and, if the National Coal Dispute is included, of 1912. For the war years, 1914–1917, the annual average was no less than 511,000, or much more than for any of the earlier periods.

The strike movements following the close of the war in 1918 were colossal. During the war itself most of the workers had voluntarily, and in the national interest, forgone their right to strike, despite the favourable conditions offered by the state of full employment. But after the war their pent-up resentment found expression in huge stoppages of work in the mines, shipyards, textile and engineering works, transport and other industries. In each of the years 1918 1921 well over a million workers were involved, the 1919 figure exceeding 2½ millions.

From 1922 to 1925 the annual number fluctuated around the half million; but in 1926 heights unknown before were reached, between two and four million workers becoming involved in strikes, apart from the General Strike.

The annual average for the period 1918–1926 works out at the enormous figure of 1,354,000, and the numbers give only a faint idea of the extent and intensity of the unrest.

The year 1926 was a turning point of great importance in the development of the industrial workers' movement of this country. The failure of the General Strike, followed up by the new discriminatory legislation of the Trade Disputes and Trade Unions Act of 1927, was a great blow to their hopes. For the rest of the inter-war period the rank and file were too tired from earlier bitter conflicts to feel like running the risk of more, and union officials were wary of losing funds in further strikes. In the years 1927, 1928 and 1933 and 1934, the numbers involved in stoppages were little over 100,000. Yet the numbers rose occasionally even, for example, in the boom years of 1929 and 1937, in each of which the total number exceeded half a million. That, it will be recalled, is modest compared with the immediate post-war years. For the whole period 1927–1938 the average annual number was 305,000—down practically to the level of the nineties.

In the Second World War workers' discipline was undoubtedly much better than during the first, and strikes shorter and more spontaneous. In spite of the greater total number of workers in industry, by the time of the Second World War we find that 402,000, the average annual number of strikers for the years 1939–1943, is well below the 511,000, the average for the years 1914–1917. In the earlier part of the second war strikers were very rare in the manufacturing industries and on no alarming scale, even in mining. Since 1940, however, they have been increasing, the number in 1943 being nearly twice that of 1940, and in the early half of 1944, especially the months preceding D-Day, the increase became serious, affecting mining most, but other industries as well.

(e) Number of Disputes

It is a significant fact that 1926, the year of the General Strike, which involved an unprecedentedly large number of workers, had almost the lowest number of stoppages occurring within its half-century period. In that year the number of individual trade disputes ending in a strike or a lock-out was as low as 323—lower, that is to say, than in any year preceding it, since 1890 or in any year thereafter, except the two years of depression just after the General Strike, up to 1944. The seeming contradiction is explained by the high average number of workers involved per stoppage—over 8,000, in fact, or many times that of any other single year under review.

The year 1926 was, of course, exceptional. For all that, it seems characteristic of British strikes that in the years involving the highest number of workers the actual number of strikes is smaller, but they are on a much wider scale. On the other hand, in the great number of scattered minor strikes occurring in other years the total number of strikes involved was very small. To this rule, of course, there were exceptions, but it is borne out, by and large, by strike statistics.

(f) Average Number of Workers per Dispute

In the eighteen-nineties the number of workers involved per dispute in an average year was 370. The greatest exception was in 1893, with its nearly 900 workers per dispute; as might be expected, the total number of strikers that year was far above the eighteen-nineties average.

Between 1900 and 1905, when the "Taff Vale" decision put difficulties in the way, the numbers on strike per dispute were slightly less than in the nineties, and the average for the period was 329.

From 1906 to 1913, on the other hand, there was a general increase both in the total number of workers on strike and in the number involved in individual disputes, the latter reaching an average of 637, or nearly twice that of the preceding period. In 1911—that peak year of strike activity—there was for the first time an average of over 1,000 people per stoppage.

The average figure for the war years, 1914–1917, was 704. It went much below that during the first three years of war, but in 1917 rose again to over 1,000 per dispute.

Great working-class militancy, reflected in strike activity at its highest, marked the years 1918–1926, the number of workers
108

per dispute becoming very high, particularly in the main strike years, 1918–1921, as well, of course, as in 1926. For this sub-period the average rose to 1,580.

The next period was one of gradual decrease—571 average—in the years 1927–1938. In the earlier part the annual average was sometimes much higher than that, but from 1932 onwards *always* well below. The strikes of the years preceding the Second World War were the decisions generally of small groups of workers, and their efforts were rarely co-ordinated.

That general tendency was still more marked, of course, during the war itself. During each of the war years the number of individual stoppages was high—higher, indeed, in 1943 than in any year between 1890 and 1942. It is also worthy of note that very few of these disputes had the support of the trade union organisations, for these were very properly using their influence to try to settle any dispute with as little disturbance to the war effort as possible. The number of workers involved in those strikes was therefore kept quite low, the average of 324 for the 1939–1943 period being lower than for any of the earlier under review.

If we were to draw two curves, one showing the total number of all workers involved and the other those in each individual stoppage, we should find the two curves running roughly parallel for the whole period 1890–1943.

(g) LENGTH OF STRIKES

The preceding paragraphs have shown certain general features governing the incidence of stoppages. It is hardly possible to find comparable principles governing their average length, for that obviously depends on many differing factors. The statistical tables show that the number of days lost per dispute per man varies greatly from year to year. On the whole, there is little consistency if the seven sub-periods (on p. 105) are compared one with another. After making all allowance for such differences, we can nevertheless venture these two deductions.

(1) In the years following 1926, and particularly after 1932, the average length of stoppages was very short. Settlement was usually reached after a few days—ten on an average for the whole period 1927–1943, a much shorter duration than in any preceding peace-time period.

(2) During the two wars trade disputes were always

settled with extraordinary speed, greater in the Second than in the First World War, when the average duration of stoppages was never less than five days a year, as compared with three between 1939 and 1943, evidence of the greater power of the unions.

(h) Causes of Strikes

Since 1890 wage disputes have been, and in most years still remain, the most important single cause of cessation of work—more important than general working arrangements, employment of certain kinds of worker, hours of labour, or even the recognition of a trade union.[1]

Latterly, however, the emphasis on wage questions has tended to give way to other causes. Whereas wage disputes accounted for over half of all stoppages in twenty-eight of the thirty-five years between 1890 and 1925, in the next eighteen years, 1926–1943, that figure was reached only in six years. This relative decline in the importance of wage disputes due to stoppages is the more significant if the absolute decline in the total number of strikers is also remembered. In recent years it is clear that wage problems are settled more often than ever before by negotiation.

Among causes of disputes and strikes more prevalent to-day are the employment of certain types of worker, usually non-members of unions, and unsatisfactory administrative personnel. To these are due recently a relatively larger number of strikes than in the earlier periods reviewed—they are now the second largest among the causes of work stoppage. "General working arrangements", unimportant in this connection between 1912 and 1921, usually take third place to-day. Finally comes the greater frequency of "sympathetic strike action". Thus, long hours of labour and the general question of trade union recognition have lost their relative importance as occasions for striking—a proof of the progress due to collective agreements and negotiation machinery.

(i) Methods of Settlement[2]

Conciliation and arbitration have proved excellent preventives of official labour disputes, often achieving the more positive aim of getting, without stoppage, the improved conditions the workers' demand. But during the last decade only about

[1] See Appendix X, pp. 252–53.
[2] See Appendix XI, pp. 253–54.

10 per cent. of all disputes have been definitely settled by the approved conciliation and arbitration methods. One obvious reason for this is that the great majority of strikes during this period have been "unofficial". The trade unions were no parties to them, and the official apparatus for the settlement of the disputes was therefore not invoked. The usual method of settlement would appear to have been direct negotiations between the workers, often represented by an *ad hoc* committee elected on the spot, and the employers' representatives. Indeed, most strikes of recent years have been settled that way, though it is surprising that a large percentage of disputes have ended by the workers returning on the employers' terms, without any negotiations taking place.

It must be remembered, when considering the statistics of the last decade, that they do not give the proportion of unofficial strikes, and the fact has an important bearing on figures purporting to show different methods of settlement and their results. Nor is there any need to draw too pessimistic conclusions from these figures, for the workers are often told by their unions during an unofficial strike to restart work. That does not necessarily imply a 100 per cent. defeat for them, for sometimes the employers were ready to accept a compromise solution. The very prevalence of that method of settlement does, however, emphasise again the increasing complexity of the disputes of recent years.

(*j*) Industries Involved

Of the manual workers in this country less than one-fifteenth have been employed in the mining industry during the last few decades; but the table recording the British strike movements of the last fifty-five years shows that in over half (twenty-eight) of these years *the number of strikers in the mining industry was higher than in all other industries in the United Kingdom put together*.

In yet another thirteen years of this period the miners, although not actually forming a majority of all strikers, still held the first place among the seven industrial groups shown in the table, and the second place in all but one of the remaining eleven years. The lowest number of strikers ever recorded per annum in the mining industry was 45,000 in 1905—a year when strikes in every trade were few—but for every other industry in our table except mining 45,000 would be a comparatively high figure.

Strike action among the miners reached its peak in the years just before, during, and just after the last war. It was comparatively low in the late twenties—*i.e.*, after the 1926 General Strike—and also during the early thirties. But every year since 1935 over 200,000 miners, on an average, were again involved in disputes.

Although over the whole range of British industry the total number of strikers during each succeeding war year has so far been well below the number in the corresponding periods of the 1914–1918 war, again this cannot be said of the mining industry. The practical influence of miners' strikes on the 1939–1945 war effort has often been exaggerated : the fact is that union officials generally managed either to localise the strikes or to get settlement by conciliation fairly quickly. Indeed, according to Professor Bowley, the country's total loss of coal through strikes has been negligible.

What the vast number of strikers in the mines during the last half-century so eloquently proves is the unhealthy, unhappy and highly dangerous conditions of this key British industry.

No conclusions can be drawn from our tables as to any correlation of strike action between different industries. In some years strikes in all industries were either uniformly many or uniformly few; but it has happened at least as often that there would be few or no strikes in, say, the metal industries, while the transport workers were continually striking.

(k) Results

Deductions about strikes are still a risky business. The value of the statistics concerning the results of trade disputes is largely obscured by the high percentage of "compromise disputes", for it is often difficult to say whether the compromise was more in favour of the workers or the employers.[1] Even so, it is a fact that the annual number of disputes which ended in a clear victory for the employers was larger in most years than the number of clear victories for the workers. This is true for the whole period under review, and it is particularly true of the time between the General Strike and the outbreak of war. For war-time itself no statistical accounts are available. Only in the two years 1931 and 1935 out of the fourteen years from 1926 to 1939 were more disputes clearly victories for the workers than for the employers. In all other recent years the reverse was true, and in 1937, 1938 and 1939—the last for which statistics

[1] See Appendix XIII, p. 256.

are available—the employers had more clear victories than the workers' victories and compromise cases taken together. One must, however, remember our remarks on p. 111 and not draw pessimistic conclusions from those figures.

our remarks on p. 111

CHAPTER VIII

COLLECTIVE BARGAINING

(a) THE TERM

THE TERM "collective bargaining", used to describe the procedure whereby employers must reach agreement about wage rates and basic conditions of labour with trade unions instead of with individual workers, was originally brought into the vocabulary of English scientific and political discussion by Beatrice Webb. It first appeared in her work on the Co-operative movement, published in 1891, at a time when this particular form of wage agreement would not have struck the casual observer as very significant. In the fifty-five years which have passed since that period "collective bargaining" has grown into a national institution, and the expression is used as a matter of course by every trade unionist and employer. It is a striking proof of Mrs Webb's prophetic vision that she should have noticed the trend of this new social phenomenon at such an early stage; and it is no less evidence of her outstanding literary ability that she coined a term which at once distinguishes this new type of negotiation from the old system of "individual" bargaining between worker and employer, and from earlier manifestations of trade unionism when strikes and lock-outs took the place of any organised negotiations.

The weaknesses of "individual" wage negotiations are obvious. From the purely legal point of view it may appear "fair" that employers and employees should meet as equals in bargaining for the use of the employees' labour power; economically, however, the employer is the "master"—and he is always stronger than his opposite number, the worker. The reason for this supremacy of the employer was the existence of a great mass of unemployed workers, often seeking employment on any terms.

Within the framework of capitalist society there would appear to be only one of two ways of remedying that "endemic" disease; through the State or through the trade unions. As is well known, even the liberal, *laissez-faire* Governments of the early nineteenth century found it necessary to prevent gross exploitation of labour, and did so especially through the Factory Acts; intervention, however, was confined throughout the nineteenth century to general labour conditions and to working hours, particularly of women and children. All through these years the State steadfastly refused to prescribe minimum wage rates. A partial reversal of that attitude began with the Trade Boards Act of 1909, but even to-day statutory regulation of wages, hours and working conditions (which will be described later in this chapter) play a relatively modest part in industrial relations. To secure improvement of wages, intervention has always been in the main, as it still is, by the workers' own organisations, the trade unions.

The idea of negotiating with the employers for better wages and working conditions appealed to workers from the quite early stages of industrial development; and collective agreements on a local basis can be found, especially in the printing trade, as early as the beginning of the nineteenth century, and even before. There were, however, powerful influences that long prevented the spread of this new industrial method. The most obvious obstacle was the reluctance of employers to "recognise" trade unions. At times the employers' objections found strong support in provisions which either rendered illegal all industrial combinations—the case until 1824—or at least kept within the narrowest limits the legal activities of the unions even in the industrial field, this particularly from 1825 to 1871. A natural result of that situation was the reluctance of some trade unionists to sit at the same table with the enemies of their organisation; generally speaking, the possibility of that ordinary legal protection of wages and labour conditions that is taken for granted to-day had hardly entered mens' minds in the earlier part of the nineteenth century.

(b) HISTORY

The history of collective bargaining in Great Britain falls roughly into three main periods. During the first, which lasted up to the Trade Union Act of 1871, progress was slow. Then, most of the contracts were concluded between small trade clubs and individual employers or groups of local employers.

The second period was that of the half-century preceding the outbreak of the First World War, which may be considered as the incubation period of the system of collective bargaining.

By 1900 the practice had become widespread in the important textile, mining and metal industries. Railways and shipping, in which trade unionism had long had a particularly hard fight against strong employers' opposition, followed suit during the first few years of the present century. In this period a marked change occurred in the attitude of the State to the employer–employee relationship. A Royal Commission was appointed, by a coincidence, in the very year Mrs. Webb first used the term "collective bargaining", "to inquire into the relations between employers and workmen and to report whether legislation could be directed to remedy any faults disclosed"; and in 1896, following the recommendation of this Commission, Parliament passed the "Conciliation Act" that amended an earlier one and empowered a section of the Board of Trade (now the Ministry of Labour) to further voluntary agreements between the two parties in industry.

The Act of 1896 is particularly important in that the State thereby became, for the first time, an interested party in industrial relations. The powers in connection with trade disputes conferred upon the Board of Trade (or Ministry of Labour) by this Act are fourfold:—

(1) to enquire into the causes and circumstance of a dispute;

(2) to take steps towards bringing the parties together;

(3) to appoint on the application of the employers or the workers a conciliator or board of conciliation; and

(4) to appoint an arbitrator on the application of *both* parties.

The idea underlying this Act and later legislation was to make the State a mediator, and not a deciding force in the dispute. Then, as now, the trade union movement accepted the State's help to reach *voluntary* collective agreements, and it can be seen that the main provisions of the 1896 Act were calculated to strengthen the cause of collective bargaining. It is, however, an essential element of collective bargaining as it has developed in Britain that bargaining must be free and voluntary, and the trade union movement does not therefore normally accept *compulsory* arbitration by the State (*i.e.*, arbitration not applied for by both parties). Only as an exceptional measure was compulsory arbitration accepted by the T.U.C. during the two war-time periods of 1914–1918 and 1939–1945, and in both cases on the explicit understanding that the voluntary principle would be restored on the country's return to normal peace conditions.

It is worth mentioning that at the outbreak of war in 1914 much of the country's economy, including most staple industries, was covered by collective agreements. Furthermore, by far the greater part of the existing agreements were on a local basis, and whatever machinery had been developed for dealing regularly with trade disputes and collective agreements was extremely flexible, and varied as between different industries and localities. Considerable variety may be advantageous, but in the light of later experience it may be said that the system as it had developed up to 1914 erred on the side of too much flexibility.

The third period—that following the First World War—has been significant mainly for the following three developments:

(1) the system of collective bargaining has extended at an increasing pace until it now covers a very wide field;

(2) the machinery in different industries for joint negotiation, conciliation and arbitration has been strengthened, and has developed a kind of standard pattern that is adopted in many, though by no means all, cases, and

(3) national, or at least regional, agreements have become the rule, and district and local agreements have been considerably influenced and modified by the general agreements.

(c) EMPLOYERS' ORGANISATIONS

One factor that made possible the conclusion of collective agreements in most industries on a national, or at any rate on a wide regional, basis was the development throughout the country of a large network of employers' organisations. By definition, collective agreements may be concluded between groups of workers on the one side, and either individual employers or groups of employers on the other; but in the national collective agreements of to-day the employers are almost invariably represented by their organisations. A short consideration of the significance of this fact is therefore essential for an understanding of modern collective bargaining.

A large number of employers' associations, chambers of commerce, etc., exist merely to deal with commercial and trading questions, and have nothing to do with the subject here treated. Those whose business it is, either wholly or in part, to represent the interests of members with regard to the demands of their workers began to play a steadily increasing part in industrial relations in this country from the eighteen-eighties onwards; but their main development falls within the twentieth century. The fact that employers began to organise themselves later than the workers for the purposes of regulating industrial relations shows very clearly how strong was the position of individual employers as long as working conditions were settled by individual bargaining. It is essentially the conditions of the workers that made it necessary to form strong defence organisations; but except to counteract strong trade unions, employers found, as a rule, little need to combine in the field of employment.

Statistics about employers' organisations dealing with industrial questions are unfortunately even less complete than those of the trade unions. The total number of such organisations in the United Kingdom in 1936 was 1,820, including about 270 national federations and about 1,550 other organisations, the latter consisting mostly of local and regional branches of the national federations, though often with a measure of autonomy within the federation. By September 1943 the number of organisations of this kind had risen to about 1,900, and at that time the ratio between national and regional or local organisations was probably much the same as in 1936. Most associations embrace employers in one particular industry, either locally or nationally, but their constitutions, functions and the powers of their executives vary greatly from one organisation to another. Above them all is the central organisation, set up after the last war, known as the "Confederation of British Employers' Organisations", and which is recognised as the employer's counterpart of the T.U.C. Its membership consists of national federations of employers in industries which cover approximately 70 per cent. of the total industrial population of this country.

The numerical strength of the employers' organisations can be gathered from the fact that their members employ an aggregate of approximately eight million workers in the United Kingdom. Their numerical strength, in other words, is comparable to that of the trade unions themselves. In some respects, however, the significance of both employers' and trade union organisations, with respect to collective bargaining, is even greater than would appear from such numerical estimates. On the one hand, the terms and conditions laid down

117

in collective agreements apply invariably to all workers in the industry, whether they are union members or not; and, on the other hand, although only members of employers' organisations are bound by the terms of any such agreements, it is undoubtedly true that in the great majority of cases non-members also abide by the terms of the agreements. Thus, the terms of a collective agreement covering a certain industry are in fact, if not in law, a sort of legal enactment for all members of the industry, whether workers or employers.

The emergence of this large network of employers' organisations accounts to some extent for the growth of collective bargaining in the inter-war period.

(d) THE WHITLEY SCHEME

Another potent factor in the development of collective bargaining was the so-called Whitley Scheme of 1917, which provided for both extending and rendering more uniform the machinery of collective bargaining. Widening the field of collective bargaining led to a considerable overhauling of trade union machinery. By a curious coincidence the scheme owes its origin, indirectly, to the shop stewards' movement, which so vigorously challenged the official trade union machine during the First World War. The wave of strikes connected with the shop stewards' movement seemed to imperil the war effort, though very often shop stewards played a positive part in localising conflicts and preventing strikes. In the autumn of 1916 a Committee was set up to report on the relations between employers and employed, under the chairmanship of Mr. J. H. Whitley, M.P., then the Speaker of the House of Commons. The recommendations of this Committee, "the Whitley Scheme", were, in the main, adopted by the Government, and the Minister of Labour was charged with putting them into practice. Inspiring it was the need to find a better and less wasteful outlet than strikes for the deep discontent of the workers.

Probably the most important provision of the scheme was a recommendation with regard to the formation of Joint Industrial Councils. The Committee in general was in favour of the "continuance, as far as possible, of the present system whereby industries make their own agreements and settle their differences themselves". It further recommended "the establishment for each industry of an organisation, representative of employers and workpeople, to have as its object the regular

118

consideration of matters affecting the progress and well-being of the trade from the point of view of all those engaged in it, so far as this is consistent with the general interest of the community".

Obviously the scheme had to be very flexible and leave room for variations as between industries; but some unification was effected through the issue, by the Ministry of Labour, following the Whitley recommendations, of a model constitution for Joint Industrial Councils which has been adopted in a great number of industries.

"Regular consideration of wages, hours and working conditions in the industry as a whole" is declared as the first function of the Council, though other tasks to which the Council may devote its attention are also mentioned, as, for instance, consideration of measures for regularising production and employment, reconsideration of the existing machinery for conciliation, collection of statistics and encouragement of research, etc. Some Joint Industrial Councils also provide in their rules for the consideration of measures for securing the inclusion of all employers and workpeople in their respective associations. As a rule, the regulation of wage rates is the most important duty of the Councils, but some whose work is described as highly successful do not deal with wage questions at all, their settlement being effected less formally and on traditional lines; conciliation in trade disputes is another important function of the Councils.

The size of the Councils differs greatly from industry to industry, and may be from twelve to seventy members. The Model Constitution merely says that an equal number of representatives of trade unions and of associations of employers shall be appointed, that they shall retire annually, and that the chairmen and vice-chairmen shall also be drawn in equal numbers from both sides of the industry. The Model Constitution further provides that meetings shall take place at least once every three months, though many Councils do not in fact follow this recommendation.

In the first four years of the scheme, from 1918 to 1921, no fewer than seventy-seven Joint Industrial Councils were established, as well as a number of provisional Councils. The number has further risen, though more slowly, in later years: an Industrial Handbook, published by the Ministry of Labour and National Service in 1944, enumerates ninety-seven Joint Industrial Councils in addition to over 100 other industrial committees of a similar character, which, however, do not fully conform to the Whitley Scheme. The system is particularly well developed in National and Local Government employment (where a number of sub-committees exist in order to work out in practice the general recommendations of the central Councils for specific grades), as well as in public utilities, dock transport and, since the war, in the retail trade. In certain other industries, such as cotton and wool, shipbuilding and some branches of engineering, the absence of Joint Industrial Councils is due merely to the fact that trade unions and employers' organisations had found, usually before 1918, a satisfactory way of bargaining that obviated the need to set up any more formal organisation. One important industry in which collective bargaining has hardly started is banking. This is because the employers' associations have refused to recognise the two main unions—*i.e.*, the Bank Officers Guild and the Scottish Bankers Association, which have formed since January 1st, 1946, the National Union of Bank Employees.

Since 1918 there has been a definite tendency for collective bargaining to be conducted on a national scale, or at any rate, in larger regional units, especially for unskilled workers. Well organised trades usually have bargaining machinery of national scope: coal-mining, where the employers long refused to deal with the Mineworkers Federation, has been the great outstanding exception to the rule, but this was overcome by setting up in 1943 the Joint National Negotiating Committee for the Coal-mining Industry. "National" bargaining does not necessarily produce complete uniformity in labour conditions throughout the country. Grading systems, which take into account the conditions varying from region to region or locality (zones), have been used, for instance, in the engineering, building, railway and other industries.

There is still ample scope for either regional trade union officials or workshop organisations both to send in proposals for national negotiations and to see that existing national recommendations are properly carried out in their own particular localities. The Whitley recommendations actually provided for Workshop Committees between employers and trade unionists, on a basis similar to those of the Industrial Councils. In most industries this provision still remains a dead letter (the recently formed Joint Production Committees are not concerned with questions of industrial relations); but there are generally Whitley Committees at the workshop level in the Government services and in railway transport, as well as in many pottery and match-making establishments, and in electricity supply and municipal transport.

(e) CONCILIATION AND ARBITRATION

Recent developments in the machinery for collective bargaining would have been much less effective had they not been accompanied by a corresponding development in the machinery for conciliation and arbitration in industrial disputes. With a view to improving the earliest machinery, the Whitley Committee made certain recommendations which were embodied in the Industrial Courts Act of 1919. That Act, though envisaging peace-time conditions, remained in force during the war, even if some of its provisions were temporarily suspended. It was, however, in the spirit of the Whitley Committee to recommend that, as far as possible, the private arrangements for conciliation and arbitration in any industry should remain valid, and that arbitration should be attempted only if both parties agreed.

As to conciliation, the private arrangements of the industry are of far greater practical importance than the legal provisions of the Conciliation Act of 1896 and of the Industrial Courts Act of 1919, according to both of which the Minister may intervene to avoid conflicts. The main "private" agencies for conciliation are the Joint Industrial Councils themselves. In the constitution of several of the Whitley Councils it is stipulated that no stoppage of work shall take place until the matter in dispute has been considered by the Council, while in others disputes are often brought voluntarily before the Councils.

Some of the more specific reasons for the fall in labour disputes and strikes are discussed in Chapter VII, but it can be said without exaggeration that but for the development of the conciliation and arbitration machinery the number of strikes and lock-outs would certainly have been much larger.

There exist five different provisions for arbitration in industrial disputes:—

(1) Voluntary arrangements within an industry to refer disputes to the settlement of a special authority came into being in some cases as long ago as 1889. Provisions of this type exist in the Civil Service, in coal-mining, in railways and in other industries; as between these, arrangements differ in detail, but the personnel of the tribunals consists invariably

of an equal number of persons representing the two sides of the industry, and an independent chairman. The provisions for State arbitration under paragraphs 2 and 4 below must not be brought into play before all private arrangements for arbitration and conciliation have broken down.

(2) Provisions in the Conciliation Act of 1896 set up the system maintained by the Industrial Courts Act of 1919, by which each of the conflicting parties may refer its disputes to a single arbitrator appointed by the Minister.

(3) The main provision of the Industrial Courts Act of 1919 is, however, the setting up of a standing independent tribunal—the Industrial Court—to which the two conflicting parties can refer their dispute. The Court is neither subject to Government control nor does it form part of the judicial system of Great Britain. The members—some of them independent, some representing the trade union and some the employers' interests—are appointed by the Minister of Labour. This enactment gave effect to a strong recommendation of the Whitley Committee.

(4) The Industrial Courts Act gives a further choice to the two parties to refer their dispute, in unison, to the decision of an *ad hoc* Board of Arbitration consisting of an equal number of representatives of the two sides of the industry, plus an independent nominee of the Minister of Labour. The Board ceases to exist when it has given its award in the case for which it was appointed.

It should be noted that under all these provisions arbitration is not legally binding, but experience has shown that the awards of an Arbitration Court to which both parties have agreed to refer have every chance of being accepted by them.

(5) Finally, there is the National Arbitration Order of 1940, introducing the principle of compulsory arbitration during war-time, which is discussed in Chapter XII.

To complete the picture, it should be added that the Conciliation Act and Industrial Courts Act also give certain powers to the Minister to investigate trade disputes, and thereby indirectly to further their settlement.

In the last resort the purpose of arbitration and conciliation is, of course, to avoid open conflicts between the two parties in industry, and, as is shown in Chapter VII, strikes have in fact become fewer in recent years. The considerable number of strikes brought to an end every year by means of conciliation and arbitration is welcome proof of the value of these methods. It must at the same time be emphasised that neither collective bargaining, conciliation nor voluntary arbitration involve, in principle, a repudiation by the trade unions of the strike weapon. The results of the awards might, indeed, be very different in many cases if there were not in the background the possibility of using the strike weapon as a last resort. The tendency towards "national" bargaining certainly makes it more difficult for large strikes to break out, but at the same time makes it more probable that if strikes become unavoidable they will become "national" in scope.

The latest developments in the field of collective bargaining have naturally influenced the structure of the trade unions themselves. Collective bargaining, especially if carried out on a national scale, becomes a complicated technical affair: it necessarily raises the question of the relative importance of the permanent machinery of the central trade union organisation in settling its general policy and developing the technique to implement it.

Important as the rôle of shop stewards and local branch officials in the whole trade union world will remain, yet the trend already evident towards national agreements in collective bargaining has had, and increasingly must have, effects on the trade union structure itself. One consequence is that trade union officials are increasingly thinking in terms of legal contracts and business bargaining rather than of strikes and the class struggle. Whether one likes them or not, such tendencies are evidently not altogether avoidable within the present organisation, and it is most essential, therefore, to improve the direct contact between the mass of members and the leaders of the unions.

(f) STATE REGULATION OF WAGES

Finally some reference must be made to direct intervention by the State to counteract low wages. The principle that the State should protect workers from low wages in sweated industries, first accepted with the Trade Board Act of 1909, was extended—following the Whitley recommendation—to still more industries, especially in the second Trade Boards Act of 1918, and later in the Road Haulage Wages Act of 1938, the Agricultural Wages Act of 1940 and the Catering Wages Act of 1943. There are fifty-two Trade Boards, established under the two Trade Boards Acts, covering such industries as boot and shoe repairing, furniture manufacture, toy manufacture, shirt-making, and many other trades where home work is tradi-tionally widespread and conditions are bad; in all, some 1,500,000 workers are engaged in the industries covered by the Trade Boards. The Boards, whose members are appointed by the Minister of Labour, can award minimum wages to the workers concerned, and there are inspectors working under the Minister to enforce their payment of those wages. Road haulage, agriculture (where similar provisions have recently been made) and the catering trade are other examples of trades with low standards of wages for many categories of workers and with comparatively low trade union membership. There are plans for strengthening the existing machinery and for its extension to other trades and industries, and the Holidays with Pay Act of 1938 provides, in addition, for statutory guarantees for a minimum holiday in sweated industries.

Such statutory provisions, affecting wages, holidays and working conditions, are particularly necessary in industries where the trade unions are not yet strong enough to assert themselves either in open conflicts or at the conference table with the employers' representatives. Ultimately, no doubt, State intervention will further the establishment of genuine trade unionism in these backward industries. Any detailed study of such provisions will not be expected in a book dealing primarily with trade unions and with the industries in which they already exert their great influence upon working conditions.

CHAPTER IX

EDUCATIONAL ACTIVITIES

THREE KINDS of educational work are carried on by the British trade union movement to-day: general adult education, political education and instruction in special trade union subjects.

The need for organised political education in the trade unions was felt from the beginning of the present century, and was to some extent met by the Movement for Independent Working-Class Education. This movement was backed by the same forces which brought the British Labour Party into being as an independent political body at about the same period.

(a) WORKERS' EDUCATIONAL ASSOCIATION

General adult education for workers was initiated in this country on voluntary lines early in 1903, when the Workers' Educational Association (W.E.A.) was formed. It was from the beginning a "workers" educational association in so far as it mainly aimed at providing education for members of the working class; but it did (and does) not conceive workers' education as anything in substance different from progressive academic education, and tries to bring to the workers "the unbiased scientific truth". On the whole, it is probably true to say that the W.E.A. was quite content to give the same kind of instruction as that provided in the evening classes of the more progressive County Councils and University Extension Courses; but it has gradually developed as a Labour Educational Institution.

The W.E.A. was not based mainly on trade union and other working-class organisations; it accepted support—financial and other—from universities and other educational organisations. With the trade union movement, however, it established closer connections after the 1914–1918 war.

Very understandably, the social sciences occupy a prominent place in W.E.A. courses, though literature and history and other subjects are also taught. The Association has published a number of useful text-books and correspondence courses, and issues a monthly called *The Highway*.

(b) THE NATIONAL COUNCIL OF LABOUR COLLEGES

The other national working-class educational organisation—which puts a special emphasis on political labour education—took definite form with the foundation of the Plebs League, in Oxford, in 1908. Its formation was the direct result of a revolt of working-class students against adult education of the traditional type.

The students of Ruskin College (which had been formed in Oxford in 1899 as a college for working men) came out on strike in protest against the uncritical way in which the teaching staff treated economics and social science. In reality the strike was not a success, for Ruskin College remained an academic institution partly subsidised by non-working-class organisations—though it is now affiliated to the W.E.A.

125

The Plebs League has meanwhile changed into the National Council of Labour Colleges (N.C.L.C.), though *Plebs* is still the name of the vigorous socialist monthly sponsored by the organisation. To-day trade unions with a membership of over four million and Co-operative Societies with a membership of about four and a half million are affiliated to the N.C.L.C. Trade unions usually pay 3*d*. a year per affiliated member, and members of such unions are usually entitled to free postal courses or direct teaching in classes. Among the affiliated organisations are the three railway unions, several district organisations of the miners, the main unions of engineers, clothing workers (including boot and shoe operatives), distributive workers, public employees, etc. The two general workers' unions are not nationally affiliated, though there is a certain amount of co-operation.

Economics, social science, history, etc., are the main subjects taught in N.C.L.C. courses. They are taught in a critical, non-orthodox spirit, and the N.C.L.C. also conducts systematic courses in Marxism. It has published a number of books and pamphlets, some of which have become standard works.

The N.C.L.C. in 1945 had 13,721 class students; 10,775 day and week-end school students; 16,540 postal students; about 400 summer school students and 59,605 students at branch lectures. The Council carried out a census of its 16,540 postal students, and found that 2,650 were trade union officers and 636 were trades council officers—a striking indication of the importance of its rôle in influencing and training officials for the movement.

(c) W.E.T.U.C.

The Workers' Educational Association has established a special Trade Union Committee (the W.E.T.U.C.) on which representatives of both the W.E.A. and the affiliated unions are represented.

The Iron and Steel Trades Confederation was the first union to agree to an educational scheme proposed by the W.E.A. in 1919. The basis of the scheme was that the Confederation should set aside a specific annual grant for the education of its own members and that it should utilise the facilities of the W.E.A. This example was soon followed by the Union of Post Office Workers and also the Railway Clerks Association, which was the first important union to establish connection with *both* the W.E.A. and the N.C.L.C. The number of affiliated unions (to the W.E.T.U.C.) rose from thirteen in 1931 to thirty-three in 1943, and these thirty-three unions represented a combined membership of about four millions. Apart from those already mentioned, the most important are the two general workers' unions; several teachers' and Civil Service unions; the main unions for shop assistants; agricultural workers; seamen; boilermakers; building trade workers; printing, bookbinding and paper workers; the Fire Brigades Union and others.

The unions of tailors and garment workers and of boot and shoe operatives are among those nationally affiliated to *both* organisations. There are very few important unions which have no contact with either of the two bodies: these include the Woodworkers, Amalgamated Weavers Association, and the National Union of Dyers, Bleachers and Textile Workers.

The educational activities of the W.E.T.U.C.—that is, of that section of the W.E.A. catering exclusively for trade unionists and organised in conjunction with the trade union movement as such—are on a far smaller scale than those of the N.C.L.C. However, it should be emphasised that these activities form only a small section of the educational work of the W.E.A. as a whole. The total number of W.E.A. students in 1945 was 93,432, and a large proportion of this impressive total were no doubt trade unionists. Moreover, leading trade unionists play an active part in this wider educational activity, and the interest of the movement is by no means confined to the W.E.T.U.C. side. Mr. Harold Clay, of the Transport and General Workers Union, is President of the W.E.A., and a representative of the T.U.C. sits on its Council..

With this proviso in mind, we can turn to the figures for the W.E.T.U.C. itself. In 1945, 121 classes were held, attended by 1,878 students; in addition, 759 students took correspondence courses. 142 one-day schools were organised with 8,129 students. Eleven one-week schools were attended by 279 scholarship students, and 939 students were granted scholarships to week-end schools.

The two organisations are open to a double criticism. In the first place, there is the very fact that there are two of them. The existence of two organisations, both catering for adult working-class education, is a·great luxury. It is true that each organisation emphasises that it offers a different type of education, but the fact remains that there is considerable duplication and it is important to co-ordinate and adjust their activities.

The second criticism is more fundamental from the trade

union point of view. Both the W.E.A. and the N.C.L.C. concentrate mainly on general education of an academic character rather than on the day-to-day practical needs of trade unionists. It is true that the N.C.L.C. has classes on chairmanship, public speaking, electioneering, etc., and even one course on "shop stewards and workshop representatives and their functions"; but neither organisation regards it as its function to train future trade union officials for their job, or to enlighten trade union membership about current trade union problems.

(d) THE T.U.C.

The T.U.C., in its Interim Report on Trade Union Structure drew attention to the existing vacuum and stressed its dangers. The T.U.C. is throwing itself, as an organisation, into the problem of adult education, and it is to be hoped that its activity will remedy the present lack of balance that exists.

The T.U.C. organises an annual summer school, lasting two to three weeks, at which 150 students were accommodated in 1945; it offers facilities for the holding of day or week-end schools in the area of each Trades Councils Federation. A most useful recent development is a summer school especially for Trades Council secretaries, the first being held in 1945, when thirty men attended. The programme of the school is specially devised to meet the needs of Trades Council secretaries. A thorough review of the organisation and work of the T.U.C. is provided, and the General and Assistant Secretaries and each of the departmental officers of the T.U.C. are acting as lecturers. Lectures are given on the structure of the movement and the relationships between Trades Councils and trade unions. Plans are on foot to expand this service very considerably.

The T.U.C. are also planning to introduce short training courses of a practical nature, such as Industrial and Trade Union History, Trade Union Structure, Organisation, Trade Union Administration and Accountancy, Industrial Relations and Negotiations and Industrial and Social Legislation. Plans are being prepared for the foundation of a non-residential college providing full-time tuition for trade union students; and in the meantime a syllabus of trade union studies at the London School of Economics for the training of trade union officials has recently been worked out. The figures of those taking advantage of this latter service are not yet available.

These activities are most welcome, and are a badly needed

supplement to the more academic approach of the general educational bodies.

(e) THE LABOUR RESEARCH DEPARTMENT

Though not "educational" in anything like the limited sense, it would be wrong not to mention in this chapter the Labour Research Department. This was founded by Sidney Webb in 1912–13, and G. D. H. Cole was associated closely with it during its formative years. The Department is a fact-finding, not a policy-making body. Its main task is the answering of day-to-day inquiries on practical questions from affiliated organisations and all sections of the Labour movement. 2,530 such inquiries were dealt with in 1945; 25 per cent. dealt with capitalists' companies and directors, 25 per cent. with local government, social services and industrial health, 15 per cent. with wages, and the rest with a wide variety of questions. In addition, the Department is "briefed" by trade unions to prepare cases in trade disputes, etc. The L.R.D. publishes two monthly journals—*Labour Research* and *Social Service News*, one weekly, *Fact Service*, and numerous pamphlets.

The Department has 1,059 Labour organisations affiliated to it, including sixty-six national trade unions, 615 trade union branches and district committees, ninety-nine shop stewards' committees and 155 Trades Councils and Labour Parties. Among those affiliated are the three railway unions, the National Union of Mineworkers, the Amalgamated Engineering Union and the Electrical Trades Union.

(f) CONCLUSIONS

The trade union movement is being called upon to play an increasing part in the nation's administrative machine. Naturally, with the Labour Party in power, its leaders have to occupy the most responsible positions in the land, and are called upon to make far-reaching decisions on policy. Locally, trade unionists are called upon to serve on Unemployment Insurance Tribunals, Industrial Accident Tribunals, Public Assistance Committees, local authorities and many other important bodies. In the workshop trade unionists are called on to assist in production, to negotiate with employers, to handle disputes. For the successful execution of these tasks—and in preparation of the still more vital and difficult task of planning and running a workers-controlled Socialist Britain—it is not sufficient that the hearts of the trade union workers should be

129

in the right place; their heads must be there as well. They must be educated, not just in the sense of being able to spell or in knowing the elementary historical events, but educated *as trade unionists*, well versed in the practical details of their job, with full understanding of the legal and technical problems they will have to meet. The solid academic type of adult education has its place—a very important one—but the trade union movement will be well advised to concentrate still more on the practical educational needs that face its workers.

CHAPTER X

TRADE UNIONS AND POLITICS

(a) POLITICAL OBJECTIVES

MANY TRADE unions affiliated to the T.U.C. are also affiliated to the Labour Party, inasmuch as in their union dues members pay a political levy. Though they are thus committed to a programme of democratic socialism, only a few unions make it clear, in so many words, that social democracy is their political goal.

For this book the Rules of forty trade unions which are affiliated to the T.U.C. (*i.e.*, of all unions with a membership of at least 25,000 at the end of 1943)[1] have been analysed to discover what political objectives, if any, are set out in them. They represent only about one-fifth of the 190 unions affiliated to the T.U.C., but they are those of real political and industrial significance. The importance of the forty largest unions is shown by the fact that they have a combined membership of 5,945,697 out of a total T.U.C. membership of only 6,642,317 —*i.e.*, nearly 90 per cent. of its total membership in 1943.

Among those not included in our analysis are some local unions, craft unions which have gained importance among certain categories of skilled workers and a few unions which, though open to large industrial groups, have in fact enrolled only a small proportion of their workers (*i.e.*, chemical workers, bakers and brushmakers).

---

[1] All subsequent statistical figures refer to the end of 1943. The unions are the same as the T.U.C. unions included in our analysis of organisational structure in Appendix IV.

We can safely say, though, that most of the smaller unions are less definite in their political aims than the bigger ones, and many of them are not affiliated to the Labour Party.

Out of the forty unions, only nine are committed to replacing the present social system by a socialist or co-operative one. Four[1] would replace the present system of capitalist enterprise by a system of collective ownership (Socialism); two of these would have the new system working under the conditions of democracy; while a third advocates complete social and economic equality between the sexes. Three other unions,[2] though not directly committed to Socialism, would replace the present competitive system by one of co-operative production and, one adds, of co-operative distribution.

One union[3] combines both aims by asking for a socialist co-operative commonwealth. Another,[4] with probably the same idea in mind, promises to support "policies which will ultimately give the workers ownership and control of industry, such as amalgamation and national guilds".

Though surprisingly few unions advocate a complete change in the social structure, these few include all the five "giant" unions, with over 300,000 members each, as well as four of the unions in the next group—*i.e.*, with between 80,000 and 300,000 members each. These four therefore account for over a third of the eleven unions in this group. Of the remaining seven in this class, only two [5] are unions of ordinary industrial workers, while the remaining five,[6] consisting of non-manual workers, agricultural workers or public employees, cannot perhaps be expected to be won over so readily to a socialist programme. On the other hand, of the unions with a membership of less than 80,000 analysed here, none specifies any objectives involving a radical change in society.

Syndicalist ideas can still be found in the Rules of British

[1] National Union of Railwaymen; National Union of Mineworkers; Boot and Shoe Operatives; General and Municipal Workers. The latter two ask for "democratic Socialism" (General and Municipal Workers only indirectly commit themselves; the union promises to secure parliamentary representation if the candidates are pledged to Socialism); Boot and Shoe Operatives demand equality of the sexes.

[2] Transport and General; Amalgamated Engineering Union; Boilermakers. (Transport and General mention co-operative *distribution*.)

[3] Tailors and Garment Workers.

[4] Electrical Trades Union.

[5] Woodworkers and Iron and Steel Confederation.

[6] Railway Clerks; Distributive and Allied Workers; Agricultural Workers; Fire Brigades Union; Public Employees.

trade unions. No fewer than seven of these[1] postulate the control of each industry (or of their own industry) by the workers employed in it; one more union[2] whose object is to encourage and afford financial assistance to co-operative and Labour establishments in its trade can be added to the same group.

Eight[3] of the remaining unions would be content, according to their Rules, with certain improvements in the conditions of the trade, in the status and in the welfare of their members or of their profession; or else they want to influence their trade through legislation, without indicating its direction. Some even promise to work for a better understanding with the employers. These aims can at best be described as reformist: those unions accept, if only by implication, the present economic structure, which they wish to modify or improve in certain aspects only.

Thirteen unions, forming another group, do not specify any desired social change, although the majority of them mention some political objectives. Four are[4] pledged to support the Labour and trade union movement (a similar pledge is also contained in the Rules of four unions with other, more definite political objectives).

Finally, a number of unions mention their concern with political questions in a more general way. A total of eleven[5] unions (including six without other political objectives) refer to the purposes mentioned in Section 3 of the Trade Union Act of 1913, where the political activities of unions are legally defined.

One[6] more union mentions political aims, but does not specify them. There remain only two[7] unions in whose Rules political aims are not mentioned (at least, among those unions

[1] Distributive and Allied Workers; Shop Assistants; Textile Workers; National Amalgamated Furnishing Trades Association; Brass and Metal Mechanics; Clerical and Administrative Workers (who mention "democratic control"), and Plumbers, Glaziers and Domestic Engineers Union.

[2] Typographical Association.

[3] Woodworkers; Railway Clerks; Painters; Sheet Metal Workers; Engineering and Shipbuilding Draughtsmen; Ship Constructors; Bank Officers; Operative Printers and Assistants.

[4] Locomotive Engineers and Firemen; Public Employees; Weavers; Foundry Workers.

[5] Those unions which have no further political objectives are: Printing, Bookbinders and Paper Workers; Card, Blowing and Ring-Room Operatives; Fire Brigades Union; Enginemen, etc.; Vehicle Builders; Bakery, Confectionery and Allied Workers. The others are: Shop Assistants; Textile Workers; Iron, Steel, etc., Confederation; Painters; Mineworkers.

[6] National Union of Seamen.

[7] National Union of Agricultural Workers; National Federation of Insurance Workers.

included in our analysis). Some of the unions not affiliated to the T.U.C. (Teachers, Civil Servants, etc.) and some of the smaller affiliated unions do not specify any political objectives.

We should finally mention that among their subsidiary political objectives, two[1] unions advocate education of a working-class character, and three[2] others the promotion of Bills in Parliament.

Here follows a summary of the position as outlined above:—

Total Unions in T.U.C.	.	.	.	190 with 6,642,317 members
Included in our analysis	.	.	.	40 ,, 5,945,797 ,,
Of these forty unions:—				
Favouring radical social changes	.	.	9 ,, 4,046,930 ,,
Pledged to support a Labour Government[1]	.	.	.	4 ,, 266,587 ,,
A syndicalist approach	.	.	.	8 ,, 575,816 ,,
A reformist approach	.	.	.	10 ,, 606,882 ,,
Political aims of Section 3, Trade Union Act, 1913[2]	.	.	.	6 ,, 283,326 ,,
Political aims generally	.	.	.	1 ,, 52,000 ,,
No political aims	.	.	.	2 ,, 114,256 ,,

40 with 5,945,797 members

[1] Excluding four unions with wider political aims.
[2] Excluding five unions with wider political aims.

Only a minority of the unions under review specify in their Rules the political duties of candidates they sponsor for Parliament or for local government bodies. The National Union of Railwaymen, in spite of its "socialist" programme, and the National Union of Agricultural Workers are both content if their parliamentary representatives "further the interest of their members"; only three[3] unions make it clear that their candidate must accept the programme and the constitution of the Labour Party. The National Union of Boot and Shoe Operatives says also that its parliamentary representatives shall carry out the decisions of the T.U.C.

As already mentioned, candidates supported by the General and Municipal Workers Union must be pledged to a socialist programme. The Weavers, the Typographical Association and

[1] Boot and Shoe Operatives and (rather surprisingly, in view of their ambiguous other aims) Painters.
[2] Iron and Steel and Kindred Trades Confederation; Railway Clerks; and Bank Officers Guild.
[3] The Amalgamated Engineering Union; Boot and Shoe Operatives; and (in their Parliamentary Representation Scheme, which is attached to the Rules) the Distributive and Allied Workers.

133

the Furnishing Trades Association all promise to further Labour representation in Parliament, but do not specify any particular policy.

(b) PARLIAMENTARY REPRESENTATION

As has been seen, the State came to play during the first quarter of the twentieth century an increasingly important part in economic life in regulating conditions of labour and relations between employers and wage-earners. Employers were able to further their own interests by using the political parties they dominated to determine the economic policies of the State. Trade unions were in turn obliged to try to counterbalance that influence, and to secure legislation more favourable to the workers. Bitter experience slowly taught the unions that they could not rely on the existing political parties, and they gradually recognised the need for a political party of their own.

The capitalist forces arrayed against Labour were formidable, and Labour had to mobilise all its strength to fight them. Trade unions began to co-operate more with existing socialist groups, and so laid the foundation of the Labour Party.

The table on page 135 shows the composition of the Parliamentary Labour Party's members elected between 1918 and 1945, and the bodies who nominated them.

This table shows that in 1918 Labour M.P.s were predominantly trade union nominees (86 per cent. of all Labour members). The position has changed considerably, and trade unions nominated only 53 per cent. of representatives in 1935 and 29 per cent. in 1945.

(c) LABOUR PARTY AFFILIATION

Trade unions affiliate to the Labour Party on both a local and national plane. Local branches affiliate to the local parties, and the national unions to the National Labour Party organisation. The affiliation of the local union branches is not given much attention in the Rules of the unions: not one of the Rules of the unions here analysed states that its local branches had to affiliate to the party, and only seven refer directly or indirectly to the question of affiliation. Five unions[1] say that local branches *may* affiliate with local Labour Parties. The Tailors

[1] National Union of Public Employees; National Union of Distributive and Allied Workers; National Union of Enginemen, Firemen, Mechanics, and Electrical Workers; Fire Brigades Union; and National Society of Operative Printers and Assistants (the latter only with the consent of the Executive Councils).

	1918.	1922.	1923.	1924.	1929.	1931.	1935.	1945.
Total . . .	57	142	191	151	288	46	152	393
Divisional Labour .	5	19	39	25	128	13	63	253
Co-operative . .	—	4	6	5	9	1	9	23
I.L.P. . . .	3	31	39	29	36	—[1]	—[1]	—[1]
Social Democratic Federation . .	—	—	4	3	—	—	—	—
Fabians . . .	—	1	2	1	—	—	—	—
Trade Unions . these were:	49	87	101	88	115	32	80	117
Miners . .	25	43	44	41	43	22	35	33
General Labour .	7	12	15	13	19	5	13	27
Textiles . .	5	6	5	3	5	—	1	2
Engineering and Metal . .	7	14	13	13	13	2	7	8
Printing . .	2	2	3	3	4	—	3	5
Railways . .	1	3	5	4	15	—	10	22
Building, Woodworking . .	1	1	4	3	5	2	3	5
Boot and Shoe .	1	2	1	—	2	—	—	3
Post Office . .	—	2	3	2	—	—	—	1
Distributive Workers, etc. . .	—	1	5	4	5	1	6	10
Pottery . .	—	—	—	1	1	—	—	—
Food (Bakers) .	—	—	—	—	—	—	1	—
Miscellaneous .	—	1	3	1	3	—	1	1
	49	87	101	88	115	32	80	117

[1] The I.L.P. has contested the elections as an independent party.

and Garment Workers Union refers to the local Labour Parties, though only in an indirect way, saying that, subject to the approval of the Executive Board, branches may affiliate with any political movement for the advancement of Labour policy; branches must not, however, affiliate to organisations which are banned by the T.U.C. All affiliations to Labour Parties and similar bodies were, of course, subject to the limitations of the Trade Union Act, 1927.

The affiliation fees to political Labour organisations are to be paid from the Central Political Fund in the case of three unions,[1] and from local political funds in the case of three others.[2]

[1] National Union of Tailors and Garment Workers; National Union of Distributive and Allied Workers; National Union of Enginemen, Firemen, Mechanics and Electrical Workers.

[2] National Union of Public Employees; Fire Brigades Union; and National Society of Operative Printers and Assistants.

(d) POLITICAL LEVY

In speaking earlier of the human wealth and the power, actual and potential, of the Labour movement, we stressed the importance of its millions of members who, fired with the right spirit and drive, can make Britain a dynamic democracy. It is in that perspective that the trade unions' political levy should be viewed. For the levy is the symbol of the political life of the unions. Here, therefore, we ask some questions.

In which union problems, apart from the election of management bodies or of officers, do members take any part or interest? If the information known to the writer is typical, the answer must be that the sense of political responsibility among the members of the unions is not very great. The limited interest of ordinary members either in organisation or in political action is reflected in the modest percentage of those paying the political levy as shown below.

When we go higher up the trade union organisation to the point where it touches the organised political life of the country, is the position better?

Hostile critics say that the block votes given in the annual Labour Party Conference by the leaders of the big unions on behalf of their thousandfold memberships are arbitrarily given, because the rank-and-file membership who pay the political levy are not seriously consulted about the problems on the Conference agenda or the way they vote. Is this criticism well founded? How many national unions see that their members have the opportunity of discussing the problems, and instructing or advising those who speak in their name at conferences? Are the means that such discussion offers of furthering the political education of the members used to full advantage by the unions' leadership?

If not, responsibility lies, no doubt, with both the leaders and the ordinary members, though the leadership cannot be held responsible for the inadequate training in citizenship afforded to the masses by the national education system. But the changes which the July 1945 elections authorise offer a new opportunity. The unions can become the school and the laboratory of the transition—at the same time economic, social and political—now under way.

The actual position in regard to payment of political levies is set out in the following table.

136

	1937.	1940.	1941.	1942.	1943.	1945.
1. Mining and Quarrying . . .	75	71	71	66	66	67
2. Railways . .	61	57	56	53	55	59
3. Transport Workers .	53	52	47	39	30	36
4. Shipbuilding . .	20	19	16	19	20	20
5. Engineering . .	28	19	18	16	13	25
6. Iron, Steel and Metal Manufacture .	36	34	35	34	29	36
7. Building, Woodworking and Furniture .	21	18	17	16	16	16
8. Printing and Paper .	34	30	28	27	26	24
9. Cotton . . .	70	67	78	80	72	70
10. Textiles other than Cotton . .	40	42	43	34	32	34
11. Clothing . .	20	23	30	23	26	27
12. Glass, Pottery, Chemicals, Food, Drink, Tobacco, Brushmakers and Distribution . .	72	60	63	56	51	51
13. Leather, Boot and Shoe . . .	47	44	41	46	45	49
14. Agriculture . .	62	69	66	68	68	78
15. Public Employees .	60	17	12	10	10	16
16. Non-manual workers	12	10	7	7	7	8
17. General workers .	71	54	44	33	33	36
Average . .	52	44	41	36	35	37

This table shows that the proportion of trade union members
affiliated to the Labour Party decreased between 1937 and
1943 from 52 to 35 per cent., or by one-third. The actual
decrease in numbers was very small—only 8,000—but the
tendency is alarming. If asked whether the Labour Party's
political education of the unions kept in step with the growth
of membership during the first four years of the war, the
answer must be in the negative. General membership of the
unions rose rapidly—the proportion of political membership
went down.

The table also shows that only in trade unions operating in
agriculture, cotton, mining, railways and the composite
Group 12 do more than 50 per cent. of members pay political
levies.

(e) COMPARATIVE DEVELOPMENT

If we compare fluctuations in the membership of the three component groups of the Labour movement during the last thirty years, we see the following results:[1] membership of the Labour Party has slumped badly since 1920; trade union affiliation to the Party has shrunk by half, resulting in a loss of over two million members. In 1942 only 27 per cent. of all trade unionists (including those unions not affiliated to the T.U.C.) in this country were affiliated to the Labour Party.

In 1920 99 per cent. of the Labour Party's membership were trade union members, as distinct from individual members. By 1937 the percentage had dropped to 80 per cent. because of the increase in individual membership, and since then it has risen to 90 per cent. as the result of the temporary loss of nearly half the individual membership of the Party throughout the war. At the end of 1946 the proportion of individual membership in the Labour Party has again risen to over 20 per cent.

The picture of the trade union movement is much brighter than that of the Labour Party. Trade union membership in 1943 reached 8,088,000, embracing more than one-third of all the wage- and salary-earners in the country; affiliated to the T.U.C. were 6,642,000, or 82 per cent. of that membership, as against 78 per cent. in 1920.

Consumers' Co-operation, which is the only group with a continuous growth, has more than doubled its membership, increasing from 3,845,521 in 1918 to 8,924,868 in 1942 and to nearly 9,400,000 to-day. Some of the politically minded Co-operators were not satisfied with outside representation in the House of Commons, even by the Labour Party, which they believed had not sufficient understanding and faith in Co-operative methods. They therefore formed the Co-operative Party, which in 1945 claimed nearly seven million members, or three out of every four British Co-operators.

Judged by figures, the Co-operative Party, with a membership running into millions, looks disproportionately more politically significant than it really is. For there are two categories of members: on the one hand the local affiliated societies, and on the other, individual Co-operators who have joined the Party—an altogether different thing from being simply a member of a local Co-operative Society. It is the affiliation of

[1] See Appendix XIV, p. 258.

138

these local societies that swells the membership of the Party to millions. Those who have individually joined the political party are still comparatively few.

The discrepancy between the growth of membership of the trade unions and Co-operative Societies on the one hand and the decline in the membership of the Labour Party on the other has become more apparent since the early years of the war. The fluctuation in membership in the three branches of the Labour movement between 1939 and 1943 can be seen from the following table:

	Compare :	
	1939–1943.	1914–1918.
Trade union movement gained in members	1,858,000	2,388,000
Trade unions affiliated to T.U.C. gained in members	1,973,000	1,900,000
Consumers' Co-operation gained in members	439,000	793,000
Co-operative Party gained in members .	1,188,000	— [1]
Labour Party's changes in total membership:		
(a) Total change of membership . .	160,000 lost	1,401,000 gained
(b) Gain in trade union members .	23,000	1,388,000

[1] The Co-operative Party was only established at the end of the First World War.

These figures emphasise the difficulties in enrolling trade union members which the Party has to face. Instead of absorbing the nearly two million new members who joined the T.U.C. during the war, it actually gained only about 23,000 of them.

We must not forget that under the 1927 Act every trade union member who wanted to join the Labour Party had to make a personal declaration to this effect ("contract in"), which rendered enrolment much harder than before. The fact remains, however, that only about 1 *per cent.* of the members who joined the "affiliated" unions during the war joined the Labour Party at the same time.

This warning must not be ignored, and new methods of political organisation, propaganda and education should be developed without delay.

CHAPTER XI

TRADE UNION FINANCE

(a) CONTRIBUTIONS

FINANCE IS the real backbone of trade union activities, and it is impossible to understand how the component parts of the trade union movement work without taking due account of their financial resources.

The bulk of trade union funds comes from the direct contributions of their members, other sources bringing in only a minor part. Those contributions, usually paid weekly, are intended to cover the cost of running the members' particular trade union, and therefore vary with different unions, in accordance with the ranges of their activities.

The main element in the relatively higher contributions of some unions is usually the welfare or benefit side of their work. Those unions which insure, even partially, against unemployment, sickness, accident, superannuation, funeral, victimisation, legal aid, travelling, emigration and other liabilities must necessarily charge a much higher rate than unions which limit themselves to strike and lock-out, legal aid and victimisation benefits.

Some unions receive extra voluntary contributions at a higher rate to cover, in addition to the general risks, special benefits, if required. It stands to reason that unions which do not operate benefit schemes can afford to ask lower contributions.

In 1939 the unions paying Friendly Society's benefits covered only $1\frac{1}{2}$ million members, or a little more than one-quarter of the total union membership in the country, according to figures published in the last Health Insurance Valuation (see p. 98).

Another factor greatly influencing the size of the contribution is the rate of members' wages and the continuity of their employment. The dues to unions of unskilled and low-skilled members are often only a few pennies per week, and even those rates are sometimes reduced for women and juveniles. Unions of skilled craftsmen, on the other hand, have much higher rates, usually not less than a shilling a week, and often more. Many craft unions impose further levies on their membership for different purposes.[1] Those periodical levies often make the average annual contribution much higher than would appear from the rules.

That divergency of rates of contribution charged and benefits paid by various unions results from the difficulty, or even impossibility, of putting the benefits on an actuarial basis—or even of predicting such risks as strikes and lock-outs with any degree of accuracy. There can therefore be no doubt, as Cole remarked in 1918, that some unions have in the past promised higher rates of benefit than the contribution they collected would justify: ". . . in the majority of the old-fashioned Craft Unions superannuation benefit is to some extent a mortgage on the future, and it is paid out of the contributions of the younger members".[2]

(b) Income and Expenditure

Having glanced at the sources of trade union finance, we may now consider how the funds are spent, and how the expenditure is distributed between defence activities, welfare and administration.

Trade union finance can conveniently be grouped under three main headings: (a) dispute and political funds, (b) welfare funds, including all kinds of benefits and insurance and (c) working expenses, covering the cost of running the organisation. Of the last of these items, it should be remembered that much of it goes on mass organisation work, which is of the greatest importance for keeping the whole body running. Organisers, delegate conferences, ballots, etc., cost a good deal of money. So do publicity and propaganda, which are the life-blood of an efficient trade union organisation.

The average contributions and expenditure for all registered unions in this country, classified under three headings, for the two decades before the outbreak of the war, are shown in the table on page 142. The figures, it must be emphasised, are average figures, with all the limitations that implies.

The analysis of these figures reveals how low are the average contributions paid by members: those contributions constitute about 90 per cent. of the income of the movement; the unions also receive allowances from the Ministry of Labour for Health Insurance and the administrative expenses connected with its distribution; but with these moneys they act simply as inter-

[1] Appendix XV, p. 258–61.
[2] See G. D. H. Cole, "An Introduction to Trade Unionism", p. 41, 1918.

Year.	Average contri-bution.	Expenses.			
		Fighting funds.	Welfare funds.	Working expenses.	Total.
	£ s. d.	£ s. d.	£ s. d.	£ s. d.	£ s. d.
1918	1 3 6	1 7	7 2	9 7	18 4
1919	1 6 1	6 10	7 11	11 4	1 6 1
1920	1 12 3	9 11	10 0	17 1	1 17 0
1921	2 2 8	13 3	1 15 6	18 9	3 7 6
1922	1 15 7	6 10	1 0 6	16 5	2 3 9
1923	1 16 0	4 3	14 2	16 1	1 14 6
1924	1 17 4	6 5	14 7	17 5	1 18 5
1925	1 15 10	1 11	16 4	15 8	1 13 11
1926	1 12 8	1 6 8	19 6	16 3	3 2 5
1927	1 16 6	1 7	16 6	15 4	1 13 5
1928	1 16 10	1 3	18 0	15 11	1 15 2
1929	1 17 7	3 0	17 9	16 6	1 17 3
1930	1 17 7	2 2	1 1 9	16 3	2 0 2
1931	1 17 0	1 10	1 4 1	16 7	2 2 6
1932	1 17 6	2 0	1 3 1	16 8	2 1 9
1933	1 17 10	1 9	1 0 4	16 1	1 18 2
1934	1 19 2	1 2	18 1	16 10	1 16 1
1935	1 18 5	2 2	16 5	16 0	1 14 7
1936	1 14 9	1 5	13 9	16 5	1 11 7
1937	1 15 8	2 0	13 4	15 1	1 10 5
1938	1 16 0	1 2	14 0	15 10	1 11 0

mediaries, and distribute the allowances among their members.

Contributions being so low, it should be easy to enrol new members, especially among the lower-paid and unorganised workers. On the other hand, the low rates impede the building up of large funds required for the development of trade union activities.

The table on this page shows that the annual contributions were particularly low in 1918 (£1 3s. 6d. per member), probably because of the great numbers of men in the Forces who did not pay their contributions. In 1921, however, the average contribution increased to over £2, which is the highest rate for the whole twenty years' period under review. In 1926—the year of greatest strike activity—the rate was, it is worth noting, only £1 12s. 8d. per annum—the lowest for the whole period.

After 1926, and during the 1930–1932 crisis, when more and more members were unemployed, the rate of average contribution increased. Trade union membership went down during these years, and the higher rates may have been a result of the fact that it was chiefly better-paid workers who kept up their membership, and that the unions gradually wrote off their lapsed members.

Prices had gone down markedly during this period, so that the real increase in contribution rates, taking cost of living into account, was much greater. During the first twenty years of the inter-war period contributions had risen in terms of 1918 prices by over 100 per cent., as the following table, which covers registered unions, makes clear.

Per member.[1]	1918.			1926.			1932.			1938.		
	£	s.	d.	£	s.	d.	£	s.	d.	£	s.	d.
Contributions . . .	1	3	6	1	12	8	1	17	6	1	16	0
Expenses:												
Political . . .			6			6			6			6
Disputes . . .		1	1	1	6	2		1	6			8
Fighting Fund (total) .		1	7	1	6	8		2	0		1	2
Welfare Fund . .		7	2		19	6	1	3	1		14	0
Working Expenses .		9	7		16	3		16	8		15	10
Total Expenses . .		18	4	3	2	5	2	1	9	1	11	0
Index of Cost of Living .	"100"			"82"			"69"			"74"		
Per member (in 1918 values).												
	£	s.	d.	£	s.	d.	£	s.	d.	£	s.	d.
Contributions . . .	1	3	6	2	0	0	2	14	6	2	8	8
Expenses:												
Political . . .			6			7			9			8
Disputes . . .		1	1	1	12	2		2	1			11
Fighting Fund (total) .		1	7	1	12	9		2	10		1	7
Welfare Fund . .		7	2	1	3	9	1	13	6		18	9
Working Expenses .		9	7		19	10	1	4	2	1	1	6
Total Expenses . .		18	4	3	16	4	3	0	6	2	1	10

[1] In all cases figures for Welfare Fund and Total Expenses exclude allowances from the Ministry of Labour, for which the unions act only as intermediaries. This applies also to the table on this page.

It can be seen that no significant change took place between 1932 and 1938 in the average rates of contributions. During the war years they went down considerably, according to the accounts of the six biggest unions, which embrace over three and a half million workers. Rising prices sharpened this decrease in cost-of-living terms.

The reason for the declining union contributions was probably that their members in the Forces did not pay any contributions during the war, and the many new members paid the comparatively low contributions of unskilled and semi-skilled workers; as was mentioned above, however, unions were able to supplement their regular dues by special levies.[1]

(c) EXPENDITURE

We can now see more clearly the use made of the income of trade unions and of their funds. Before analysing the figures on

[1] See a very interesting article by D. B. Halpern in the *Bulletin of the Institute of Statistics*, No. 14, Vol. 5, "The Trade Union Movement since the Outbreak of War." According to Mr. Halpern's information the average figures for the six largest national unions (Transport and General Workers Union, National Union of Municipal and General Workers, Miners Federation of Great Britain, Amalgamated Engineering Union, National Union of Railwaymen and National Union of Distributive and Allied Workers) are as follows:

Per member.	1938.			1942.		
	£	s.	d.	£	s.	d.
Contributions	2	0	2	1	14	9
Expenses:						
Political			8			6
Disputes			6			—
Fighting Fund (total) . .		1	2			6
Welfare Fund . . .		14	3		9	4
Working Expenses . .		16	7		14	2
Total Expenses . . .	1	12	0	1	4	0
Index of Cost of Living . .		"74"			"96"	
Per member (in 1918 values).						
	£	s.	d.	£	s.	d.
Contributions	2	14	4	1	16	2
Expenses:						
Political			11			6
Disputes			8			—
Fighting Fund (total) . .		1	7			6
Welfare Fund . . .		19	4		9	9
Working Expenses . .	1	2	5		14	9
Total Expenses . . .	2	3	4	1	5	0

pp. 142–43, we would like to start with similar information published by G. D. H. Cole nearly thirty years ago (in 1918), dealing with the expenditure of 100 principal trade unions during the decade before the First World War (1904–1913). This information shows that

	%
Dispute benefits absorbed	14·4
Unemployment benefits	24·2
Other Benefits and Grants	40·3
Working and miscellaneous expenses	21·1
	100

The figures of that period were much influenced partly by rising industrial unrest and partly by bad trade, which greatly increased outlay in dispute and unemployment benefits.

Another factor causing great variation in expenditure was the amounts which different unions spent on management and working expenses. The low average figure of working expenses for the period of ten years (21 per cent.) has increased to the end of the period (1913) to over 27 per cent. The unions of unskilled workers showed, however, an expenditure often nearly three times as high as this average: the National Union of General Workers 61·3 per cent., National Union of Railwaymen 62·4 per cent., Dock, Wharf, Riverside and General Workers Union 74·3 per cent. and the Workers Union 40·9 per cent.[1]

What was the position during the two decades preceding the Second World War?

The heavy demands made on the unions by strikes in the years following the First World War reached a climax in 1926—the year of the General Strike—when the average dispute benefit was £1 6s. 8d., or amounting to nearly 80 per cent. of the average membership contribution for the year. The unions could not possibly have paid such high benefits for much longer, and comparable benefits were never paid again. The highest dispute benefit paid in any year after 1926 equalled an average per member of 2s. 1d. in 1939—a mere fraction of the total outlay—and in most other years it was much less. During the war of 1939–1945 the unions paid negligible sums in dispute benefits (see p. 147).

The other part of the "fighting" expenses—the contribution to the political fund—was in most years a bare sixpence per

[1] See Cole, "An Introduction to Trade Unionism", p. 142.

member a year, although in the early twenties, when large numbers of trade union members paid the political levy, it occasionally rose as high as 1s. 1d. After 1926 it never rose above 11d., and has since been further reduced owing to the fall in "political" membership.

Although in the early thirties it was no longer necessary to make large payments out of the "Fighting Funds", economic conditions were very critical, and fairly large amounts had to be spent on welfare; under this heading came unemployment, sickness and accident, funeral, superannuation and other benefits. By the late thirties the situation was better, and during the war got better still, as the numbers of the unemployed went down. Yet it is probably true that many workers to-day still look on the unions as insurance and social service agencies, rather than as fighting units. The "welfare" and "insurance" character of the unions would become still more marked if we included among the income and expenditure statistics the sums received from the Ministry of Labour and paid out in benefits to trade union members.

More than half the comparatively small outlay of 1918 consisted of "working expenses" (in which are included grants to federations, etc., as well as "other outgoings"). The cost per member on the score of working expenses soon rose to almost double the 1918 rate, and then from 1920 to 1938 remained fairly stable at between 15s. and 18s. 9d. With an even sharper rise over the 1918 figure of "other expenditure", "working expenses" at the outbreak of the 1939 war did not exceed half the total of the trade unions' outlay. To judge from the accounts of the "big six", "other expenditure" during the war decreased, but not to any appreciable extent the working expenses. Now, therefore, working expenses are apparently over 50 per cent. of the total. The special expenses of the "fighting years", 1919–1926, and of the depression and crisis, 1930–1935, put the heaviest strain on the finances of the movement. Yet, in spite of the rather lower membership dues, the income of unions exceed their expenditure considerably. This has enabled them to increase reserves and become much stronger financially, and correspondingly better equipped to tackle the more ambitious tasks they might set themselves.

(d) War Years

The following table shows the total income and expenditure of the registered and reporting unions which account for 85 per cent. of the total trade union membership in this country during the years 1938–1944.

	Number of unions.	Number of members.	Income from Members.	Income from Other sources.	Total income.	Expenditure total.
1938	521	4,920,837	8,915,619	859,315	9,774,934	7,715,310
1939	522	5,072,977	9,031,030	863,138	9,894,168	7,719,031
1940	513	5,416,519	9,200,672	908,755	10,109,427	7,874,851
1941	516	5,980,851	9,486,651	948,901	10,435,552	7,593,912
1942	522	6,584,259	10,516,218	1,122,337	11,638,555	7,808,401
1943	520	6,896,317	11,197,635	1,169,564	12,367,199	8,525,983
1944	520	6,831,001	11,491,262	1,323,663	12,814,925	8,957,550

Those figures show that the funds of the unions increased during the war by nearly £20,000,000.

The following table gives the expenditure on the main branches of activity during the same period in the percentages of total expenditure.

	Dispute benefit.	All other benefits.	Political fund.	Working expenses.	Other outgoings.	Total.
1938	2·0	45·0	1·5	44·4	7·1	100
1939	2·1	44·5	1·5	45·9	6·0	100
1940	0·8	46·0	1·3	45·7	6·2	100
1941	0·2	40·0	1·5	51·2	7·1	100
1942	0·2	37·0	1·5	54·1	7·2	100
1943	0·2	36·2	1·4	54·7	7·5	100
1944	0·3	35·5	1·5	55·3	7·4	100

Expenditure on strike pay is seen to have dwindled to a merely nominal figure, since more of the strikes which took place during this period (the larger part of which falls within the war years) were unofficial, and therefore involved the unions in no expense. The expenditure from the political fund during 1938–1944 amounted to an average of only 5d. a year per registered member, but it must be remembered that it was only 35 per cent. of the total trade union membership that were paying political levies.[1]

[1] The figures in the two tables on this page have been supplied by the Office of the Registrar General of Friendly Societies.

(e) FUNDS

Appendix XVI, pp. 261–62, shows the accumulated trade union funds in Great Britain for the period from 1890 to 1942, and the average amount per member is seen to be:—

1890	.	.	.	£2 2s.
1900	.	.	.	£3 2s.
1910	.	.	.	£3 10s.
1920	.	.	.	£2 6s.
1930	.	.	.	£3 2s.
1938	.	.	.	£4 2s.

These figures reveal that in nearly fifty years from 1890 to 1938 the funds have practically doubled, rising by £2 to £4 2s. per head. Recent figures published by Mr. Halpern for the six largest unions show that their average funds per member—£4 15s. in 1938—had risen by 1942 to £5 8s. When, however, we compare such increase in funds with the changed cost-of-living index, it becomes evident that the real increase is very modest.

From this analysis of the financial position of the trade unions it follows that since dispute benefits represent so very small a part of their expenditure, it would be difficult for them to finance strike movements on a very large scale. They are able to stand by for a long time and to give some help in local disputes, but, should those swell to national proportions, the unions would not find it easy to finance a long-term struggle. Realisation of that situation has had a direct and important influence on the whole tactics of British trade unions, as has been seen in the chapter dealing with strike activities during the last fifty years.

The financial problems with which the unions will have to deal in the coming years are in many cases different from the problems of the past. To begin with, the new National Insurance legislation means handing over to State institutions the larger part of Benefit and Friendly Society activities that have in the past formed the great part of the work of many unions. Among the consequences will be a reduction in members' subscriptions for these purposes, and a reduction of administrative work on the benefits' side, with a corresponding release of staff. Obviously an enormous amount of difficult actuarial work and organisational adjustment is involved.

Readjustment will also be needed to the extent to which the

unions participate in the country's economic planning. A planned economy with nationalised and regulated industries will require the unions to strengthen very considerably their central and regional apparatus and further to develop their research and planning organisation. The growth in the unions' working expenditure during the last twenty years has been in part due to an increase in the central and district machinery of the large national unions. The research and planning machinery, as well as the intensified education programme, which are urgently called for all mean that more money will be needed.

This raises the question of where this money is to come from. This increase is most likely to come from an increase in membership subscriptions. These still stand at an average of 8*d.* per head a week, but may in some cases be reduced after the transfer of insurance activities to the State. A penny more a week from each member would produce over £1,500,000 per annum, and might provide the funds required.

Further, now that the Trades Disputes and Trade Unions Act of 1927 has been repealed, more unions can affiliate to the T.U.C. Incidentally this should place much larger funds at the Labour Party's disposal, through the political levy. We should now see a radical change from the position which obtained in 1944, when, out of the 6,300,000 trade unionists affiliated to the T.U.C., only 2,300,000 paid the political levy towards the Labour Party's funds. The need for speedy political education among trade unionists is obvious. Clearly what is called for is a combined effort in the way of education and membership campaigns, which will be of incalculable value to the Labour movement in its industrial, political and co-operative aspects alike. With its increased income from the political levy the Labour Party is likely to be in a stronger position to participate in such a drive through the National Council of Labour.

PART THREE

TRADE UNIONS AND THE WAR

CHAPTER XII

LABOUR SUPPLY AND DISPUTE MACHINERY

(a) GENERAL

THE WAR had a profound effect on the conditions in which British trade unions had to work. From the beginning the unions pledged themselves to support the fight against Fascism, and as early as 1939 the Prime Minister, Mr. Chamberlain, asked the representatives of the T.U.C. to co-operate with the Government in waging the war. On that occasion, it may be recalled, the Prime Minister emphasised the overwhelming importance that such co-operation was bound to have, and Sir Walter Citrine declared after the interview that the significance of the British trade unions had never before been accorded such clear official acknowledgment.

While contributing to the war effort the unions could not, and did not, abate their general concern with the conditions of labour. The General Secretary of the T.U.C. formulated the war-time duties of the unions in these terms:—[1]

"(1) to contribute all we can to the national war effort;

(2) to defend the workers against all forms of exploitation during the war;

(3) to prepare the Trade Union Movement at all points to be able to play its part in post-war reconstruction".

Clearly this war-time situation would often require quite new policies and machinery and involve much modification in pursuing those traditional tasks. Let us now examine how they were carried on in the conditions of a world war.

This examination falls into three parts. The first deals with labour supply policy and the machinery for settling labour disputes. The second analyses how the unions protected wages

[1] "T.U.C. at War", which is a useful summary of T.U.C. activities in 1939–1945, compiled by Sir Walter Citrine.

and general conditions of labour during the war; it compares the movements of wages and prices, with the new welfare arrangements, which in so many ways improved the standard of living, and traces the general influence of war conditions on other spheres of trade union activity. Finally it gives an account of a new activity for trade unions, which is of the greatest importance for the future—their active participation in the organisation of war production.

(b) LABOUR SUPPLY POLICY

"Security of employment"—that first and fundamental aim of trade unionism—no longer presented any difficulty. With a war to wage and a very inadequate war machine to equip, mass unemployment gave way first to full employment, and later to an actual shortage of man-power in every industry. Many trade union practices designed expressly to maintain employment could safely be—and were—temporarily relaxed. Indeed, it soon became the central task of national policy to mobilise man-power with little regard to the unions' traditional restrictive practices—a task that could be smoothly carried out only with the active co-operation of trade union leaders, who enjoyed the confidence of the workers and knew the conditions in their industries.

The appointment of an outstanding trade union leader—Mr Bevin—as Minister of Labour and National Service was one of the most significant contributions of the trade union movement to the national labour supply policy, and it greatly facilitated the success of that policy. The movement itself took direct part in preparing the measures necessary for the mobilisation of man-power. A National Joint Advisory Council to the Minister of Labour and National Service, consisting of an equal number of trade union and employers' representatives, was formed soon after the declaration of war. In its original form the Council came to an end in 1940 after Mr Bevin had become Minister, when its duties were taken over by the Joint Consultative Committee—a smaller body consisting of seven members from each side of the Joint Advisory Council.

The Committee met regularly under the chairmanship of the Minister himself, and though officially it was only an "advisory" body, it is probably true to say that the Minister has never acted against a well founded objection put forward by either side of the Committee on a major question of Labour policy and legislation. Problems such as the supply of labour, industrial relations connected with scheduled occupations, the application of the Essential Works Order, the formation of the National Arbitration Tribunal—these and similar questions could hardly have been handled in a way satisfactory to the workpeople without a regular consultation beforehand between the Minister of Labour and the representatives of the trade unions. Trade unionists were also asked to serve on other consultative bodies connected with the Ministry of Labour, as, for example, the Women's Consultative Committee, Factory and Welfare Advisory Board, Engineering Industry Advisory Panel, a consultative committee for the recruitment of nurses and midwives, etc.

Nevertheless, although trade union leaders devoted so much of their energy to the mobilisation of man-power, they could not close their eyes to the danger of mass unemployment reoccurring after the war. Security of employment, usually under the slogan of "Full Employment", has become the corner-stone of the post-war plan of every political group, a goal to which the Trade Union movement would be the last to take exception. Generally speaking, the T.U.C. was in sympathy with the employment suggestions of Sir William Beveridge: it did, however, stress more than he the need to accord to trade unions the fullest liberty, and to individual workers, freedom to choose their employment. T.U.C. policy in this matter is discussed in more detail in Chapter XVI.

(c) LABOUR DISPUTES MACHINERY

The peace-time function of trade unions next in importance is to secure high wages and favourable conditions for the workers; and we have already seen that the General Secretary of the T.U.C. promised "to defend the workers against all forms of exploitation during the war". The trade unions accordingly refuted the contention that higher pay for civilian employees was unjust to the soldiers, sailors and airmen. They suggested that levelling should be upwards—soldiers' pay being raised to bring it more into line with civilian pay—that the trade unions were thus fulfilling their trusteeship for those workers, who would expect decent wages after demobilisation.

Moreover, the wages and conditions of some categories of workers were so miserably low at the beginning of the war that output itself was bound to suffer. This was the case for practically all miners and agricultural labourers, to say nothing of certain others not quite so essential to the war effort. Obviously, therefore, a certain adjustment of the wage level was of urgent importance to the war effort itself—hence the first enactment of a minimum wage for agricultural workers at the rate of £3 5s., raised on March 4th, 1945, to £3 10s. and in 1946 to £4, as well as a minimum wage for miners.

Nevertheless the conditions of the wage struggle are admittedly different in war and peace. It might in theory have been possible to raise the wage level in all industries substantially if the unions had decided to use, or even to threaten to use fully the strike weapon. But such action would obviously have endangered the war effort—strikes reducing the output of essential goods, and wage increases and rising prices setting in motion the inflationary spiral—and would have been for other reasons inacceptable to the British workers.

The trade unions had therefore to act with caution, and kept, in the main, to the traditional methods of collective bargaining, coupled with conciliation and arbitration, rather than using strikes to enforce their will in labour disputes. Tentative arrangements made at the beginning of the war had to be given more definite shape after the invasion of France and the Low Countries, and the following recommendations were made unanimously by the National Joint Advisory Council to the Ministry of Labour on May 22nd, 1940:—

"(1) In this period of national emergency it is imperative that there should be no stoppage of work owing to trade disputes. In these circumstances the Consultative Committee representing the British Employers Confederation and the Trades Union Congress have agreed to recommend to the Minister of Labour and National Service the arrangements set out in the following paragraphs.

"(2) The machinery of negotiation existing in any trade or industry for dealing with questions concerning wages and conditions of employment shall continue to operate. Matters in dispute which cannot be settled by means of such machinery shall be referred to arbitration for a decision which will be binding on all parties and no strike or lock-out shall take place. In cases where the machinery of negotiation does not at present provide for reference to such arbitration, the matters in dispute shall be referred for decision to a National Arbitration Tribunal to be appointed by the Minister of Labour and National Service. The Minister shall take power to secure that the wages and conditions of employment settled by the machinery of negotiation or by arbitration shall be made binding on all employers and workers in the trade or industry concerned.

"(3) In any case not covered by the provisions of paragraph (2) any dispute concerning wages or conditions of employment shall be brought to the notice of the Minister of Labour and National Service by whom, if the matter is not otherwise disposed of, it shall be referred within a definite time limit to the National Arbitration Tribunal for decision, and no strike or lock-out shall take place. . . ."

The outcome of this recommendation was the passing of the Conditions of Employment and National Arbitration Order in July 1940 (later amended), according to which disputes were to be settled by negotiation and, if necessary, by arbitration. Lock-outs and strikes were prohibited unless the difference had been reported to the Minister and had not been referred by the Minister for settlement, and it was obligatory for employers in every district to observe terms and conditions which had been settled by collective agreement or by arbitration for the trade concerned in that district. The Order also provided for the recording of departures from trade practices during the war, with a view to facilitating the operation of legislation for the restoration of those practices after the war.

The essential new departures contained in these recommendations and Orders were first the *de facto* renunciation of the strike weapon by the trade unions, and second, as a necessary sequel to this renunciation, the introduction of compulsory arbitration as a last resort in labour disputes. All peace-time provisions for arbitration in British labour disputes are entirely voluntary in character, but obviously, if there is no resort to strikes and lock-outs, there must be some other final authority to settle disputes which prove incapable of voluntary settlement. The trade unions had therefore to accept compulsory arbitration during the war, but they made it very clear that once it was over they would not surrender their established rights.

There remained one important loophole in the "no strikes, no lock-outs" principle. Union officials were not permitted, according to the 1940 Order, to call on the workers to leave their places of work, but there was nothing to prevent the workers themselves from organising "unofficial" strikes. That is to say, the organisation of a strike, and the strike itself, were not illegal, but could receive no support from the union or recognition from the Ministry of Labour.

(d) Unofficial Strikes[1]

An unofficial strike is one that takes place without official sanction of the Executive Committee of the trade union concerned, and in which, therefore, the strikers are not entitled to strike pay from the union funds. That—the widest possible definition—is not entirely satisfactory, for several reasons. There are various possibilities. One is where the National Executive Council of a trade union cannot, on technical grounds, sanction a strike which they nevertheless feel to be morally justified. Another is where the strike is backed by local officials whom the Executive do not wish to repudiate, yet cannot publicly uphold. Causes of such strikes vary. Sometimes, in loyalty to their trade union principles, but in violation of the 1940 Order, workers will strike against either the employment of a non-unionist or against the revocation by the employers of a well-established trade practice. That being a violation of the agreed negotiating machinery, the union cannot openly give its sanction, even if considering it justified. Thus, though on a strict definition nearly all the strikes during the war from July 1940 onwards were unofficial, the strikers often had moral support and sometimes union backing from either national or local resources. When such support was given is often hard to say—a fact to bear in mind in reading Appendix XVII.

A second and psychologically important fact to keep in mind is that workers will sometimes strike on one pretext, though the purpose is to strengthen their representatives' bargaining power in a dispute taking place for other reasons. Even when the union officials must repudiate such a strike as illegal they cannot ignore the help it affords them in seeking favourable results in the other issue.

Although they greatly increased in number during the war as a result of the Condition of Employment and National Arbitration Order, unofficial strikes were by no means the product of the war. They are much more the product of the very negotiating machinery set up by the unions and employers to avoid trade disputes. Such negotiations are almost necessarily, though sometimes unnecessarily, slow, and their results are often compromises—not always good ones. On both counts they give

[1] See Appendix XVII, pp. 263–65.

155

rise to dissatisfaction, and hence to the tendency of the workers to short-circuit matters by direct action. The unofficial strike is often the result of the workers' revolt against the delay in removing grievances.

The characteristics of an unofficial strike are its short duration and the small numbers involved. Usually it is confined to one works or one pit, and in substance to one particular issue, such as the reinstatement of a dismissed shop steward, the rate for a particular job, or the provision of a canteen, rather than on wider questions like *general* wage rates. It is thus not possible to give anything like a comprehensive list of all the unofficial strikes of the war years, but the list in Appendix XVII covers some of the more important ones.

In some of those strikes, as can be seen from the list, a large number of men was involved, and because of this they are not entirely typical of the unofficial strike. Such a strike is essentially a workshop matter and is a spontaneous and, usually, short-lived affair called by the shop stewards to support them in a particular issue before the management.

It seems that unofficial strikes—the illegitimate child of industrial conciliation—have become a permanent part of our industrial life, because industrial conciliation has also come to stay. What should be the union's attitude to them? It is no use ignoring these strikes or treating the men who take part in them as enemies of the working class movement: such an attitude only tends to weaken the union in the eyes of the workers. On the other hand, unions cannot be expected to recognise any and every strike that takes place: such an attitude would be a complete negation of the whole machinery of industrial conciliation so laboriously built up. The solution would seem to lie in an overhaul of the negotiating machinery with a view to the speedier settlement of disputes through the recognised channels. The biggest single cause of unofficial strikes is the workers' feeling that their claim, whatever it may be, will drag on before one tribunal after another and that the union will be fobbed off and stalled, and their case never decided. The way to stop unofficial strikes is to remove completely all causes for such disillusion, which in some cases has a perfectly legitimate basis, by an effective increase in the speed of dealing with disputes through the normal negotiating channels.

During the war unofficial strikes, particularly in such important industries as mining and engineering, were numerous, though most did not last long and most were supported only by
156

small numbers of workers. To some extent the "unofficial strike" served a useful purpose in putting constant pressure on union officials from their own rank and file and forcing them to advance the workers' demands with more energy than they might otherwise have done. On the other hand, they tended to endanger the war effort—the more so since they increased as the risk of invasion receded. The peak of unofficial strike activity was reached in 1943 and in the early part of 1944, and they were partly initiated by small irresponsible political groups.

It was in the special circumstances of those months that the Government decided on further measures against strikes. An Order in Council, issued on April 17th, 1944, provided that "no person shall declare, instigate or incite any other person to take part in, or shall otherwise act in furtherance of, any strike among persons engaged in the performance of essential services or any lock-out of persons so engaged".

Yet this Order did not, even temporarily, do away with the right to strike. On the contrary, the Order contained the provisos that nobody should be liable for punishment (a) because he ceased work or refused to continue to work or to accept employment, or (b) because of any act done at a properly constituted trade union meeting. However, "enticement to strike" was punishable if carried on outside an official trade union meeting, and this measure naturally caused a great deal of uneasiness among union members, even though it was accepted by the great majority of the national trade union leaders. The difference of opinion within the movement found lively expression in the famous "Bevin–Bevan clash" in the House of Commons. Even those who, like Mr. Bevin, defended the measure nevertheless agreed that it should be abolished as soon as possible, and in fact this Regulation was rescinded immediately after victory in Europe, little more than a year after its issue.

CHAPTER XIII

WAGES AND CONDITIONS

(a) WAGES

IT MAY be claimed that the war-time wage policy of the trade unions was on the whole successful because it fulfilled the following conditions:—

(1) Wages to a certain extent kept pace with the cost of living, though some categories of workers fared much worse than others.

(2) The workers received additional remuneration for the special effort made in the form of longer hours, more piece-work, or in work calling for responsibility rather than mere mechanical skill, etc.

(3) Wage-earners who were particularly under-paid before the war received a compensatory increase in pay, especially if their work was important to the war effort.

(4) On the other hand, wages had not risen enough to lead to a great increase in prices, and therewith an uncontrollable inflationary movement.

It must be made clear from the outset that the actual earnings of the workers and the level of their wages differ considerably, as the earnings include not only wages, but overtime, bonuses and other forms of remuneration which were introduced during the war to stimulate their war effort.

Fortunately, the statistics of actual workers' incomes are more complete for the war years than they were in peace-time.[1] The most reliable information is now to be found in the periodical inquiries of the Ministry of Labour. Before the war these were made at quite irregular intervals, but they have appeared half-yearly since July 1941.

The inquiry of July 1944 dealt with nearly six million workers. Like previous returns, it covers practically all manual workers in the manufacturing and building industries and public utilities, and certain categories of transport workers. It is true that such important industries as agriculture, coal-mining, railway work and dock labour are not included, but it is certain that if they *were* included the percentage of war-time increases in manual workers' wages would not be materially different.

The main results of the most recent inquiries can be summarised as shown on page 159.

For convenience the data for October 1938 and July 1944 are given in the form of an index (viz., the 1944 earnings as percentages of the 1938 earnings), also shown on page 159.

The earnings of women and girls have apparently risen somewhat more quickly than those of men and boys. One of the more fortunate results of the war is therefore, that at least

[1] Most of the material is contained in *Ministry of Labour Gazette*, February 1945. See also A. L. Bowley, in *London and Cambridge Economic Service Bulletin*, April 1945.

In the first pay-week of :	Men.		Youths and boys (under 21).		Women.		Girls (under 18).		All.	
	s.	d.	s.	d.	s.	d.	s.	d.	s.	d.
Oct. 1938	69	0	26	1	32	6	18	6	53	3
July 1940	89	0	35	1	38	11	22	4	69	2
July 1941	99	5	41	11	43	11	25	0	75	10
Jan. 1942	102	0	42	6	47	6	26	10	77	9
July 1942	111	9	46	2	54	2	30	3	85	2
Jan. 1943	113	9	45	1	58	6	32	1	87	11
July 1943	121	3	47	2	62	2	33	10	93	7
Jan. 1944	123	8	46	10	63	9	34	3	95	7
July 1944	124	4	47	4	64	3	34	11	96	8
Jan. 1945	119	3	44	1	63	2	33	8	93	9
July 1945	121	4	45	6	63	2	35	1	96	1
Jan. 1946	114	1	43	4	59	10	34	3	92	7
July 1946	—		—		—		—		100	5

	Men.	Youths and boys.	Women.	Girls.	All.
Oct. 1938	100	100	100	100	100
July 1944	180	181	198	189	181½

temporarily, the gap between men's and women's incomes has become smaller. This is hardly surprising, and the difference in the percentage increase between the two categories may at first sight appear smaller than expected; but it should also be remembered that women's working hours during the war were, on the average, not much longer than before, while in the case of men the increase in wages is largely due to the longer working week.

The over-all average increase of 81½ per cent. may be considered a very substantial rise, especially compared with the 37 per cent. for the same period in the official cost-of-living index. But the several factors contributing to this increase must be considered separately if its real significance is to be realised.

First and foremost, it is essential not to confuse this average increase in weekly earnings with the increase in wage-rates—that is, the rate fixed by collective agreements for a certain amount[1] of work of the same type. A worker may increase his income, for instance, by increasing his output by working overtime, or by getting a better job, or by getting better results out of his piecework, etc.[2] Such efforts, if made by many workers, may raise the average weekly earnings very considerably; but it is the increase or decrease of wage rates—a matter for which the trade unions are *mainly* responsible—that is the real index of the rise or fall in the price for the same kind and amount of work.

For the categories of workers included in the Ministry of Labour inquiries the wage rates proper rose between October 1938 and July 1944 by 35½ per cent. Rates for some of the under-paid workers not included in the inquiries rose much more: those for coal-miners and agricultural labourers in particular were practically doubled.[3] Among the industrial workers, those employed in the textile and clothing industries fared rather well, as well as some engineering workers. Wages of printers and compositors—among the best-paid workmen before the war—increased during the war by barely 25 per cent. On the whole, therefore, and in spite of many exceptions to the rule, it seems safe to say that the wage movements during the war diminished to some extent the difference in the wage levels between highly paid and badly paid industries and occupations, as well as between men and women.

Among other factors contributing to the great increase in average weekly earnings there are two whose relative importance is easy to calculate—namely, longer hours and the shifting of workers from such industries as textiles to war industries on higher wage-level. Before the war the average industrial male worker worked rather less than forty-eight hours a week: that average rose to over fifty-three during the war, and dropped to slightly over fifty-one hours in the first pay-week of July 1944.

The working hours of women, youths and girls also rose temporarily during the war, though in 1944 they were no longer substantially above the 1938 level. The trade unions, in the first few years of the war, did not as a rule oppose longer work-

[1] Increased either in length of time or quantity of output.
[2] Or by increasing his output under the difficult system of payment by result.
[3] It should be taken into account that agricultural workers and miners were not able to the same extent as many workers in the manufacturing industries to achieve higher wages by being upgraded, by working longer hours, etc.

ing hours, partly because of the national emergency, and partly also (according to H.M. Inspector for Factories) because longer hours are one of the surest ways of getting a more adequate wage. There was a reaction, however, in the second half of the war, as it came to be realised that after a certain number of hours of effort no first-rate work could be done. The average working hours were about 4 per cent. longer in July 1944 than in October 1938—with a corresponding gain in the pay-packets.

The second factor was the gain through the shifting of workers from one industry to another. Clearly some of the specific war industries (especially engineering) paid wages much higher than were usual in those industries from which they attracted workers. This alone would account for the wage increase in question.[1]

Another factor is the sharp rise in the war industries in the ratio of administrative to operative personnel. Yet another combination of factors made inevitable the higher wages gained during the war. More piecework enabled workers to get more actual pay without any change in the rates. Further, some overtime got a higher rate; and special payments or bonuses were made for work on Sunday, at night, or on holidays. Again, a number of workers got more responsible or better-paid jobs within their own industries by improving their qualifications. These different factors, which cannot be separately assessed, had the cumulative effect of raising considerably the total level of earnings. The increase may be put at as high as 21 per cent.

As a result of all these developments, some categories of workers were able to do, during the war years, much better than they could have hoped to do before. But stories of workers making "a fortune" out of the war are in most cases grossly exaggerated. The industrial group with the highest earnings in July 1944 was "motor vehicle, cycle and aircraft manufacture and repair", where men got on an average of nearly £8 (£7 19s. 11d.) per week. Some of the foremen and highly skilled engineers, of course, earned considerably more, but it must not be forgotten that the "wealth-makers" were by no means numerous, also that they were mostly highly skilled specialists who had to work very long hours

[1] The gain through the re-distribution of industries would even be as high as 8 per cent., but some of this gain was compensated by the substitution of women for men workers.

every day, and finally that they were subject to the same income-tax[1] payments as every other citizen in similar circumstances.

It is possible to conclude that, on the whole, the incomes of the workers showed a handsome, though by no means gigantic increase, and that the lower-paid categories of workers fared, on the whole, comparatively well. The question arises whether these increases were so high as to endanger the policy of price stability which was proclaimed by the Government and supported by the Labour movement.

Sir John Anderson, the Chancellor of the Exchequer, suggested on April 25th, 1944, that the proclaimed policy of maintaining the cost-of-living index on a level of 25 to 30 per cent. above pre-war had been endangered by the rising wage level. "In 1941 (he said), wage rates were 21 to 22 per cent. above the level of September, 1939. In 1943, the increase had reached 35 to 36 per cent. on the average for the year. This is the increase in wage rates. Earnings have, of course, increased a good deal more. Thus, during the period over which the cost-of-living index was rigidly stabilised wage rates rose by about 15 per cent."

Sir John's argument raises the important problem of the so-called cost-of-living index. The argument is, indeed, unanswerable, provided that the movement of the cost-of-living index really reflects a movement of the same size in the actual costs of living of an average working-class family. Against this it is argued by trade unionists that the present cost-of-living index is seriously out-of-date and cannot possibly serve as a yardstick for the actual price movements of the goods and services obtained by working-class families in the 1940's. It is at present, however, compensated by food subsidies.

It can easily be shown that the objections of trade unionists to the existing cost-of-living index are substantially correct. The index now in use is based on a calculation of working-class expenditure in 1914, at the outbreak of the First World War. The index figures, in the words of the official publication, are "to show the average percentage increase in the cost of living prevailing in working-class families prior to August, 1914, *no allowance being made for any changes in the standard of living since*

[1] The incidence of taxation was such that it paid some men better to lay off work for a day or two to prevent their earnings being liable to a higher income-tax rate.

that date, or for any economies or readjustments in consumption and expenditure since the outbreak of the war".

The deficiencies of the index are the more serious, as the working-class budgets, on which it was based, were probably very low, even if measured by 1914 standard of living. It is, for instance, generally acknowledged that a considerable part of the working-class people are usually able to spend at least something like half their income on goods and services other than food: but the official cost-of-living index is based on the assumption that food expenditure amounts to 60 per cent. of the total. This assumption is the more astonishing since such "luxury" foodstuffs as fruit, vegetables other than potatoes, beer, sweets, preserves, breakfast food, tinned food, biscuits, and food taken in restaurants are not included. The budget is similarly austere about items other than food. Nor is any allowance made for education and amusement, or for postage, doctor's fees, insurance, trade union dues, etc. As for electricity and wireless, they did not even figure in a working-class budget of 1914.

These deficiencies were serious enough before the war. Since the war, and more particularly since 1941, the Government has accepted a policy of stable prices, effected mainly by paying subsidies to producers. The goods included in the official index are mainly staple goods[1] whose prices are on the whole successfully stabilised; and the Government can influence the index in such a way as to exclude any changes at all. In 1942, for instance, when the price of clothing was coming down owing to the introduction of utility wear, the Government decided to raise the prices of certain foodstuffs just in order to keep the index stable. The foodstuffs in question were anyhow in very short supply, and were therefore intentionally over-weighted in the index; thus, the price increases did not really matter, and it was therefore possible to balance the fall in clothing prices without tears, so to speak. It can easily be seen that, in such circumstances, the index is no longer a fair measure of the actual price movements. Nor is it denied that some of the prices outside the index have risen more steeply than those in the index itself. This is true with regard to the prices of foodstuffs, and still truer of non-food prices. Furthermore, working-class families must now sometimes buy more expensive articles—pork in-

---

[1] The foodstuffs which are included, and which alone form 60 per cent. of the whole prices, are the main rationed foods (beef, mutton, bacon, tea, sugar, butter, margarine, cheese, eggs) and bread, flour and potatoes.

stead of beef or mutton, for instance—merely because the cheaper varieties are unobtainable. As regards dwellings, which constitute a relatively much larger proportion of working-class expenditure, it must be remembered that the index includes only the rents and rates paid in respect of unfurnished working-class dwellings, which are all subject to the Rent Restriction Act; many war workers, however, were compelled to live in furnished rooms where the rents were allowed to rise by leaps and bounds. Other war workers had to travel much longer distances every day than they had to do before the war, yet the index does not take this into account. Nor is any consideration given in the official index to the deterioration in quality which has doubtless taken place in regard to many goods during the war. It is difficult to give any numerical estimates of the actual rise in the cost of living which has taken place during the war. All impartial observers will agree, however, that these costs have risen by much more than the roughly 30 per cent. indicated in the index; and it can certainly not be maintained that the actual cost of living has remained virtually unchanged since about 1941.

Sir John's argument was, therefore, hardly valid, the more so since he himself agreed that in many cases wage increases were needed either to compensate for anomalies in certain industries or because of the growing efficiency of labour.

On the whole, therefore, though the price-wage mechanism was perhaps not so stabilised during the war as might have been desirable, it is by no means true to say that this comparative instability was the result of unreasonable demands on the part of labour. Certainly the price mechanism would have been far more upset if the workers had been allowed to spend all their income on current consumption; but such action was successfully prevented by a number of counter-measures, among which high income-tax, rationing and the national saving campaign were the most conspicious.

(b) WELFARE ARRANGEMENTS

In war even more than in peace it seemed essential that trade union policy for securing high wages should be accompanied by arrangements for the general well-being of the working population. A high money wage is obviously reduced in value through measures taken to reduce spending, and the trade unions had to see to it that the workers received at least a certain minimum of goods and services for their money.

Furthermore, many new welfare problems arose from special war-time conditions: the recruitment of female and juvenile labour; the transfer of workers to new places; the increased tempo of work, especially during such crucial periods as after Dunkirk, the black-out and many other war time arrangements—all those made life harder and sometimes more dangerous. These conditions called for vigilance and for active intervention by the unions in the interests of the workers. The necessity of such vigilance can be illustrated, for instance, by the growing number of reportable accidents in factories, fatal and non-fatal, during the first few years of the war. The number of such accidents was 180,103 in the last full pre-war year (1938), and it was as high as 314,630 in 1942—i.e., 75 per cent. higher, in the fourth year of the war (1942). It was slightly lower (311,144) in 1943.[1]

From quite early in the war the T.U.C. took a very proper interest in these problems: it set up a special Rationing and Price Committee with a view to giving competent advice to Government Departments on all questions of the supply of food and essential commodities, and its advice was indeed often asked. Trade unionists also took an active interest in the administration of rationing and food supply at lower levels: it was arranged that every Trades Council could ask to have representatives present at local Food Committees, and those Committees had to admit them provided that the T.U.C. vouched for their *bona fides*.

The Mineworkers and other unions suggested that special rations should be granted to heavy manual workers, but the T.U.C. and the Rationing and Price Committee were not in favour of this demand, partly because of the administrative difficulties connected with differential rations, and partly because extra rations given to special workers might, if used by their families, fail to achieve their purpose. As an alternative the trade unions favoured the opening of workshop canteens where the workpeople, and they alone, could get cheap and nourishing meals. Extra rations were granted only to certain categories of workers for whom the provision of factory canteens was impracticable. The most important of such groups are agricultural labourers, who receive special cheese rations

[1] These and other facts in this section have been taken from "Annual Report of the Chief Inspector of Factories for the Year, 1943", Cmd. 6563. Useful material is also contained in "War-time Developments in Factory Welfare", *Fabian Quarterly*, No. 46, 1945.

the whole year round and further additional foodstuffs during the harvest. Although this scheme looks satisfactory on paper, it seems that many agricultural workers never got their harvest rations because their employers did not bother to make the special application.

The Rationing and Price Committee has used its influence to secure special rations for workshop canteens in an attempt to improve the nutritive value of the food served. In thousands of factories special Canteen Committees were established, operated sometimes in connection with Joint Production Committees, thus enabling trade unionists to keep an eye on the arrangements. According to H.M. Chief Inspector of Factories, the number of factories with canteens was as high as 11,630 in December 1944. Canteens exist in nearly all large factories; due, however, to the technical difficulties involved, they were lacking in many of the smaller factories, as well as at docks, on building sites, etc. Things are better in collieries where canteens are officially stated to be either in operation or in preparation in 98 per cent. of all establishments.[1]

Useful as was the part played by works canteens during the war, it took a long time to educate workers to make full use of them. Special efforts were made to provide canteen meals for youths, but nevertheless "it appears that some young people do not use the canteen facilities which have been made available at most of the larger industrial establishments. They are too often content with scanty meals which do not provide sufficient nourishment, and they need to be educated to make full use of the facilities in factory canteens, which provide adequate hot meals during the dinner hour break. This is all the more important when so many mothers are unable to cook suitable meals at home because they themselves are engaged on full-time or part-time employment on war work." (From the White Paper on "Youth Registration in 1942".)

War economy, of course, covers every side of the economic life of the nation—not only labour supply and munition production. The unions have also taken interest during the war in distribution and similar problems, and there has been co-operation between the unions and the Government with regard to rationing of food, clothing and other consumers' goods.

The T.U.C. Rationing and Price Commission has also been active about the provision of goods other than food, and was

[1] Ministry of Fuel and Power, Statistical Digest, 1944, Cmd. 6639.

largely responsible for getting delivery of working clothes. In the small but important matter of alarm clocks, long reserved for war-workers only, distribution was helped by the trade unions, their officials testifying to the needs of special workers.

The shop stewards, rather than the trade union officials themselves, started at the beginning of the war a movement for the appointment of welfare officers to deal with the special problems of the numerous transferred workers, juvenile and female workers, etc. Early in the war, however, the unions took the question up, Mr. Bevin, the Minister of Labour, showing particular sympathy with the idea. Consequently, the number of Personnel Managers or Welfare Supervisors attached to factories with more than 250 persons increased from 1,500 before the war to 5,378 in January 1944. Necessarily, many of the new officers had to come from the ranks of unqualified people, but the Ministry of Labour also introduced a number of special courses at technical colleges and universities in which up to 1944 between 700 and 800 people were newly trained in factory welfare and personnel management.

According to Factory Inspectors' reports, many welfare officers still had to work under such great handicaps as insufficient support from the factory directors, lack of secretarial help, insufficient training, etc. On the other hand, many examples are quoted of welfare officers helping to solve difficult problems alike on the human side and in matters of physical welfare (washing facilities, ventilation, lighting, etc.). The frequent results in the form of a decidedly higher output show that improved workers' welfare benefit the management as well as the workers. The importance during the war of sufficient holidays for overworked people was another important aspect of welfare work. It should be remembered that in March 1938, when an official inquiry into the question was held, only about 3 million manual wage-earners were enjoying holidays with pay, under collective agreements: some 1,100 new arrangements made after that entitling workers to paid holidays either by collective agreements or statutory orders raised the numbers benefiting in 1944 to some 10 million manual workers, and many non-manual as well. The usual holiday period is between six and twelve days and the qualifying period is mostly twelve months' previous employment.[1]

[1] Ministry of Labour, February 1945.

The preceding narrative does not claim to be complete, but perhaps it gives an idea of the many services the trade unions rendered in war-time to help the workers in conditions of increasing hardship. The aim of some of these measures was higher output, constituting *ipso facto* a contribution to the war effort. But the unions inaugurated many other measures, especially on production policy, which did not concern welfare at all, but were designed primarily to further the war effort.

The Secretary of the T.U.C. himself advocated, among the war-time tasks of the movement, preparations for the post-war period. This aspect of war-time trade union activity, although important, was carried on mainly at the higher levels, and naturally did not affect the everyday work of the average trade union member. The post-war plans thus worked out by the T.U.C. and the national unions are described in Chapters XV, XVI and XVII.

It remains to examine briefly what happened during the war to such other trade union tasks as social security, education and work in the political field.

Generally speaking, these three have all been maintained during the war, though on a reduced scale. We have seen when dealing with trade union finance how payments under the headings of social insurance diminished during the war years—a not surprising consequence of the high level of employment. Educational activities had to be sharply cut down because of the long working hours, the preoccupation of the workers with Civil Defence and other duties, the black-out, the shortage of teaching staff, etc. Similarly, the political activities throughout the Labour movement were more or less in abeyance under the political truce. The essential point is, however, that the apparatus for all these trade union activities—educational, political and social insurance—was kept intact during the war years, so that the activities themselves could be fully resumed as soon as the opportunity arose.

CHAPTER XIV

TRADE UNIONS AND NATIONAL PRODUCTION

IT SHOULD now be clear that during a modern war of defence there is less call for militant action to secure the traditional objectives of the trade unions than there is normally in peace-time. The war against Hitlerism, however, created in Britain particular problems of general economic policy in the solution of which the Labour movement had new rôles—consultative, executive and operational—greater than ever before.

From the beginning trade union leaders started to support actively the general economic and production policies of the Government, aiming at the same time to maintain and improve the conditions of labour. The rank and file was enthusiastically behind this positive attitude, and from 1941 onwards exerted increasing pressure for full and vigorous participation of their own representatives in the management of factories connected with war production. This two-way movement, from above or from below, brought into being during the war years a wide, if incomplete, network of worker representation at every level and key point in the national scheme of war production—from the high strategical level of the ministerial direction of the war effort, through various stages of regional organisation, right down to the workshop.

(a) PRODUCTION POLICY IN THE EARLY PART OF THE WAR

The obstacles to the full utilisation of the experience of trade union leaders—in the *strategic direction of war production* as distinct from the more specialised problems of labour policy—were quite serious in the earlier period, as there was no even fairly satisfactory machinery for co-operation before the early half of 1942. This may have been because, until then, the Government production machinery itself was a patchwork of very doubtful utility, and in the absence of such adequate machinery it was all the more difficult to secure the co-opera-tion of the trade union leaders. It will be remembered, for instance, that at the beginning of the war munition production for the different services was in the hands of a variety of Ministers, that a co-ordinating "Production Council" was appointed only in 1940, and a Minister of Supply only after Pearl Harbour—in 1942. There had not even been regional organisation of the Departments responsible for munition pro-duction, and only after the formation of the Churchill Govern-ment were the first decentralisation measures in the Ministry of Supply carried out. It took two more years before the regional organisation took final shape.

A committee under the chairmanship, significantly enough, of Sir Walter Citrine, General Secretary of the T.U.C., was

169

appointed in 1942, after the Ministry of Production had been formed, to advise on the best methods of regional organisation, etc., and it was on the basis of this Committee's recommendations that the Production Executive and the whole mechanism of war production was reorganised.

The unhelpful attitude of the employers' organisations early in the war was a further obstacle to co-operation on a production strategy. Joint councils of trade unionists and industrialists to advise the Ministry of Supply, the Air Ministry and the Admiralty—that is to the individual Ministries responsible for munitions production—might have been formed in 1939. But the employers' organisations were not interested in having them set up, presumably because there were sufficient industrialists "on loan" to the various Government Departments to make possible full control from their point of view without any definite organisation. Thus the only bodies which could at first be formed were Trades Union Advisory Committees to the Ministry of Supply and the Air Ministry. Joint committees on both national and regional bases, representing employers and trade unionists, were formed during 1941—at about the same time as the movement for Joint Production Committees in the workshops was starting on a large scale; nevertheless in the first few months of their existence these committees were somewhat ineffective just because there was no Ministry of Production to co-ordinate the whole effort.

(b) Production Committees: 1942–1945

I. *National Level*

Since the reorganisation of 1942 the joint advisory machinery to the Production Executive consisted of organisations on both national and regional levels; it was also linked to the new Joint Production Committee at workshop level. The National Production Advisory Council to the Minister of Production was composed of six representatives of the T.U.C., three of the F.B.I., three of the British Employers' Confederation, and eleven vice-chairmen of Regional Boards, of whom six were employers' vice-chairmen and five workers' vice-chairmen. The Minister of Production (as chairman) and the other Ministers concerned with war production also attended the meetings of the Council as and when necessary. The duties of this Council were to advise the Minister of Production "on general production questions (excluding matters which were normally handled by the joint organisations of trade unions and employers in connection with wages and conditions of employment) and on such production matters as arose from the proceedings of the regional organisations". According, however, to Sir Walter Citrine, who originally suggested the formation of this Council, the trade union and employers' representatives received much valuable information, but were very rarely consulted about production difficulties or ways to overcome them. Moreover, as the war went on, interest in the Council fell off; at first it met monthly, but early in 1944 the Minister suggested that quarterly meetings would suffice. As a result of trade union pressure he finally agreed to bi-monthly meetings.

This picture would be incomplete without mention of some further organisations, also on the national level. Trade unionists, together with other experts, sit on an Industrial Panel upon which the Minister of Production may call whenever investigation is needed into some particular firm or a specially difficult production problem. Joint Industrial Councils of industrialists and trade unionists are also attached to the Ministry of Supply and the Admiralty to improve co-operation in the ordnance factories and dockyards, and with the Ministry of Aircraft Production there were less formal consultation arrangements. Finally, the Ministry of Fuel and Power, though not under the supervision of the Production Executive, has also developed consultative machinery. The National Coal Board, with functions somewhat similar to those of the Production Advisory Council, has as its members the two vice-chairmen (one employer and one worker) of each of the eight Regional Coal Boards, and various other members.

II. *Regional Level*

In each of the eleven production regions there was set up a Regional Board, consisting of the Ministry of Production's Regional Controller acting as chairman, of the regional representatives of various other economic departments and, *most significantly*, of an equal number of employers' and of workers' representatives respectively; the latter were appointed by the Minister of Production after consultation with either the British Employers' Confederation or the Federation of British Industries, and with the T.U.C. Further, district committees in the most important centres of war production also include representatives of both sides of the industry; and there existed, independently of the production machinery, for every mining

171

region, a Regional Coal Board, appointed by the Minister of Fuel and Power from representatives of the coal-owners, miners, managers and technical staff. The purpose of these regional organisations is, in the words of the original Citrine Committee, "to assist the Minister of Production and the supply Ministries to make, in a co-ordinated manner, the fullest and most efficient use of the actual or potential resources and manufacturing capacity of the regions for the purpose of carrying out production programmes, whether approved or in contemplation". It seems that the regional organisations had in many cases carried out very useful work, although T.U.C. critics are of opinion that the efficiency of some of these organisations had been impaired through lack of enthusiasm on the part of the authorities.

III. *Workshop Level*

The Joint Production Committees in the workshops differ from the national and regional production machinery, for, although the State has shown definite interest in them, they remain voluntary organisations. In a statement submitted to the International Labour Office, Mr. Jack Tanner, President of the A.E.U., sums up the significance of the J.P.C.s in the following words :—

> "The J.P.C.s are of exceptional importance in war-time industry because they have released the latent dynamic factor of the workers' initiative and brought into play the almost inexhaustible reserves of knowledge, experience, inventive capacity and practical genius of the industrial worker. The J.P.C. movement was initiated by the workers and their organisations. The committees were only set up and developed by constant and unremitting pressure from the workers' side. This is their essential feature, distinguishing them from all previous movements to establish worker–management co-operation. The present movement does not derive from the superficially similar one of the 1914–18 war and to trace such a relationship, or to identify the J.P.C.s of to-day with the workshop movement of the last war, is to miss their character and significance altogether."

There are no hard-and-fast rules about the constitution or tasks of the committees. As they have grown out of very different conditions, they naturally differ greatly from one workshop to another. Nevertheless, they have gained a semi-official

172

status, and their development has been stimulated in two important industries by national agreements which provide for the setting-up of such committees. The first agreement, which was made on February 26th, 1942, with the Ministry of Supply, provides a model constitution for the establishment of J.P.C.s in all Royal Ordnance Factories; the second agreement—with the Engineering and Allied Employers' Federation, which followed on March 18th, 1942—provides for the setting up of similar committees in all private munitions and metal-working establishments where at least 150 workpeople are employed; committees in smaller workshops may be, and often are, set up by mutual agreement.[1] In many collieries, too, there are Pit Committees; there are also Yard Committees in nearly all private shipyards, and Joint Site Committees in most of the larger building sites working under contract with the Minister of Works, etc. The number covered by all these committees is estimated at probably over 3,500,000 workers.

Usually, though not always, there is the same number of representatives of the workers as of the management in the Joint Committees. The former are in many cases also shop stewards, though quite intentionally the two offices are not made identical. One reason for this separation is that the committees would easily become unwieldy if *all* the shop stewards in a big factory joined the workers' side of the committee. More important, however, is the consideration that J.P.C.s should not concern themselves with questions of wages and labour conditions. Furthermore, the most democratic method of electing representatives on the workers' side, and the one which at the same time secures the greatest publicity for the J.P.C. idea, is the ballot: and in fact this is the method generally used for appointing the workers' members on the J.P.C.s. Every adult worker, whether man or woman, can be elected if a trade union member; there is a further provision that he or she must have been two years in the workshop, but this provision (which may easily work against the election of women) can be waived.

An odd provision which greatly detracts from the practical value of the J.P.C.s is that "white-collar" employees—*i.e.*, the clerical, technical and scientific staff—are not allowed to take part in the ballot. Most valuable suggestions for the improve-

[1] Towards the end of 1944 the number of Joint Production Committees was 4,500, including 1,600 in establishments employing less than 150 workers.

ment of production methods might undoubtedly come from these specialised workers.[1] Trade unions in general, and those catering for "white-collar" employees in particular, have tried hard to abolish this provision, but the employers have so far stuck to their point that "salaried employees are not workers," except the shipbuilding employers, who agreed to the representation of draughtsmen on the Yard Committees.

The following list of topics on J.P.C. agenda was published by the Ministry of Aircraft Production. It is admittedly very limited, and also the minutes of only two meetings from each of sixty-three firms have been published. Even so it gives a rough idea of the kind of problems discussed.[2] From the trade union side come many complaints of employers trying to side-track the committee on questions of welfare and absenteeism; but it is nevertheless an acknowledged fact that many of the committees have done a very useful job.

This has been clearly recognised by the trade union move-

[1] In the U.S.S.R. managerial and technical employees represent one-third of all members of the Production Committees. See "Our Soviet Ally", London, 1943, article by N. Barou, "Soviet Trade Unions", p. 128.
[2]

Subject.	Items discussed.
Technical questions	266
Organisation	141
Labour supply	85
Supply of equipment, components, etc. . . .	60
Progress reports	59
Fuel economy and scrap drives . . .	51
Specific cases of "bottle-necks"	47
Total: Technical and production subjects . .	709
Welfare	198
Absenteeism	45
Hours	44
Wages	27
Total: Welfare and other personnel subjects . .	314
Production committee machinery . . .	37
Miscellaneous	77
Total: Other subjects	114
TOTAL	1,137

ment, as the following resolution unanimously adopted by the 1945 Trades Union Congress clearly shows.

"This Congress recognises the importance of the part which Shop Stewards and Joint Production Committees played during the war, and is convinced that the workshop machinery should be definitely established as a primary measure of Post-War Reconstruction. It is convinced that it is essential for the General Council, after consultation with the Unions concerned, to make recommendations for strengthening and expanding the functions of this machinery in harmony with the respective Unions so that it can adequately extend Trade Union organisation, supervise agreements and act effectively on questions of welfare, safety, and production."

IV. *Co-ordination between the Three Levels*

Special provisions have been made in the collective agreements for questions that cannot be settled within the J.P.C., and it is here that the workshop organisation comes into contact with the regional and national machinery of the Production Executive. Generally speaking, the problem in dispute is to be referred to the Regional Board for investigation and decision, but the method of submission is somewhat different according to whether the two sides of a J.P.C. can agree or not on joint terms of reference. If they agree, the joint submission is made directly to the Board from the J.P.C.; if not, each side (the workers and the management) may submit their case to their trade union or employers' organisation, which may then forward it to the Regional Board. Complaints from the actual workshops helped to enliven the work of the Regional Board, and also of the District Committees, which may be commissioned by the Boards to investigate the problem, even though the number of submissions has on the whole been very small.

The T.U.C. has, along with the appropriate unions, formed special District Production Committees to deal with complaints from the workers' sides of the J.P.C.s and also to co-ordinate the work in various local factories and propagate the J.P.C. idea; the local Trades Councils are not supposed to concern themselves with the establishment of Joint Production Committees. The national organisation appointed by the T.U.C. for the co-ordination of this side of trade union activities is the

National Advisory Committee for the Engineering and Ship-building Industries.[1]

(c) POST-WAR PLANS

The collective agreements only provide for Joint Production Committees to be set up during the war; but, as shown in Chapter XV, the T.U.C. itself intends to maintain its interest in production matters after the war, at least in the nationalised sector of the industry. A very far-reaching resolution was moved and carried by the Trades Union Congress at Blackpool in October 1944:—

"That this Congress declares itself in favour of continuing in the post-war period the Joint Production Committees established during the war and the method of electing same, and of extending this principle into wide spheres of production, industry and commerce generally to suit peacetime needs. Congress regrets that the Engineering and Allied Employers' National Federation persists in excluding technical and administrative workers from participation on the workers' side of these Committees and instructs the General Council to take immediate steps to remedy this position."

In the field of production trade union experience during the war may prove to have been invaluable for the Labour movement. It can be said that the Joint Production Committees were one of the most significant social–economic developments of the war period in Britain. There, in many cases, the workers had a definite job to do, and made good use of the joint machinery to see that the job was done. At the higher levels, the functions of the Advisory and other committees were never adequately defined; nor did the trade unions have a sufficiently clear policy of their own with regard to war production.

On most major issues of industrial war economy the trade unions were rarely prepared definitely to take the lead. To enable them in future to take their rightful place in the reconstruction of industries or the increase of their productivity the movement would be well advised to improve greatly its own organisation for technical and economic research.

It was valuable to sit in on "fifty-fifty" committees and learn, as trade union representatives did during the war, about production plans for things like mulberries and tanks or planes

[1] We add at the end of this chapter a list showing the most important features of the new production machinery.

176

even when initiated by the Government or employers. But how much more valuable for rebuilding Britain on socialist lines would it be if trade union representatives were to come with their own well-prepared programmes. Such programmes are needed not only on the national, but on every level where Joint Production and Working Committees already exist or ought to be created. That can be realised when the trade union movement, rendered more confident by the knowledge of its indispensable contribution made during the war, and thus more aware of its even greater rôle and possibilities in the peace, equips itself with an efficient modern technical and economic research organisation commensurate with the political mandate the electorate gave to Labour in 1945.

War-time Production Machinery

Note.—Only the machinery connected with the Ministry of Production is outlined here. There is similar machinery with the Ministry of Fuel and Power, and there are some less essential committees in connection with the Ministries of Supply, Aircraft, Production, Admiralty, etc. Independently of the production side, there exists a fairly complete consultative machinery with the Ministry of Labour; and there are some provisions for participation of trade union representatives with the Ministries connected with rationing.

Level.	Trade union organisation.	Production machinery.
National Level.	T.U.C. *National Advisory Committee for the engineering and building industries.*	*Minister of Production.* *National Production Advisory Committee.* Members: Representatives of T.U.C. (6), F.B.I. (3), B.E.C. (3), Chairman Regional Boards (11). *Industrial Panel.* Members: T.U.C. and other experts.
Regional Level.		*Regional Boards* (in 11 Regions). Chairmen: Controllers of M.O.P. Members: Regional representatives of other economic departments—equal numbers of trade union and employers' representatives.

Level.	Trade union organisation.	Production machinery.
	District Production Committees.	*District Committees* (only in important districts). Members: representatives of trade unions and employers.
Workshop Level.	*Workers' side of J.P.C.s.*	*Joint Production Committees* (in all larger engineering and other workshops). Members: Usually equal numbers of workers' representatives (mostly elected) and management's representatives.

PART FOUR

THE FUTURE

CHAPTER XV

THE FUTURE OF TRADE UNIONS

INTRODUCTION

THIS BOOK was well advanced before Labour secured its Parliamentary victory in July 1945. It would have been hard to rewrite it fully in order to relate its conclusions and suggestions to the future of a Labour Britain. The obstacles were twofold: the economics and social mechanics of the transition period would require a special and detailed study quite beyond the limits of our investigation; and—not less important—the trade unions themselves have not yet made up their minds about all the changes required in their policy and organisation by the coming of a Labour Government elected on the new programme of nationalisation and planning.

It would be premature to do anything more now than indicate the general direction that such changes should seek to follow, and that is what we have attempted to outline in the last part of this book.

It is interesting, however, to compare the views of the T.U.C. and those of the employers' organisations on the part to be played by trade unions in the post-war period. These were published before the end of the war, and show very clearly how far apart were these two groups in their plans for the future of trade unionism. It, however, shows that both parties wanted the State to leave them to settle their differences in the traditional manner.

(a) CAPITALIST VIEWS

Capitalist organisations and writers in this country have hardly yet had time to recover from the victory of Labour and to adjust their own thinking to the resulting changes. During the war, however, blue prints of *capitalist planning* were coming

179

fast from many willing hands. They came from groups, institutions and individuals occupying leading positions in the economic life of the British Empire—the Federation of British Industries, the Chambers of Commerce, the "120 industrialists", Mr Courtauld, Unilever, Ltd., and others. All these plans have one feature in common: they did not expect a Labour Parliamentary majority, and visualised the economic transition from war to peace under private capitalist control. It is instructive to see the place accorded to the trade unions in these statements, which reveal three main approaches:—

(1) The extreme individualist group still believes in the capitalism of the nineteenth century—*i.e.*, in unlimited competition—and advocates full freedom for the economic conflict of workers and employers; State interference, and especially State capitalism, it considers anathema. So detached is it from the realities of modern monopoly capitalism that it is hardly taken seriously, even by the rest of the employers.

(2) The group represented by the "120 industrialists" accept State capitalism, but believes that industry should be left to govern itself and each industry should be accordingly "organised". In each separate industry the "120" industrialists are quite ready to make a deal with the workers through their trade unions. They stipulate, however, that the "direction" of industry shall be left in the hands of the enlightened, benevolent and progressive capitalists, who best know how to organise trade and industry, and who will be good to their workers and employees, sharing with them as much as they can afford. Notwithstanding its niceties, this silk-glove approach is designed to retain exclusive direction of each industry in the hands of employers alone, and is a kind of capitalist syndicalism.

(3) The group represented by Unilever, Ltd., produced a report which is more significant than all the other capitalist blue-prints. It has all the trimmings of capitalist democracy. As one newspaper said, "It is a kind of economic New Deal in British conditions". A New Deal in a country where the labour organisations are not strong enough, or not prepared to take responsibility for the political government of the community, may be a progressive approach. For this country, however, such proposals are a different matter. In the necessary adjustment of the inequalities of the British

economic system the organised labour forces in industry and trade must, and are quite fit to, play their part. Unilever's "New Deal" would effectively prevent the workers' organisations from taking due responsibility for the conduct of trade and industry; it would try to keep them in the subordinate position which they still occupy.

The Report tries its best to camouflage its real approach: it states that "industry is not taking part in the general direction of economic life", and this is left to the State. The main problem in the economic sphere is the question of capitalist investment, and this "lies with the Government".

The Unilever Report does not advocate the organisation of industry on compulsory lines, as suggested by the "120 industrialists". That is too crude for the enlightened capitalist democrats of Unilever. Representation in Parliament by nearly 400 Conservative members was quite sufficient for the protection of their interests, and it would be of interest to see the suggestions of the Unilever Report readjusted to the conditions now that a Labour Government has come.

According to capitalist plans, the main question in their relations with trade unions is the readiness of the unions to become junior partners of monopoly capitalism, and to share the spoils with it. This is not a new idea. It originated in Germany in 1927–1928 under the title of "economic democracy", and some of the German socialists fell for it. For that "political innocence" they paid dearly in the concentration camps of Fascist Germany, which owed its victory to the political demoralisation of the German Labour movement through its collaboration with national capitalism.

The increased competition in world markets and the shrinkage of the fields of colonial exploitation would make economic and political collaboration between British capitalism and British trade unions very difficult, and would entail great disadvantages for British Labour.

(b) TRADE UNION VIEWS

1. *Main Objectives*

The rôle to which capitalists would confine trade unions in post-war reconstruction was seen in the preceding summary of authoritative pronouncements. Some idea of the trade unions' view of their rôle in the organisation of post-war Britain can be found in the Interim Report on post-war reconstruction published by the T.U.C. in 1944, though one must not overlook the fact that the T.U.C. apparently did not expect the "landslide" of 1945.

With its traditional trade union approach, the Interim Report sets out as the main objectives for that crucial period : (a) to assure adequate opportunities for suitable employment and to maintain and improve wages, hours and conditions of work, and (b) to extend the influence of organised labour over industrial policy and development. To these a third task is added, arising out of war-time experience : the participation of the workers and their trade unions in the management of industry.

Bitter experience has taught the unions how closely interconnected in modern industrial society those three objectives are : better wages and working conditions, for instance, are not just a matter of collective bargaining for higher pay in terms of money; they affect at the same time the cost of living, the general level of prices and so forth. "We are", says the Report, "concerned with increasing the size of the real national income and with the share of it which should accrue to workpeople in terms of goods and services, conditions of work and leisure, as well as opportunities for individual and social development."

The trade unions' share in responsibility for State economic activities is specially important, if only because those activities should include, according to the Interim Report "(a) the determination of wages and working conditions; (b) the control of prices; (c) the control of monopolies, etc.".

Let us see how the Interim Report proposes to reach these main objectives, starting with the problem of guaranteed employment.

2. *What Kind of Full Employment?*

While adopting the slogan of full employment, the Report emphasises that the "right to work"—a right which the unions have always tried to get firmly established—is not just a claim for a job of *any* kind.

"We are concerned to ensure that every worker shall be able, within limits determined only by the need to safeguard the reasonable freedom of others, to *choose* freely work which he prefers and for which he is trained, at rates of wages and in conditions commensurate with his skill and the nature of the work."

Sir William Beveridge's definition of full employment as a state of affairs where there are more vacant jobs than unemployed men, is therefore acceptable to the T.U.C.

"Except that [in the words of the Report] by 'vacant jobs' we mean jobs on terms and conditions not less favourable than those negotiated by Unions which, in any 'free society' would be free to determine their own policy and to pursue their normal activities; and further, that the T.U.C. could not at any stage commit itself in advance to approve or to acquiesce in the methods to be adopted to reach full employment simply because those methods can be shown to be well fitted and even necessary to the achievement of that objective."

The general attitude of the T.U.C. is summed up in the words that "the task of the Trade Union Movement is at one and the same time to inspire the Government to pursue a proper employment policy and to protect work-people against unnecessary encroachment upon their freedom of action".

The language used by the Report in this part is very vague. It is evident that a "free society" apparently means a Parliamentary democracy, where trade unions may determine their own policy and pursue "their normal activities". It is more difficult to see what is meant by "normal activities", but these also it must be left to the unions to decide. If, however, trade union policy or activities conflict with the interests of other groups of the population, then such conflict can, and should, finally be resolved by Parliament. For if the trade unions want to avoid Government interference in their activities, if they prefer to rely on their own bargaining powers and deal directly with the employers' organisations, then they must be ready to give adequate guarantees that their members will uphold agreements which the unions have made on their behalf.

In principle the unions would be prepared to do so, in the interests of Full Employment, but they would only give such assurances and guarantees under certain conditions and with qualifications. The main conditions seem to be price control and greater legal freedom for the unions.

The first condition is formulated as follows: the Government would have to convince the trade unions "that in genuine pursuit of a policy of full employment it is determined to take all other steps that are necessary to control prices"; and the Government would also have to convince the movement "of the need to secure equivalent guarantees that wage movements will not be such as to upset the system of price control".

The second condition the Report formulates in even greater detail:

> "We are bound to insist that in all circumstances Trade Unions should retain their present freedom from legal restraints upon their right to frame policy and pursue activities in support of that policy and should even be given greater legal freedom in those respects than they now possess. As voluntary associations of workpeople they must, in their policies, interpret the wishes of workpeople and their actions must be designed to protect and advance workpeople's common interests. Otherwise, though they may continue to exist as organisations, they will cease to be Trade Unions."

Clearly the part of the Report which deals with industrial policy and management must be considered first, before conclusions can be drawn as to whether under conditions of planned economy trade unions can retain their essential characteristics or powers.

3. *Industrial Policy and Management*

With regard to the Interim Report's second main objective of trade unionism—namely, to increase the influence of the workpeople in industry, etc.—the T.U.C. has so far made only tentative suggestions for the new machinery of public control; these embody various ideas from previous T.U.C. reports, as well as a number of new points.

On the national level, the T.U.C. still favours the proposal of a National Industrial Council, originating in the National Industrial Conference of 1919 and endorsed by the Melchett–Turner Conference. Such a body, which should be representative of all parties in industry and economic life, "would provide the Government with detailed industrial experience upon which to draw in the formulation of policy. It would also materially assist in the application of economic policy to industry".

The T.U.C. envisages an economic future where a large proportion of industry will emerge from private control, so that the question to be faced becomes whether the Governing Boards of socialised industries should be mainly constituted through Government appointments, or to what extent trade union representatives should act as members of these Boards.

184

This problem has occupied the minds of trade unionists for many years and has been given different answers at different times. The Interim Report points out that "ultimate control over the policy and direction of a public industry must be exercised by Parliament as representative of the community in general. Public control must be secured through the definite responsibility of a Minister to Parliament for the industry's affairs. This in turn must be ensured by placing the administration of the industry in the hands of persons responsible to the Minister for that administration." Persons composing the Governing Boards "should be selected for their competence efficiently to administer the industry" in the public interest.

The idea of having on the Boards workers' representatives who would participate in an advisory capacity only, the T.U.C. rejects, since such representatives would be without any real influence. Nor would it be in the interest of the trade unions to appoint to the Boards representatives who would be responsible to the Minister, and who would therefore lose their independence.

It is, however, in the interest of efficiency in the industry itself that there shall be on the Boards at least some persons who have gained wide experience in the trade union movement, and who shall ensure that the view of the workers receive full consideration by the management.

It is suggested that this end "might best be secured by nomination by workers' organisations of candidates from whom the Minister shall select a number of the Board members. The T.U.C. as representative of the viewpoint of organised workers in general, might well serve as the best channel for this, particularly since, in cases where a number of separate unions each have a substantial membership in the industry, it would be difficult to determine the responsibility of the Minister concerned to the different unions. The T.U.C. would, of course, consult with the appropriate Unions about nominations. On the other hand, while those appointed should hold office for a definite period, it seems proper that they should surrender any position held in, or any formal responsibility to, the Trade Union".

It is further suggested that, in addition to the Governing Boards, Consultative Councils should be introduced in publicly owned industries, which could regularly and frequently meet with the Boards to discuss policy. On such Councils it is suggested that the trade unions should be directly represented.

4. Socialised and Regulated Industries

The Interim Report suggests that on the workshop level, the wartime experiment with Joint Production Committees, which has proved successful, should be carried over to the peace. It is, however, only in the field of socialised industries, where the workers have a genuine interest in efficiency, that Work Councils should be set up to watch over technical, administrative, financial and commercial matters. The Trade Unions concerned should, however, always be consulted about the form and scope of such Councils; and they should undertake "the general duty of surveillance of the effective functioning of consultation at all levels and of direct representation to the Government where the machinery is inadequate, is perverted or is ignored".

Questions of wages and labour conditions should still remain the province of the trade unions; "the consultative machinery of public industry should not be prejudiced by association with wage disputes"; nor should the workers be denied their right to be heard freely on matters concerning their conditions of labour, even in a socialised industry.

Finally, the T.U.C. hopes that trade union organisation in socialised industries will extend to administrative and technical personnel; under socialist conditions the traditional division between management and workers would no longer hold good.

The T.U.C. is further of opinion that even the industries which will remain under private management are nevertheless in urgent need of public regulation. Such regulation should, for instance, counteract monopolistic tendencies, should further unification and efficiency (as in the cotton industry), and secure a regular supply of good-quality products at reasonable prices for the general public, etc. It is assumed that in all such industries Industrial Boards will have to be set up, and that the trade unions will there co-operate along with representatives of the employers and of neutral parties, such as the consumers. The composition and the function of these Boards, as well as their relations with the Government, will probably vary from industry to industry, according to their several economic functions. The T.U.C. abstains from formulating any detailed suggestions for their working. Generally speaking, however, these Boards should concern themselves with "the internal organisation of the industry". That pretty well implies general planning of a given industry with a view to maximum efficiency of production, measures for concentration and specialisation of production, standardisation, measures for technical education, research into marketing and export requirements and so forth. There might also be included the promotion of general welfare services for the industry's employees.

Two important functions should be definitely excluded:—

(1) Negotiations on wages and conditions of employment. "In most of these industries there is established machinery for the settlement of disputes, which has proved its value and need not be disturbed."

(2) "On those matters which directly affect interests other than those internal to the industry the Boards should not be empowered with final authority. Any proposals to fix minimum general prices or restrict production or entry into the industry should be subject to stricter examination by an appropriate body and to approval by the Government, possibly by Parliament."

5. *Conclusions*

Such policy as the Interim Report advocates suggests that the General Council of the T.U.C. has been content to stop at a halfway house, not realising that the introduction of full employment would radically change the whole industrial scene. With the fear of unemployment banished would vanish at the same time one of the great forces in capitalist society— the force that contributed as much as any other to urge work-people to establish trade unions and remain in membership in order to ensure employment. Under conditions of full employment new and powerful incentives will be required to sustain the membership of trade union organisations. These incentives will have to be not merely defensive, but of a positive and creative kind.

Full employment in modern industrial democratic society will demand planning on a greatly extended scale, and in the State planning organisations it is essential to ensure that the interests of the workers shall be represented by their trade unions and Co-operative Societies. Strangely enough the Interim Report does not even mention this problem: it insists that the whole scope of questions connected with conditions of employment—wages, hours, etc.—should be left to *free* agreement between trade unions and employers' organisations. The unions "find it necessary to make it quite clear that we are not in any circumstance inviting the State to impose a system of compulsory arbitration in wage disputes". This leads the unions to the logical conclusion that they cannot consent to making it "a criminal offence on the part of workmen to refuse to accept the terms and conditions of wage settlement". It is difficult, however, to see how in an organised and planned society compulsory arbitration can be avoided, unless the trade unions and the employers' associations can assure the State that their methods of settling working conditions and wages will not upset the operation of the plan.

Doubtless there is every justification for the demand that trade unions, as voluntary associations, should maintain, in the interests of their members, their freedom of defence and attack during the transition period from capitalism to planned economy. It is this very necessity that led Lenin to emphasise clearly in the early days of the October Revolution[1] the dual position of the trade unions during the transition period from Capitalism to Socialism.

The T.U.C. has not so far worked out *any* positive suggestions for giving the necessary guarantees that agreements will be observed and that, thus, the wage level can be maintained without introducing compulsory measures. If individual unions or groups of workers were to act on their own without authorisation by their unions or by the T.U.C. it would be difficult to avoid such compulsion. The unions are aware of the difficulty of the position. They suggest, however, that society should rely on them to keep up the balance of industrial relations. "We should in all cases insist", says the Report, "that reliance must be placed upon the ability of unions to secure the general compliance of their members and that the possibility of individuals or small groups refusing to conform to general settlements should not be made the excuse for the imposition of legislative sanctions."

The past experience of unauthorised strikes and industrial

[1] As far back as 1920 Lenin rightly emphasised the special position of Soviet trade unions during the early stages of the transition period in the U.S.S.R. "Our present State is such", he said, "that the working class, organised to the last man, must defend itself and we must use the Labour Organisations for the defence of the workers from their own State as well as for the defence of the State by the workers. The defence of the one and the other is to be realised through the unique interweaving into the same texture on the one hand of our State measures and on the other of our understanding and unity with the trade unions."

disputes does not make it too easy to share the optimism of the Interim Report; we cannot refrain from observing that trade union machinery was sometimes too slow or bureaucratic to register and respond to the discontent that finally led to open conflicts, or to deal with these conflicts efficiently and in time.

These facts ought to be faced courageously and with an open mind. They reveal: (a) that in many unions the tide of industrial democracy is at a low ebb and that effective measures are urgently needed to stimulate the interest of the membership in the day-to-day activities of their unions; (b) that the multiplicity of unions and the competition between them for members and power lead to a great waste of social energy and impair the solidarity and achievements of the whole movement; (c) that the power which trade unions exercise in this country is far less than it could be, because of the limited existence of industrial unionism, and because of the competition of different types of unions. This has to be adjusted, if the unions are ever to become one of the real foundations of a planned economy; (d) and that voluntary self-discipline in the movement, as well as the bonds between individual unions and the T.U.C., ought to be strengthened without delay.

If all these shortcomings are to be met as they should be, then the Trades Union Congress and its General Council must be granted much greater authority by its constituent bodies, and be given the task of making the organisation and methods of the whole trade union movement commensurate with their aims and responsibilities. It is no use taking cover under such terms as "normal functions", for in our days trade unionism has to deal with an entirely new distribution of social forces and a new organisation of industry. These new political and economic facts make essential quite a new interpretation of *what should become normal for our time*.

If "freedom of action" for the unions is to be protected "against unnecessary encroachment" by the State, then the State had to be assured in return that the trade unions can themselves enforce the acceptance by their individual members of obligations freely entered into by their own organisations. If we are advocating the end of chaotic competitive capitalist economy, then the trade unions, conditional on the optimum integration and mobilisation of their forces, can themselves constitute one of the most important guarantees that this organised economy will not become a totalitarian one. They cannot, however, play this great part without thorough readjustments. It is no good claiming in one part of the Interim Report maximum freedom for organised labour while showing in another part that "organised" labour is still so much in the grip of outworn traditions, faulty methods of organisation and out-of-date machinery that it dare not face drastic reorganisation for fear of a "split" among its members.

A study of the Interim Report on Post-War Reconstruction shows that another coat of paint will not fill up the cracks in the structure of British trade unionism; it calls for nothing less than thorough rebuilding and readjustment.

British trade unions rightly want to remain free and voluntary organisations, and not to become powerless parts of the State machine. Can they maintain their freedom without adjusting their industrial organisation; without raising to a much higher level the education and political awareness of their members; or without improving beyond recognition their research organisation and the training of trade union officials and leaders? Genuine democracy demands much higher standards of individual understanding, culture and discipline from every one than does the all-powerful totalitarian State. The goal of voluntary and free unions in a democratic but organised and planned society will be reached only if the trade union members rise to the present task with conviction, courage and imagination. Only so can Labour maintain its traditional place as the leading force in British Democracy.

CHAPTER XVI

THE INDUSTRIAL PLANS OF THE NATIONAL UNIONS

THE TRADES Union Congress having shown its attitude to the future in the industrial and general plans formulated in 1944, which we examined in the preceding chapter, it would be interesting to see in what ways its constituent national unions envisage the future planning of their own industries. The main proposals made in the Reports which a number of them have published will, therefore, repay study. Many of these unions' proposals followed the T.U.C. 1943 resolution in industrial post-war reconstruction, and were submitted to its Economic Sub-committee, which prepared the general statement on trade union policy. Their main purpose was to harmonise the particular policies of the trades and industries concerned with the general policies of the T.U.C. and the Labour Party. Some of their arguments for nationalisation, such as the wickedness or incompetence of Capitalism, have of course been outpaced by the 1945 elections and the Labour Government's subsequent legislation.

In many of the unions, on the other hand, there had been a strong pressure from below to ensure that any pronouncements on behalf of the union on post-war policy should be submitted for study and discussion of the rank and file. Plans so prepared, embodying the experience of the problems under discussion of men in the industry itself, were naturally full of constructive suggestions. The two groups of problems emphasised in the reports are, as might be expected: (1) suggestions for the reform of the industry itself as an industrial unit; and (2) the wages and conditions of the workers.

While an exhaustive account of all these plans cannot be given here, an attempt will be made to describe how the more significant among them envisage those general problems in their respective industries.

(a) COAL-MINING

The century-old demand of the miners for nationalisation of coal as a condition of decent living has at long last been granted. This has not meant, however, immediate or automatic improvement of their conditions, and to this point the Mineworkers Federation gave urgent attention when preparing the Report. The men are being called upon by the Government to increase output, and at the same time are being told that, owing to its financial state at the time of transfer, the industry cannot now, or for a long time to come, afford them any substantial improvement. Concentrating on this issue, the National Union of Mineworkers has launched a campaign for the Miners' Charter consisting of twelve main demands.[1]

[1] 1. Modernisation of pits, taking the Reid Report proposals as a standard; compensation to redundant workers; aim at a general day-wage system.

2. Training for youth and definite promotion schemes, with facilities to qualify as technicians.

3. New safety laws for modern conditions, especially to suppress disease.

4. Adequate compensation for injury and disease.

5. Wage standards not to fall below those of any other industry.

Though the demands are primarily for better wages and conditions, emphasis is placed on the necessity for modernisation and for the rationalisation of the industry on the lines of the Reid Report. The miners may well be excused—if not, indeed, thanked—for not adding yet another to the many proposals for modernisation made from time to time, and for contenting themselves with the Reid proposals, which are on lines they have long advocated.

That apart, the most important general issue is whether modernisation should come first and the improvement in wages and conditions wait until the industry can afford to meet them, or whether the latter should come at once and be financed for the time being by a subsidy. The miners emphatically demand the latter course and, therewith, that the points of the Charter be implemented immediately.

(b) Iron and Steel

Each of the two bigger unions in this industry—the British Iron and Steel Trades Confederation and the National Union of Blastfurnacemen—has put forward its own particular plan.

(a) The British Iron and Steel Trades Confederation makes its main plank the need to end the insecurity of employment which has always been such a problem in this trade. To achieve this, it proposes greater centralised direction and organisation of the industry with increased State control. The plan upholds the principle of State control and public ownership, but the union would seem to be satisfied—subject to increased State control—with some alternative planning, possibly even the continuance of the present cartel—the British Iron and Steel Federation. If that is a fair reading of their viewpoint, then it is, in fact, indistinguishable from that of the Federation itself. The plan in this connection is somewhat verbose, and it is difficult to pin it down to any very clear state-

---

6. Restoration of seven-hour day underground, forty-hour week on surface and five-day week without loss of pay.

7. Guaranteed week to continue when Essential Works Order is withdrawn.

8. Two weeks holiday and six public holidays with pay.

9. Pensions for miners unable to work in the industry after fifty-five, and subsidiary pension from the industry in addition to ordinary pensions.

10. New towns and villages built so as to end segregation of miners, with cheap transport facilities.

11. Reorganised health and welfare services.

12. Compulsory medical examination, with right to training for other work at full wages if found unfit for mining work.

ment of policy.[1] For this reason the extracts given below are somewhat lengthy.

The plan argues that the industry must be thoroughly modernised and to some extent re-located. It advocates the increased use of home ores and the development of the integrated plant. It faces up to the possibility that increased rationalisation and mechanisation are liable to cause some falling off in the total demand for labour in the industry, but thinks that this will be compensated for by the increased demand that will arise with the consequential fall in costs and with the Government's full-employment policy leading to a higher standard of living.

The most striking feature of the plan is the absence of any comment on the subject of wages. This is the more surprising because at the moment the wages position is very uncertain, and one would have thought that for this reason, if for no other, their members would have appreciated a statement of union policy on the matter. The method of calculating wages in the trade is that of basing them on the selling price of steel: as that price goes up wages go up, and vice versa.

During the war this method had been suspended and a cost-

[1] "The survey made in the preceding pages of the position of the iron and steel industry has emphasised the necessity for a further advance in its organisation. A study of the industry's problems made by the Union in conjunction with the Trades Union Congress in 1935, led to the conclusion that conditions were ripening for its socialisation. Trends of policy in industry before the present war, and the developments of the war years as they have affected the industry, seem to us to fortify the case for socialisation. In this section, therefore, we will set forth the proposals to which our Union was a party, embodied in the T.U.C. Plan for Socialisation of Iron and Steel, made a decade ago."

"Steelworkers are not hidebound political theorists. They apply their commonsense to the problems that confront them. They have seen the iron and steel industry re-established and reconstructed in this country by Government assistance, direction and control. They fear unregulated private enterprise, many of them having suffered from its consequences in past years. Therefore they ask that further steps shall be taken to perfect the machinery of direction and control within the industry and it is their considered view that a public corporation can best serve the interests of the community and expand the output of an industry which is an essential part of our national economic system."

"The organised workers in the iron and steel industry pin their faith to an expanding industry organised and controlled by a public corporation or some similar form of controlling agency imbued with the ideal of maximum service to the community rather than profits for private enterprising shareholders. The workpeople believe that the industry can stand on its own feet if given a chance, and will be able to produce as economically and efficiently as any in the world if properly organised for the task."

of-living sliding scale temporarily put into force. What is the union's policy now? It is in a dilemma. It advocates modernisation, which should mean reduced prices, and at the same time, in fact, it contemplates the return to the selling-price sliding-scale, which, with lower prices, would mean lower wages. In fact, the union has an interest in high steel prices, and is quite content with the present cartel set-up which secures them. This fact may well account for the somewhat hazy way the statement of future policy is put, with its rather tentative support of nationalisation and its complete silence on the subject of wages generally. On the question of modernisation it is quite sound and, though somewhat less precise, in line with the technical proposals contained in the Federation's plan for the industry published as a White Paper.

The Confederation's plan contains a strong plea for amalgamation of the unions in the industry.

(b) The National Union of Blastfurnacemen, on the other hand, faces the question of wages quite frankly. It advocates the return to the previously existing selling-price sliding-scale, which also applied in pig-iron production, until its temporary suspension in 1940, with slight modifications which are not of any general interest. It supports the T.U.C. policy for the reduction of hours of work by stages and an extension of the present one week's holiday with pay to two weeks, in view of the onerous nature of the work.

With regard to the position of workers who lose their employment because of mechanisation or closing down of plant due to centralisation or some other long-term cause, its plan is very instructive. It advocates the setting up of a pensions fund to cover the entire industry, to be partly contributory on the part of workers employed, to compensate by weekly payments the workers rendered redundant in this way.

This is a valuable suggestion. Any scheme of modernisation is bound to bring in its train redundancy, either temporary or permanent, and is liable, therefore, to be met by the instinctive opposition of the workers, who, whilst they may appreciate its necessity from the national point of view, are not unnaturally most mindful of its effect on themselves. Such a scheme would go some way towards meeting these proper objections and help to alleviate the sufferings of the workers actually concerned. It is a proposal which, in some form or other, merits far wider consideration.

On the question of the future economic control of the

industry, the union faces frankly the effects of the industry being in the hands of a monopoly and, altogether apart from the national interest, takes the view that this monopoly is contrary to the interests of its members. It categorically supports, without any hedging, the T.U.C. policy, which was in favour of the nationalisation of the iron and steel industry.

On trade union organisation the union strongly opposes any return to negotiating wages on a district basis, and proposes the continuance of the present method of settlement on a national basis. The plan proposed an approach by the union to the Confederation for a discussion of the points of policy raised in it, and the close working together of the two unions in matters of common interest.

(c) ENGINEERING

The National Engineering Joint Trades Movement (N.E.J.T.M.) prepared in April 1946 a plan dealing mainly with the rôle of the industry in national reconstruction. Its thesis was that the contribution of the engineering industry must be part of a planned effort involving trade union participation at all levels. It was not therefore specially concerned with wages, but with general matters of high policy: that does not mean that the unions concerned were not at the same time taking a very strong line on wages and conditions. In fact, proper working conditions are essential to the successful execution of the Plan.

The National Engineering Joint Trades Movement advocate the setting-up of an Engineering Advisory Board consisting of an equal number of representatives of both sides with an independent chairman, to assist the Minister to draw up a practical plan with a view to:—

(1) Defining the tasks and targets of the various sections of the industry so that manpower and capacity can be adjusted to priority requirements in an orderly manner.

(2) raising efficiency;

(3) minimising the misuse of trained labour and capacity and ensuring full employment.

The arguments presented in the Report run on the following lines. The products of engineering provide the foundation for efficiency in most other industries. At the same time, and largely for the same reason, they offer the most promising export prospects.

The question of equipment and re-equipment comes first. In the factories of Britain at the outbreak of the war the machine-tools had been on active service on an average for over twenty years. It is not, then, surprising that before the war output per worker in the U.S.A. was somewhere between 50 and 35 per cent. above that of Britain.

What is needed from the engineering group of industries, if home and export demands are to be met, can be obtained only if their production fits into a national plan. That requires that priorities be decided, targets for the several sections and their products be fixed, Government allocation to be made of capacity and resources to the different parts of the programme —a man-power budget.

All such decisions are left to-day to the firms, combines and trade associations of the industry. Therefore production falls behind, bottle-necks occur and, despite labour shortage in some places, there are pockets of unemployment, and a tendency to sacrifice the more necessary to the more profitable production.

How completely any plan is lacking, or even any general out-look, is shown by the fact that workers are drifting away from the industry, though in some sections there is redundancy and the ranks of the unemployed are increasingly filled by engineer-ing workers. Thus the sections called general—*i.e.* electrical, marine and constructional engineering, motor and aircraft, carriage and wagon—have lost more than a million and a half workers since the middle of 1945. By the end of 1946 it is estimated that the total employed will drop to about 1,650,000, as against 1,500,000 in 1939, nearly 3 million at the peak in 1943, and 1,827,000 in January 1946. On February 11th there were 83,000 engineering and vehicle workers in a total of 388,000 unemployed.

Among the shortcomings to which the Report draws atten-tion are these. Before the war the value of the mining machinery produced was about £3 million, whereas the Coal Mines Bill expects in its five-year development plan, which emphasises intensive mechanisation, machinery to the value of £150 million. The position is similar as regards the output of agricultural machinery, which before the war was of about the same value as that of mining machinery. The National Farmers Union put the post-war requirement at £20 million, exclusive of output for export.

To achieve the higher production necessary, development must be planned and based on priorities, while rings and

196

monopolies must be curbed both in engineering and in industries such as steel which furnishes its raw material. Engineering products which represented in 1913 12·3 per cent. of Britain's total exports had risen steadily—to 15·4 per cent. in 1930, 18·4 per cent. in 1935 and 24·6 per cent. in 1938. The future world demand is above all for engineering products to raise through industrialisation the output per head of countries which imperialist exploitation had caused to lag behind. Thus would world supplies of raw materials and foods that now are scarce become more plentiful.

The argument that the diversity of the engineering industry renders harder its effective planning ignores the fact that its ownership is highly concentrated. So small a number as 511 firms, having over 500 workers each, employed in 1935 67 per cent. of the total number of workers. Hence, "the industry can be effectively guided and controlled through these firms which are sufficiently limited in number to be individually contacted. Most of them are large enough already to have their own plans for production and capital investment which can be directly influenced by the Government planning authority. The activities of most of the smaller firms—as sub-contractors, supplying components and services—revolve round the larger few which dominate the industry."

Many of the strongest employer groups, the unions point out, are not interested in efficiency, and their interest in output is to restrict it in order to keep up prices and thereby profits— an attitude fundamentally opposed to the aims of the Labour Government. Therefore "without the full co-operation of the organised workers . . . at all levels including the highest, economic planning . . . cannot possibly be effective". If the boundless enthusiasm, drive and initiative of the men and women on the job are to be won for the economic aims of the Labour Government, then the Government must be prepared to set up the kind of machinery that permits the organised workers to participate in economic planning and in carrying those plans through. The unions represent the people whose livelihoods are concerned, who suffered so bitterly between the wars because of the neglect of proper planning and control— and they are the people who are determined to see the Labour Government's plan implemented.

It is the ingrained recognition of the fact that a high standard of living is based upon a corresponding high level of production that impels the unions to demand a genuine plan

197

for engineering in which they shall themselves actively participate. Of the higher production, on which higher standards of living for all workers, engineering and others alike depend, a new wages structure is an essential part.

(d) TRANSPORT

The T.U.C., considering public ownership of transport a matter of urgency, prepared, in consultation with the unions concerned, a comprehensive plan for the future management of the whole industry—road, rail, canal, coastal shipping, internal airways, and ports and docks. Although issued as a T.U.C. publication, it represents the view of all the unions concerned.

The plan lays down these three pre-requisites: (1) the several sections of the industry should be operated as one system, (2) there should be no competitive struggle between the various transport services, (3) the industry must be operated at the highest level of efficiency. The working of British transport during the war, when a depleted staff carried out very great tasks with antiquated equipment, is cited in support of the first two of those requirements.

Alongside the lack of co-ordination between the various forms of transport before the war there developed a combined rates structure without any corresponding co-ordination of operations that was virtually becoming a transport monopoly, with all the vices and none of the virtues of that state of affairs.

The unions claim that full nationalisation is the only effective alternative, and, to that end, advocate, as a first step, the retention by the State of all services it then operated—the main-line railways, London Passenger Transport Board, main canals, that part of road transport under the Ministry, road haulage organisation, coastal shipping and internal airways. Power should be acquired to take over other sections as and when the time is ripe.

The form of organisation followed that proposed as a model in the T.U.C. Interim Report on Post-War Reconstruction—namely a National Transport Authority responsible to Parliament on matters of principle and subject to its over-riding authority, but responsible for the detailed running of the industry. Sub-boards would be appointed to operate each section of the industry, and the war-time administration would be continued. Compensation would be on the basis of reasonable net maintainable revenue, and displaced staff would be

198

compensated. Freight rates would be standardised and made the responsibility of the National Transport Authority.

The plan deals principally with administration rather than with details of any necessary technical improvements, while recognising throughout that far-reaching reforms are required. For the unions, nationalisation of transport and co-ordination of its several branches precede any technical modernisation whatsoever.

(e) POTTERY

Localised and special in many of its characteristics as the pottery industry is, the National Society of Pottery Workers has published a report on its reconstruction, advocating nationalisation as the ultimate solution of its troubles and recommending a short-term programme.

Among the outstanding facts of the industry are these. Before the war 85 per cent. of British pottery was made around Stoke-on-Trent. This concentration made the district depend too exclusively on the industry. Nearly half of its insured workers of that period were pottery operatives, and as there was little alternative employment, conditions of life, including wages, remained low.

The national industry employed nearly 80,000 workers, of whom 55 per cent. were women workers and girls : of the total, 67,000 lived in the Potteries. In the months of 1939 before the war those unemployed rarely numbered less than 4,500, and still more were on short time. Of the 327 factories in the area, ten employed over 800 operatives each, ten between 600 and 800 each, eighty-six from 200 to 600 each, seventy-one from 100 to 200 each, and 150 factories less than 100 each. "Technical efficiency was low and the factories for the most part obsolete : not so much the small units producing specialised ware, for which it is quite likely there will always be a place in the industry, but simply old and dilapidated factories, producing under more or less primitive conditions the kind of common-grade ware that could be better done by mass-production methods". It is not only the small factories which are in need of reconstruction. The vast majority of the factories are "badly constructed, inefficient and a menace to the health of the workers employed in them".

The war required concentration, and fully half of the factories were wound up; but because the firms were left a free hand as to which to liquidate, it was not always the less

199

efficient that disappeared. Of the 30,000 still at work in 1943 no fewer than 28,000 lived in or around Stoke.

Pending nationalisation, the short-term programme that the Pottery workers recommend means adapting the methods of Government control so far employed, but with entirely new aims. The Board of Trade is urged to establish a Pottery Advisory Board representing workers and employers equally, and with a neutral chairman. Pottery would be made only under licence, laying down standards of efficiency and working conditions, including (1) observance of the Lead and Dust Regulation, the Factory Acts, or other statutory standards; (2) wages agreements and conditions jointly agreed by the unions concerned and the manufacturers' federation; (3) an agreed apprenticeship scheme; (4) compulsory presentation of any statistics or other data dealing with the running of the industry that may be required.

The workers' wages hitherto have been low and the ways of fixing them complicated. Eighty-five per cent. are paid by piecework. Rates for skilled craftsmen in 1938 varied between 1s. 2½d. and 2s. 2d. or, not more, on the average, than 1s. 6d. an hour. Women's wages were between half and two-thirds of that for work equal to that of a man. It is true their average output was lower, but their piecework rates themselves were always lower for the same work. A new system must therefore be introduced, including a just basic time rate adapted to the type of work and a scale of piecework prices allowing the average worker a minimum percentage above the time rate. A Pricing Committee in every department should settle the piecework prices.

In view of the high death and disability rates in the Stoke district, due especially to silicosis, a new Lead and Dust Regulation, to be enforced within a specified time, is recommended; and therewith more inspection and a forty-hour week within three years after the war.

(f) COTTON

In 1943 the President of the Board of Trade invited some workers' and employers' organisations to submit, jointly or severally, plans for post-war reconstruction. Probably the most complete, as well as the first, of the schemes announced came from the United Textile Factory Workers Association, which includes every union in the cotton industry.

The Report recommended its socialisation for the threefold

reason "to meet foreign competition, satisfy the aspirations of the workers to a better life and make the industry a national asset". Owners were to receive compensation and interest-bearing Government securities, redeemable either after a period of years or later at a fixed price to be issued. When socialised, the several sections of the industry would be grouped horizontally under a General Board—appointed by the Board of Trade—of fourteen members, with an independent chairman of proved ability in industrial management.

Aiming at both industrial efficiency and improved working conditions, the Report maintains that the pre-war practice of meeting competition by wage reductions must be replaced by the industry itself guaranteeing every adult worker a living wage. Owing to the poorer wages, conditions and prospects the cotton industry offered, it, like mining, was always short of young beginners.

For the reorganisation recommended the Report makes these points: inefficient undertakings should be wound up and the mills modernised; separate units in the spinning and weaving sections should be combined and weaving units made big enough for mass production of standard cloth.

The industry being so largely dependent on exports, the question of their organisation bulked large in the Report. It suggests the setting up of an International Control Board, which would allocate to each country its quota of piece-goods for the various markets, and fix prices. Any country exceeding its quota or seeking to under-cut would suffer sanctions in the form of being deprived of its raw materials. An International Bureau of Standards to deal with infringements of copyright design and cloth standards would work on the same lines as the National Standards Bureau already proposed for this country.

The Association suggests an investigation into a system of rebates on export goods, whereby the prices of export goods would be lower than that of home-consumed goods (in other words, subsidising exports at the expense of the home market). It does not, however, commit itself in advance to supporting any such scheme.

(g) Printing

The Printing and Kindred Trades Federation in its Report deals almost exclusively with matters of concern to the workers in the trade. The problems of the efficiency of the industry or its place in the national life are hardly touched. Within these limits, however, the Report is full and careful.

Exploring the possibilities of employment in the immediate post-war years, it emphasises the necessity of enabling blitzed printing-works to start again, and to ensure the ample supplies of paper and other materials required. It recommends Government assistance in the matter of refresher courses for men leaving the Forces, and rehabilitation of disabled ex-Servicemen to fit them for their trade.

It is suggested that the services which the Federation render its affiliated unions could be greatly expanded. A Federation Reference Department, a Legal Advice Service and education facilities (through Summer Schools and so on) are among the services mentioned. There is a call, too, for membership drives, especially in non-union houses.

As to wages, the Report puts forward a four-fold policy: (1) further efforts to reduce the wage gap between London and the provinces; (2) piecework to be a matter for individual decision by each union—for opinion is much divided; (3) the principle of "the rate for the job" in female labour; (4) where women are employed on work not normally done by men, to secure for them adequate wages and a clear definition of the extent and scope of their duties.

As regards hours, the demand for the forty-hour week and two weeks holiday with pay is to be pressed immediately.

Still closer working arrangements between the unions is advocated and the creation by the Federation of its own conciliation machinery to replace the T.U.C. Disputes Committee, for settling inter-union disputes.

The Report makes, in conclusion, various detailed proposals with a view to securing healthier and safer conditions in printing shops.

(h) Boot and Shoe Industry

In 1943 the National Union of Boot and Shoe Operatives published a statement on the Organisation and Employment Policy which, in its view, should be followed by the Boot and Shoe Industry after the war. It followed this statement, which was mainly concerned with the economic planning of the industry and the conditions of workers employed in it, by a further statement, in 1944, setting out an educational policy for the industry, which dealt specially with the recruitment and training of young people. These two statements are naturally closely related—recruitment of young people into an industry is to a large degree a function of the wages and conditions prevailing—and the two statements can therefore properly be considered together.

The union was perturbed at pre-war developments. The boot and shoe industry showed increasing use of mechanisation at the expense of the craftsman, and there was a corresponding fall in numbers employed, as output per head rose; it showed a high level of unemployment, increased monopolistic control and, with it, increased exploitation of the consumer as evidenced by the widening gap between wholesale and retail prices.

The solution of this was nationalisation, but as it was recognised that the industry would come low on the list of industries to be taken over, the union proposed the setting-up of an Industrial Board, made up of an equal number of representatives of employers and workers, presided over by an independent chairman. This Board would be responsible for the general planning of the industry, with especial attention to maintaining full and continuous employment, the control of costs and prices, the maintenance of quality standards, the development of research, the elimination of monopolies and the development of markets, both export and home.

The union did not recommend that this Board should have power to determine wages, hours and conditions. These, it was proposed, should continue to be determined by the conciliation machinery already established.

As to these factors, the union advanced a number of demands. Hours should be arranged with the primary objects of securing the regular employment of the maximum number of operatives and the regular production of the planned quantity of footwear. It was demanded that the industry should work a forty-hour week of five days for forty-eight weeks a year, that such hours should be adjusted over the whole of the industry so as to maintain full employment and the planned production, that the holidays should be paid for, and that overtime be abolished.

As to wages, the statement did not go into the question of the actual rates to be paid, but laid down certain general principles, which included (a) a minimum basic rate equal for men and women, (b) no reduction in such basic rates consequent upon a decrease in the standard hours of employment, (c) payment of full wages during sickness, (d) a substantial increase in the basic rates for juveniles and full adult basic rates to all workers at twenty years of age, (e) piecework is recognised as inevitable, but must be based on an agreed output for each operative, to avoid physical over-strain and other harmful factors which frequently arise under piecework conditions.

The union put very great emphasis on the proper education, training and recruitment of young persons, if the industry is to maintain proper standards of life for the operatives and provide efficient service for the community. It advocated the increased use of Juvenile Employment Committees, operating under the authority of the Local Education Committee, that greater regard should be paid to the youth's school record and aptitude, and that the Committee should pay more attention to the standards of employment in the industry or firm in which they contemplate placing young people. It was vital that the industry itself should provide a code of "agreed standards" to govern the employment of young persons. It advocated increased correlation between the curriculum of Continuation and Technical Schools with the day-to-day practice and technique of the industry, and the increased provision of Technical Schools. The union proposed detailed plans for getting youths acclimatised to factory life and learning thoroughly about the trade they were entering.

The union advocated the general setting-up of Workshop or Factory Committees. These Committees must not in any way usurp the powers and responsibilities of the union's officers, and their proposed rights and duties appear somewhat limited compared with those in many other industries. They include: (a) the application within the undertaking of the measures to secure full production laid down by the Industrial Board, (b) the development of factory and social amenities, (c) the maintenance of the agreed standards of young persons.

(i) POST OFFICE

The Report of the Post Office Workers Union differs from all the others because it contains on the one hand a series of statements about the need of abolishing the wages system and the operation of industry though guilds based on service to the community, and, on the other, a number of most thought-provoking proposals of practical relevance. The Report advocates the immediate introduction of workers' control of an uncommon type.

In its shorter-term policy, the Union of Post Office Workers advocates that the Post Office should be run, subject to periodic reports to and final control by Parliament, by a Board on which the unions concerned are fully represented, the unions running the service jointly with the Administrative side—*i.e.*, it advocates a large measure of workers' control. This Post Office Administrative Council would operate through Sectional Councils dealing with technical and departmental matters, subject to the over-riding control of the Council. Such Sectional Councils and the local administration would conform to the same principles.

The other proposals suggest:

(1) that the section of the Trade Disputes and Trade Unions Act, 1927, which bars the Union of Post Office Workers from membership of the T.U.C., should be repealed (a prayer already answered by the repeal of the Act);

(2) that the Labour movement formulate its policy on workers' control and call a series of conferences to consider (*a*) extended amalgamation, (*b*) joint control schemes by each union, (*c*) "A plan for a National Industrial Authority" and (*d*) "The integration by legislation of trade unionism into the democratic life of the community".

CHAPTER XVII

"RE-ORGANISATION" [1]

(*a*) 1942–1944

WAR CONDITIONS and the discussions on social and economic reorganisation after hostilities end have helped to stimulate within the trade union movement a willingness to reconsider and modernise its own organisational structure. Striking evidence of this tendency is to be found in the formation, on January 1st, 1945, of the National Union of Mineworkers, to replace the former loose federation of some thirty regional organisations. In a wider field, the problem of reorganisation has been discussed and studied by some recent sessions of the Trades Union Congress and by the General Council of the T.U.C.

[1] "Interim Report on Trade Union Structure and Closer Unity." See T.U.C. Report 1944.

When the question was discussed at the Trades Union Congress, in 1942, Mr. F. J. Burrows (National Union of Railwaymen) moved a resolution which aimed at having the organisational structure of the unions investigated, and having measures formulated for any necessary improvements and reorganisation. The resolution reads as follows:—

"This Congress calls upon the General Council to make a complete examination of the following two points, and to report their views and recommendations to the next Annual Meeting.

(a) To report upon the present structure of affiliated unions in order to determine:—

(1) Where competition and overlapping exists,
(2) Where such structure is uneconomic,
(3) Where policy is diverse within an industry.

(b) To report upon the advisability of the alteration of the constitutions of the Unions where it can be shown that their present basis of improving the conditions of employment of their members is ineffective from the point of view of general progress both now and in a visualised Socialist economy."

We cannot do better than repeat Mr. Burrows' argument for the necessity for such an investigation.

"The seriousness of the situation seemed to demand that trade unionists, in addition to fighting the enemy, should examine their own organisation to make it in every respect ready to meet the tremendous calls that would be made upon it. It would not be an adequate answer to the resolution to say that the trade union structure had been capable of meeting the demands made upon it in the past. Were they dealing solely with the past, there would not be agreement that the prevailing trade union structure was the best which the movers could create. There would be agreement, however, upon the point that they need take no shame for the structure which they had created. Surely, however, it was a duty devolving upon them to look for ways of adding to its strength."[1]

Unfortunately the Congress decided by a comparatively small majority not to undertake such an investigation.

[1] See Report, 1942.

The conviction has, however, been growing that a general overhaul of trade union structure might help to make more effective the struggle towards political and economic objectives. It is significant that the Congress of 1943 unanimously carried a motion asking the General Council to re-examine the organisational problem of the movement, although in 1942 it had rejected a similar motion.[1]

This resolution appears, on the face of it, far-reaching indeed. It calls for nothing less than a complete re-examination of the structure of British trade unionism: the problems of amalgamation, and of the avoidance of overlapping and competition, are treated only as special cases of a wider issue. It is doubtful how far the majority of the 1943 Congress realised the full consequences of its own resolution; but it would appear from the wording that the General Council was given a mandate enabling it to consider, among other things, the problems of local organisation (whether branches were to be based on the places of residence or on the places of work); the place of shop stewards within the movement; the position of the local Trades Councils; as well as the problems of the amalgamation and co-operation of existing unions.

Following this resolution the General Council referred the question of trade union structure and closer unity to its own special committee. This committee examined the problems involved and, as a result, called a number of inter-union industrial conferences to consider possible improvements in the structural organisation of special industries. Twenty-four such conferences, attended by representatives of over 100 affiliated organisations and covering twenty-two trades, had been held up to the time of the annual Trades Union Congress at Blackpool in October 1944. Others were still to be held, and the General Council presented to this Congress therefore only an Interim Report; there is, however, little likelihood of any further fundamental alterations before the Report receives its final shaping.

[1] The 1943 resolution reads:—

"Congress, having in mind the still wider functions and responsibilities of the Trade Union Movement in the post-war period, calls upon the General Council to take immediate steps to examine Trade Union structure and to report subsequently to Congress with regard to: (a) uneconomic overlapping and competition, (b) what amalgamations are desirable, (c) structural or other changes necessary to ensure maximum Trade Union efficiency in the future."

(b) "THE INTERIM REPORT"

As a result of its deliberations the General Council fully acknowledges, in principle at least, the need for sweeping changes. The problem is stated as follows:—

"The question the Movement will be called upon to answer at any stages and on many subjects will be as to whether the Trade Union Movement alone, in a changing world, can retain its pre-war ideas of organisation." This question, it is added, should be put primarily from the point of view of achieving greater trade union effectiveness, but there are many other reasons for an urgent reconsideration of the "pre-war ideas". For instance, the Movement will probably challenge "vested interests . . . in plans for reorganisation of industry". It would obviously be weakened if, owing to antiquated forms and methods, it kept a structure unwieldy and too complicated to mobilise. By so doing it would diminish its fighting powers and impede rejuvenation. It is worth remembering, too, that trade unions employ a considerable number of people, and that some of their members and officials act as employers in local government and elsewhere; they can therefore appreciate the usefulness of modern trade union organisation from the viewpoint of a good employer. The Report quotes the statement of one influential group of employers to show that shortcomings in the trade union movement are "also an embarrassment to the employer who is prepared to co-operate with the trade unions". The conclusion is unequivocally summarised in these words:—

"The Trade Union Movement in a changing world cannot retain its pre-war conception of organisation if it is to prosper and efficiently fulfil its ideological and practical functions."

However, while accepting the necessity for basic changes, the General Council rejects in so many words any "structural" reorganisation of the movement as a whole, mainly because of its impracticability. "Basic alteration of Trade Union structure is impracticable", declares the Report.

In this the Council is merely reiterating the finding of earlier T.U.C. Reports on the questions of organisation; indeed, as far back as 1874 Congress adopted resolutions on the basic problems of organisation, which in one form or another have been continuously under review by the General Council since 1924.

In that year Congress, still under the influence of the war and the immediate ensuing period, with its revolutionary tendencies, mass strikes and growing shop steward movement, passed the following remarkable resolution (known as the Hull resolution):

"(a) That the time has arrived when the number of Trade Unions should be reduced to an absolute minimum.

"(b) That the aim should be as far as possible organisation by industry, with every worker a member of the appropriate organisation.

"(c) That it is essential that a united front be formed for improving the standard of life of the workers.

"(d) And accordingly instructs the General Council to draw up

(1) a scheme for organisation by industry, and
(2) a scheme which may secure unity of action, without the definite merging of existing Unions, by a scientific linking up of same to present a united front."

A scheme for revitalising the machinery of the T.U.C. itself had already been envisaged in 1921, when it was planned to have six permanent Group Committees on which representatives of six groups of unions should sit, and which should "cultivate the closest possible contact" between the T.U.C. and the individual organisations of the movement. These two schemes —the one for the setting up of industrial unions and the other for the reorganisation of the T.U.C.—might well have modernised the whole structure of the movement, provided, of course, that they had been intelligently and courageously carried out. Unfortunately, however, the resolute and "adventurous" spirit that had prompted these suggestions died away before they could be translated into practical terms. As a matter of fact, the present Interim Report states that the Group Committee system "has never been fully developed", although the T.U.C. machinery for consultation has been partly improved by the formation of certain Advisory Councils; these were established to deal with problems directly concerning women workers, non-manual workers, the nursing profession, local government, the tobacco industry, engineering and shipbuilding, etc.

The fate of the Hull Resolution, with its recommendation of industrial unionism, is still more disappointing. The inquiry that followed the Resolution took over three years to complete, and the final Report was made only in 1927, the year after the General Strike, when the movement had lost the heart needed to carry through any sweeping reforms. At that time the T.U.C. resigned itself to the "impossibility of a body such as the T.U.C., composed of all types of unions, reaching agreement on any specific form of organisation. It was recognised that the most which the General Council could achieve would be to facilitate negotiations for amalgamations and for various forms of closer unity." (Quoted from the summary given in the 1944 Report.)

Two main reasons are given why "the General Council considers that in passing the Hull resolution Congress placed upon it an impossible task", namely:—

"(a) The resolution, which is composite in character, was based upon resolutions and amendments containing opposing principles and was merely a compromise in wording which left a wide divergence in policy.

"(b) The varying structure and method of working of unions, the differing circumstances in the various trades and industries, and the impossibility of defining boundaries make the general application of any particular scheme impracticable."

It would appear that these considerations still guide the policy of the General Council, for the 1927 Report is quoted with apparent approval. In principle, they only state that the numerous unions, with their divergent history and organisational structure, have not arrived, and in fact cannot arrive, at a genuine general understanding about the best possible organisational structure of trade unionism. In these circumstances, if the General Council should suddenly press for any general organisational scheme in the whole movement, there is, in their opinion, real danger of a schism in British trade unionism (similar to that which occurred, for instance, in the U.S.A.), and in their opinion nobody could seriously advise the Movement to take such a risk.

The 1944 Report includes the following remarks on the question of trade union unity:—

"Fortunately, in this country, it has been possible to avoid the deeper schisms which have developed between Unions and groups of Unions in other countries. This is in large measure due to the existence of Congress during the period of the most extensive growth of Trade Unionism, and its unchallenged operation as the national co-ordinating body on questions of general principle. In addition, the existence of Congress disputes machinery has led Unions to seek a solution of their acute inter-Union problems through that machinery. Without the provision of any real constitutional power, Congress, through its General Council, has assumed a wide range of co-ordination and leadership on general questions, which the Unions have accepted with approval, until the Unions now place added responsibilities on the General Council over an ever-widening field."

As it is, the T.U.C. is in the main content with recommendations concerning greater co-ordination within the movement, without dealing with the direct reorganisation of unions themselves. It repeats the recommendation (already made with insufficient effect, about seventeen years previously) "that the Unions themselves must strive for closer unity and resolutely pursue that end, probably making some sacrifices on the way, until it is achieved". Already in 1927 it was pointed out (and experiences since then have confirmed this apprehension) that there are quite a number of obstacles which very often make amalgamation of unions, under present conditions, within one industry very difficult. These obstacles in their approximate order of importance are: fear of loss of trade identity and autonomy; marked differences in scales of contributions and benefits; unwillingness to pool resources with a union in a weaker financial position; conflicting ideas about bases of organisation, wage policy and general affairs; difficulty in transferring officials affected. In addition, difficulties arise from the law which requires that 50 per cent. of the membership must vote on the question of amalgamation and that those voting for the amalgamation must exceed by at least 20 per cent. those voting against.

A compromise is suggested in those numerous cases where unions within one industry cannot make up their minds to promote amalgamation. Unions belonging to one industry should, in such cases, closely co-operate, and should agree, as a half-way measure between complete independence and amalgamation, to form *federations* which should take over the main "economic functions" of trade unionism. These functions are: negotiations of wages, hours and conditions of work, and the formulation of industrial policy. Furthermore, federations should have considerable facilities for research and adequate statistical and technical services, in order to carry out these functions efficiently.

The unions should, the 1944 Report says, have complete autonomy in all other respects; in particular regarding the recruitment of non-members, the general protection of members in their employment, the collection of contributions, payment of benefits, educational work and general servicing of members. The unions are advised (although in general terms only) to consider now how far their internal machinery has attained maximum efficiency; and special attention is directed to the need in many unions for improvement in educational services. More important is a recommendation strictly to observe the existing Congress resolutions and rules against "poaching" members, and to supplement these measures as far as possible by the provision of joint working arrangements, the determination of spheres of influence, recognition of cards (which as a war-time measure has been generally adopted and which naturally commends itself for the time after the war), and the setting-up or improvement of inter-union machinery for composing differences.

At the top of the movement, the T.U.C., the Report proceeds, should develop the closest possible relations with the federations, so as further to improve their economic efficiency. The main recommendations for the improvement of its own machinery are that the system of Advisory Committees should be developed to cover each industry, service or related group, and that the federal body in an industry or service should be associated with such an Advisory Committee along with representatives of the General Council. The educational and research facilities of the T.U.C. should be extended.

There seems to be a clash between two principles. On the one hand, the T.U.C. wants to avoid anything which might break with the old-established structure and traditions of British trade unionism, whereby the unity of the movement might be endangered; on the other hand, the General Council expressly acknowledges that the movement "cannot retain its pre-war conception of organisation if it is properly and efficiently to fulfil its ideological and practical functions". To us, however, these two principles are not necessarily in such conflict that one or the other must be completely sacrificed. The legal standing of Congress was not at first assured and perfect, but its leadership and authority gradually grew in power and in range. It is evident that during the present decisive period it should assume responsibility for guiding the movement along lines which the new conditions demand, instead of being mainly guided by the movement's own "historical tradition". The General Council might well have used the mandate which it received at the 1943 Congress to establish certain guiding principles of trade union organisation which would help the trade union movement to prosper in a new and changing world. Quite possibly Congress would still have had to introduce the reorganisation gradually and to postpone the application of some of these principles, or might have adopted them only in those industries in which the transformation were urgently required. There would have been no immediate danger of a schism unless Congress had decided to go ahead with its schemes even against the will of a considerable opposition.

On the other hand, even if the suggested new principles of organisation had not been immediately adopted in any part of the movement, their formulation alone would have been a guide for the future development of British trade unionism, by which unions already so inclined might steer their courses. Such a statement would have helped to focus on certain basic ideas the discussions about trade union re-organisation which have commanded constructive interest throughout the last two decades. Thus, too, could Congress, with its General Council, have fulfilled its duties of democratic leadership entirely in accordance with its own history and in its best traditions.

Unfortunately, the "half-way house" decisions suggested by the Report and accompanied by timid remarks and explanations, such as "a federation is in effect a loose form of industrial unionism", will only put additional strain on the T.U.C. Immense energy and determination will be required to put them into operation and to make them a working charter. We believe that a straightforward policy on the lines advocated by the 1924 Resolution would be easier to achieve and better in its effects.

(c) SUGGESTIONS

To encourage discussion of lines of trade union adjustment called for by changes in the economic, social and political field, we would like to put forward the following suggestions:—

1. Because of the high number of wage- and salary-earners who are still not members of any trade union the first task of British trade unions should be to impress upon these the move-

ment's material and moral value with sufficient force and persuasiveness to induce most of them to join. A vigorous national campaign should be launched, especially in trades and industries where membership density is weakest.

2. In all unions the interest of the members in their organisation should be so stimulated and enforced as to enable them to participate actively and intelligently at workshop level in the daily problems confronting the union. The ordinary member must be helped to feel his due share of responsibility for the policy and strategy of his union, and to take part in formulating them, as well as in carrying them out. Only in this way can discipline become both democratic and enjoyable, the tendency to "unofficial" strikes and breakaways be averted, and any energy behind them directed into constructive action.

3. Most trade unions as organised to-day have neither the structure nor the power to achieve these aims. On the one hand, there are great numbers of wage- and salary-earners in many industries still non-trade unionists; on the other, the trade union movement affords little outlet for the young forces. Some unions have made special efforts to facilitate the promotion of younger officials (Electrical Trades Union), others are still ignoring the problem. The position of young workers in trade union organisation should be tackled as a high priority task.

4. The renovation and remoulding of the trade union system and many of its links to meet the conditions of modern planned society have become the more urgently necessary with a Labour Government in power. Without them the prospects of democratic socialism succeeding in this country are not very promising.

5. Although, officially speaking, the movement is centralised in the T.U.C., this centralisation is restricted, and exists more in theory than in practice. The T.U.C. has not sufficient authority or influence over the affiliated unions to secure the necessary discipline. Under a Labour Government the movement will have more opportunity to act as the representative body of organised workers, and it cannot effectively represent the affiliated unions if it cannot ensure that decisions taken by majority vote shall be honoured and effectively applied or enforced. But such increase of power for the T.U.C. will require certain structural changes which should give full guarantees that the majority of the General Council represents the majority of the affiliated unions and has behind it a democratic majority of the whole movement.

6. Without any planning, but yet with irresistible force, re-adjustments are already taking place throughout the trade union system, and these are in the direction of industrial unionism. In this matter the social and economic developments of the twentieth century are facts forcing the hands of the unions, whether they like it or not. Industrial unionism is going to become an indispensable instrument of the workers for the achievement of democratic planning, and therewith the transition from capitalist to socialist economy. The trade unions and the whole Labour movement should face this fact, and should prepare for a scientific, efficient and rapid rebuilding of their organisation. It can be done in a variety of ways, starting with amalgamation and federation, which would prepare the way for the gradual, unchallenged, handing over of the membership of the general unions to industrial unions.

7. The maximum amalgamation of craft unions should be initiated and encouraged by the Trades Union Congress, and wide co-operation and federation should be advocated as between the national unions embracing members belonging to the same factory or economic unit paving the way towards industrial unionism.[1]

The speed and effectiveness of trade union reorganisation in this country will depend largely on the ability of the industrial unions to offer the craftsmen a place in their organisation, which would give then an assurance that their special interests would be protected.

8. It ought, of course, to be clearly recognised that the development of powerful general unions embracing wage- and salary-earners employed in different industries and trades is at variance with the traditional trend of development of present-day monopolistic Capitalism and with attempts made so far to build a planned democratic economy.

These unions, which have played a great part in organising unskilled and semi-skilled labour, should continue their activities as spearheads of trade unionism, for the enrolment of that great mass of British wage- and salary-earners who still remain outside trade union organisation.

The general unions should, however, agree to hand over gradually to those unions, which will be rebuilt as industrial

[1] "The Report on Trade Union Structure and Closer Unity", published in full in August 1946 by the T.U.C., is a welcome step in the right direction; it makes useful and workable propositions for further amalgamation and federation in many industries and trades.

unions, those of their members who belong to the specific industry.

In such a way the general unions will help the British trade union movement to rebuild itself on an industrial foundation, and their great experience and drive in catering for the unorganised workers will not be lost to the movement. Simultaneously they will have time gradually to adjust their organisation and personnel and redistribute it among the growing industrial unions.

Comparatively small and pioneering organisations catering for the technical and managerial personnel will have to go through a similar process, no doubt, as regards their membership, and to re-distribute it in the course of time among industrial unions.

Inside the Labour movement there are at present tens of thousands of scientists and technicians who are not coming to the forefront because traditional forms of organisation bar the way. These men rarely sit on the Joint Production Committees, and, ironically enough, only if sent there by the management.

9. If the reorganisation necessary in this country were to take place on the lines of industrial unionism, these intellectual and scientific forces of the Labour movement would join with the operatives in raising production required for higher standards of life. At the same time they would not be benevolent middle-class onlookers, but would by their work naturally qualify to be among the representatives of the mass of wage-earners in building up the edifice of industrial democracy.

10. Trade union organisation with regard to the branches of the unions needs to be rebuilt on functional lines, and not remain only on its present geographical basis: in general, members should belong to the trade union branch in the economic unit, shop, factory, mine, ship, etc., where they are employed and not in the locality where they live. The collection of membership fees, thus simplified, could be re-arranged accordingly.

11. (a) Shop stewards should be recognised as an indispensable element of the trade union movement, and trade unions which have not yet adopted the practice of having them should be encouraged to do so. The shop stewards would thus serve as a firm bridge between the national unions and their local membership in each industrial unit; they should be given proper standing inside the local and regional organisation in the way initiated by the Amalgamated Engineering Union.

The fact that the greatest majority of strikes during the last ten years were unofficial strikes shows clearly that trade union machinery has not a sufficiently strong grip on the mass of workers, and that the latter often feel the need to influence union policy through direct action.

Shop stewards can serve well as a direct contact between the union administration and the masses, and help in organising in the workshops themselves all the manifold sides of trade union activity.

12. The Trades Councils should expand their activities and influence and reorganise their finances so as to become effective local and regional organisations. The introduction of a planned economy will enhance the importance of regional and local units for planning and production purposes. The trade union movement will have to adjust its organisation to these new developments and changing needs, and create efficient local and regional bodies able to represent their combined membership.

CHAPTER XVIII

THE NEW SCENE

(a) THE TRANSITION PERIOD

WE HAVE seen in earlier chapters what great changes have come during our generation in the main work of the trade unions as well as in the forms of their organisation. Such matters as the furtherance of stable employment, the fight for wages and better conditions, improvements in social security provisions and the right to engage in political organisation all took on a new significance. Gradually the workers' organisations, besides having to adjust themselves to developments in these matters which were, and remain, their principal purpose, were at the same time confronted with great changes occurring within the economic and social structure of the nation.

As this book was nearing completion, the political complexion of the country suddenly and fundamentally changed: the people elected to power a Labour Government with a working majority, and thus set in motion the transition from a predominantly capitalist Britain to one aiming at establishing democracy and Socialism in our time. Much that has been said in this book must now be read in that new light, which, far from invalidating the main arguments advanced, renders them, it will probably be admitted, all the more urgently relevant.

That the political victory was long overdue is proved by the social structure of the population, which could not but favour policies that only Labour had the will and, technically speaking, in a wide sense, the power to apply. For of every hundred occupied persons sixty-nine were manual workers, twenty-five non-manual workers and only six were either people working on their own account or capitalists. Considering that a country of that social composition was for practically the whole of the inter-war period under Conservative Government, can the Labour movement seriously claim to have made full use of the resources residing in its political, trade union and Co-operative organisations? Whatever the answer, a new question becomes inescapable. Can it now adapt and co-ordinate those resources so as to secure for the Labour Government the support that will render easier some of the difficult and complicated problems of the transition? For there is no denying the difficulties ahead, and Labour theorists of all shades have in the past so concentrated on the criticism of Capitalism that unfortunately not enough hard thinking has been done about the strategy of transition and the technical and cultural organisation of the socialist future.

What are the main difficulties ahead? To begin with, there is the mentality engendered by an all-pervading Capitalism. Ordinary people do not change a life-long outlook overnight. They remain the products of a decaying capitalistic society, with its acquisitive spirit expressed in greed and monopolies, in unemployment and insecurity, in ignorance and disease, frustration and mutually destructive ambitions. All these make for habits of mind and life in which monetary rewards must long remain a principal incentive to work, unless the movement, rising to its great opportunity, offers deeper and more sustaining incentives. And it has the means to hand.

Granted that a people's outlook does not quickly change, the period of transition to the mental atmosphere of a socialist society might last a generation or two. But by using the means just referred to, the time lag between the coming of a Socialist Government and the achievement of a socialist society can be shortened and the transition period rendered a happier creative time.

218

This means that those men, women and youths who constitute the mass membership of the trade unions and the Cooperatives, as well as the Labour Parties, and who in varying degree are now mostly passive members, must be rendered more actively aware of the purposes and possibilities of their movements. They can, and should, be taught to find in the movements they form and finance ways of personally helping to fashion a socialist Britain—one where a finer quality of life will be the goal, and a revitalisation of these organisations by making them dynamic and democratic, through and through, will be one of the surest means.

To that end a proper division of work and responsibility between the three branches of the movement should be worked out, and the National Council of Labour has never had a more magnificent opportunity. Their joint resources and efforts can provide the required education in democracy theoretically to the extent necessary, but much more by developing in actual practice the art of democratic planning, and by encouraging voluntary organisation and local initiative in every sphere of public life. A courageous enlightened system of education will encourage to study, reflect and express their views at every level of social organisation.

This, coupled with improved overhead social engineering, will weaken the dead grip of the past and develop a new sense of solidarity with one's fellows. The first duty of every Labour organisation and of its individual members in this time of transition is to rise above the ingrained inertia and complacency in our political and social habits and to think things out afresh. To the trade union movement, above all, the coming of a Labour Government offers a kind of a new life and status. Signs are not lacking that it may soon proudly rise to the occasion.

The election of a Labour Government must therefore be of great consequence for the activities of the trade union movement. Is that movement ready to face its new tasks?

(b) Is There a New Outlook?

Curiously enough, we have to face new and radical changes while many unions still cling to organisational features which are more in accordance with the social conditions of the last century than with our own. Craft unionism, though it started losing ground some fifty years ago, has out-lived two world wars, survived through our generation, and looks as if it might still carry on even in the transition period to democratic socialism. How far can it stand up to the demands that this new era is making?

If during the twentieth century the unions adapted themselves very slowly to new demands from outside, they had at least the excuse that they were without any responsibility for the country's political life. But, considering its close connection with the Labour Party to-day, the trade union movement cannot escape a great deal of responsibility, however indirect, for the policies and enactments of the Government. Yet, apart from one pledge, no definite proposals have been submitted to the electorate as to the rôle of trade unions in the shaping of Socialism.

That one pledge is that British Socialism is to remain democratic. In other words, the essential rights of the human personality are to be respected, parliamentary institutions are to continue to function, and the freedom to choose one's job—largely suspended during the war—is to be restored as soon as possible. The Labour movement is in general determined that the spectre of a "British Gestapo", which was the main bogey which the Tories overworked during the election, shall never become a reality. In that connection it is sometimes argued that a State-controlled economy would be easier to manage if the Government were to monopolise all the powers of the State and pay less attention to the rights of the individual. Apart, however, from the fact that such methods have little chance of succeeding in this country, the Labour Party neither sought nor received a mandate to organise a dictatorship of the proletariat or of the Party. The British elector cherishes his political freedom, and the Government has no intention of misusing the mandate it was given.

Democracy has been called the "less convenient" way of carrying out a fundamental change of policy, and certainly the idea of democratic Socialism is not an "easy" one to grasp in all its implications. For not only must its programme be seriously worked out, but its strategy and organisation must be continuously checked in practice and re-examined. It must be so conceived, organised and interpreted to the public as to keep alive both the interest and the willing effort of the people in every sphere of social and economic life.

Thinking out the problems of transition is especially urgent with regard to the industrial organisation of the workers. Little progress in that direction can be reported so far: the T.U.C.

has hardly moved ahead of the principles enunciated two years ago in its "Report on Post-War Reconstruction" (1944). At a conference called on March 6th, 1946, to receive "a comprehensive survey of the economic situation of the country and the measures which the Government considers it necessary to deal with this", and addressed by the Prime Minister, the Foreign Minister and the Minister of Labour the following resolution was passed:

> "The conference declares its determination to do all in its power in accordance with the policy laid down by the T.U.C. and in agreement with the principles set forth in the General Council's Report on Post War Reconstruction, to accomplish the speedy reconversion of industry to peace-time needs, to increase production and to utilise the nation's manpower, financial and productive resources, in order to ensure full employment, and a steadily increasing supply of goods and services to meet the needs of the people and the demands of the export trade".[1]

The resolution is followed by a number of decisions on the various aspects of reconversion, which are examined below.

It is noteworthy that, apart from a diplomatic allusion to them by the Minister of Labour, the actual problems of organisation are hardly touched in the "Statement",[2] which does, however, recognise serious weaknesses in trade union organisation. After reinforcing Mr. Bevin's pledge about "the restoration of cherished traditions"[3] or "of pre-war trade practices", Mr. Isaacs pointed out that "on the subject of industrial relations, he asked the Trade Unions to look at their machinery for the settlement of grievances in those cases where there was undue delay. Compulsory arbitration would go when the trade unions wanted it to go. He particularly hoped *that demarcation disputes between unions would not be brought to the Ministry of Labour or to the Government.*" Could there be any more convincing proof than that, by its former chairman, that the authority and powers of the T.U.C. must urgently be reinforced and the

[1] "T.U.C. Statement of Policy on Problems of Production", March 6th, 1946.

[2] Referred to in the following pages as "Statement".

[3] Mr. Bevin said that "in a similar conference in 1940 he had made certain promises on behalf of the then Government which have been kept. Every step that was open to him to make provision for the restoration of those cherished trade union traditions which had been taken away, had been taken" ("Statement", p. 2).

machinery for settling of grievances overhauled if they are to avoid that "undue delay" which is the most important cause of unofficial strikes?

We believe that trade union organisation can be most successfully adjusted to fulfil those conditions by moving in the direction of industrial unionism; more important than any belief is the fact that such adjustment is already taking place, but often in instinctive and roundabout ways.

Is it not doing so precisely because the combined effect of the social, the economic and the political changes that have taken place during the present century make imperative a change-over from craft and general unionism towards functional, industrial unions organised on the industrial locality or place of work basis, alike in individual enterprises and throughout a whole industry? Would not such unions be able not only to improve more quickly labour conditions, but also—and better still—to contribute to the everyday running of industry in ways that prevent bad conditions from coming about? For that possibility to be realised, however, trade unions must become organisations inclusive of all the wage- and salary-earners in each industry or group of industries, and must get away alike from the narrow limitation of craft unionism and from the all-embracing approach of the general unions.

(c) Nationalisation and Regulation

Labour's programme provides for the early nationalisation of some basic industries, particularly mining and public utilities. In these trades the unions are strong and have always been particularly militant. The different sections of industry are so interconnected that nationalisation of the basic industries must greatly influence all the rest.

It is well to remember that mere nationalisation or any other form of State control is not in itself the socialist goal or the ultimate object of its economic or social policy. What is fundamental in the case, for example, of the mining industry, whose human, psychological problems are particularly acute, is that nationalisation will put an end to the strained relations between managements and workpeople which have been among the causes of low output. Once it is nationalised it will be better able to carry out the various recommendations made from time to time for raising its technical and economic efficiency, more especially those of the Reid Report.

The question thus arises, what part are the unions to play in this "struggle for efficiency"? Considering the close relations between the Labour Party and the National Union of Mineworkers, the latter would presumably wish to support the Government's mining policy and improve the lot of the miners. Just as clearly, too, any open conflict between miners and managements would be much more dangerous politically after the industry is nationalised than before. A strike would be full of political dynamite.

Mining has here been taken as an illustration, because the most vital problem lies there. In principle, however, the same argument applies to any industry that is nationalised, though less cogently to any for which the State has taken only limited responsibility.

Even in the case of industries remaining for the time being under private enterprise, like textiles, the influence both of the State and the trade unions in their general direction and planning must steadily increase.

There is much evidence that both trade unions and employers would like to be left alone by the State to arrange their relations through existing machinery and methods. This is clearly shown by their attitude to a "national wage policy", with which we will deal in the next pages.

In adopting this attitude both sides overlook the closely interwoven texture of modern economic life. It is so interconnected and indivisible that it will be impossible to do without planning on a national scale and to rely exclusively on sectional (or industrial) arrangements, whether in matters of supply, of capital, of labour, of wages, of general policy or any other really important issue. However comprehensible in employers this evasive attitude to national planning may be, it is less understandable as a part of trade union policy.

But the fact remains that with the exception of the paragraph indicating that the country needs "planning of our foreign trade as a whole"[1] the "Statement" does not even mention the need for planning and planned economy.

On the other hand, Mr. Bevin "specially reminded the conference that as Minister of Labour he had introduced the

[1] "The problem here is to secure and pay for the imports we need in order to maintain our standards of life. But this problem neither can nor should be solved simply by attempts to expand our export trade, and least of all by the traditional methods of cut-throat competition. On the contrary, it demands the public regulation and planning of our foreign trade as a whole."

principle that a manpower budget should be prepared each year. The Labour Government had carried this a stage further and incorporated with it an economic budget."[1] It remains to be seen how these "budgets" will be incorporated into a national plan.

A beginning of some kind of voluntary planning and co-ordination in separate industries between the employers' organisations and trade unions can be seen in the recommendation to establish National Production Advisory Committees.[2] Neither side, however, is considering anything more than bi-partite voluntary consultations on different levels. It is evident, however, that to the extent that the country is to adopt a planned or regulated economy, it will have to find a special place in its planning machinery for the representation of workers' and employers' organisations.

It is clear, too, that democratic planning must increasingly rest on the productive unit itself: each factory, mine, dock-yard, department store or Co-operative Society must be so organised internally and so integrated in the overall planning process that it will evoke, and give scope to, the team-spirit of the workers, and at the same time meet the needs of the management and the policy-making bodies. In developing such organisations it will be wise to make the utmost use of existing nuclei at different levels—shop, factory and industry. To-day there is on all three levels only a very modest beginning of efficient organisation for this purpose, but a beginning which will have to win recognition by the workers and their unions and by the employers, and extended along the whole industrial front. Deliberate furtherance of this tendency, which arose less from deliberation, than from necessity, or at least convenience, can make industrial planning become at the same time part of the process of democratisation.

(d) PLANNING

National planning is still in its beginning, and its form and machinery are undefined. It is impossible, therefore, to indicate the exact functions of trade unions in a British planned economy. But whatever form this may take, if planning is to be democratic, and is to command the whole-hearted under-standing and support of the workers themselves, the trade unions will have to be consulted about these plans and invited to collaborate at all levels with the planning organisation.

[1] See "Statement".   [2] Ibid., p. 14.

If unions are to take their place effectively in this planning machinery they must be organised on an industrial basis. That is not to say that nothing can be done until Industrial Unionism becomes a fact. With the present organisation, in addition to some of the national unions, the best-organised federations would be able to undertake the task of presenting the plans to the affiliated unions and discussing them with their members, and to convey their views to the planning authorities and to the Government. Some of the federations have gained considerable experience in negotiating wages and in other fields, and reinforced by strong research departments, they should be able to play an important part in industrial planning.

Full federations (see p. 56) existing in railway transport, in shipbuilding and engineering, in the building and printing trades, as well as in iron and steel, could play an important part in mobilising their affiliated unions for the development of democratic planning.

The position in other industries, where one strong union is dominating the field (such as mining, or boot and shoe, or tailoring industries), seems to be even more favourable.

Let us take the mining industry as an example. In this industry trade union density is very high and the great majority of workers (over 85 per cent.) are organised in the National Union of Mineworkers. The Union is therefore highly representative, and carries full authority with the miners.

The industry is nationalised. It will have to be replanned without delay. The Coal Board will have to decide what pits will continue to work and what should be closed down; it will have to take decisions on capital re-equipment and on the re-distribution of man-power.

It is essential that the representatives of the National Union of Mineworkers should be kept informed and consulted by the planning authorities about the coming changes. It is essential that when a general overall draft plan is ready, it should be discussed in detail at a National Conference of the Union, and that plans for each region and for each economic unit should be presented to, and discussed by, the men employed in it in conjunction with their Union. Such procedure will raise the interest and the understanding of the mineworkers for their own industry, and will increase their sense of responsibility for its future.

In order to play its part properly, the National Union of Mineworkers will have to prepare scientifically, technically and

225

economically for this new task, and it will have to reinforce its research department in such a way that it would be able to advise the executive and the area and branch committees on any question connected with the planning and running of the industry.

The Union will also have to establish close collaboration with the unions which organise the managerial and technical personnel in the mines, and secure their full participation in the discussion and preparation of mining plans on all levels.

It is clear that unions will have to realise that they have to grow beyond their present position as negotiating and bargaining organisations, and it is evident that the whole problem of trade union participation in planning has to be studied by the T.U.C. and by the national unions without delay.

The next Congress should be able to give the movement proper direction.

(e) National Wages Policy

The attitude of the T.U.C. to a "national wage policy" is typical of the stand it has so far taken with regard to national planning.

It seems openly to criticise and resent any attempt to discuss the subject publicly.

"The T.U.C. is aware of the Statement and has from time to time considered the arguments used in support of a National Wages Policy. Singularly none of these demands have been advanced by any of our affiliated unions, or, as far as we are aware, by employers organisations. Much of the argument is academic and unconvincing and leaves out of consideration the reality of the present state of development of British industry and of the Trade Union Movement." [1]

Mr. Bevin in his address to the Conference uses even stronger and more definite language.

"'I have met many people [he said] who had the idea that somehow wages ought to be fixed at a certain level by the State.' In his view that would be fatal, but he asked the General Council to make a clear pronouncement on the matter. The Government policy was to leave the Trade Unions and the State to settle wages where the State was the employer, and to leave the Trade Unions to settle wages with

[1] See "Statement", p. 10.

226

the employers where they were dealing with private employers, and to create conciliation, arbitration and anything else they like in order to settle wages. He [Bevin] thought that the more the Trade Unions went to the arbitration court instead of settling things themselves with the employers, the more they undermined their own authority." [1]

That is certainly the "traditional" approach. The State should be kept out of the direct negotiations between employers and trade unions. Whenever it must be brought in it undermines the authority of the "contracting" organisations. This is a perfect expression of the "bargaining-power" mentality necessary in the past, which trade union leaders incline to carry over to the present. They fear that without it they would have no ground to stand on, and that will remain true until the movement makes clearer what they can count on. That uncertainty as to the future probably explains the unions' hesitation and their attitude and declarations. Once, however, a democratic Labour Government has had time to find its feet there is no doubt that the State will evoke more confidence and enthusiasm than when run by other parties: is there enough evidence of such a possible change in attitude?

In the T.U.C. "Statement" a whole page is devoted to the National Wages Policy. Reviewing the efforts made during the war, it notes with satisfaction "that it has been found neither necessary nor desirable to modify the normal practices of wage settlement", because the existing machinery for wage negotiations has operated successfully during the war. [2] The "Statement" points out that the T.U.C. has voluntarily agreed to the prohibition of strikes and lock-outs and the establishment of the National Arbitration Tribunal, and only recently has the T.U.C. decided not to disturb this practice for the time being.

The Wage Councils, which are empowered to enforce the terms of wage agreements on all employers in the industry concerned, can remain in force until 1950.

"The T.U.C. [says the "Statement"] will continue its efforts in these directions, but will neither seek nor agree to the imposition of legal restraints upon the right of Trade Unions to formulate their wages policies and to pursue activities in support of those policies". [3]

[1] See "Statement", p. 4.   [2] Ibid., p. 10.   [3] Ibid., p. 11.

227

The T.U.C. argues further that "as regards the distribution of work-people amongst the various industries and services, the alternative to freely negotiated collective agreement is not the imposition on industry of a wages policy, but the compulsory direction of labour", which the T.U.C. cannot contemplate, to be continued in peace time.[1] And Mr. Isaacs emphasised in his speech that "it was the Government's purpose to get rid of all labour controls as quickly as possible".[2]

Although the Ministers addressing the Conference made it clear that any initiative in the direction of a National Wages Policy must come from the T.U.C., the "Statement" asserts that "the T.U.C. has no intention of making any such approach to the Government to seek the determination or enforcement of any policy or practice which would substantially modify the present position or impose limits upon the rights of the Unions to engage in and to consummate collective bargaining".[3]

(f) Full Employment

The fact that the Labour Party has made "full employment" its main slogan is of the utmost importance. In this the Labour Party is by no means alone, for every political party in this country, and indeed in democratic countries all over the world, has subscribed to the idea. It means that the State guarantees to every citizen both the right and the possibility to work. If, for one reason or another, employment cannot be offered immediately, the State undertakes to maintain the unemployed workers until it is available. That policy, if realised, can confer upon social and economic life a security it has hitherto lacked.

But the economic consequences will be felt in many ways. (a) To begin with, the wider opportunities of suitable training will offer the worker a wider choice of jobs. The main factors determining choice of employment in a capitalist society were three—its stability, wages and working conditions. What most made a worker choose one job rather than another was how long it was likely to last. That was perfectly natural after the bitter experience the workers had between the two wars, when unemployment, even among trade union members in this country, was very high: they would rather have a lasting job at a lower wage than higher wages that might soon stop altogether. The policy of full employment will remove that strongest motive and will leave in operation only the two others—the remuneration and

[1] See "Statement", p. 11.   [2] *Ibid.*, p. 5.   [3] *Ibid.*, p. 11.

the working conditions. Of these, the latter will count for far more than ever before, and consequently the importance of welfare work in factories and other places of employment will greatly increase.

(b) A full-employment policy must also have profound, though double-edged, effects both on efficiency and on the incentive to work. On the one hand, the worker need no longer fear that greater efficiency and output will endanger regular employment in his actual job or in another one equally attractive; nor that it will result in his wage being cut. Thus, the old spectre that haunted wage-earners ever since labour-saving machinery was introduced—that the machine and his own greater efficiency would soon make himself or his mates superfluous—will be gradually eliminated as the policy of full employment bears its promised fruit.

(c) On the other hand, that policy must at the same time deeply influence the incentive to work, for if unemployment, or the fear of it, has been a major incentive in making people find work and stick to it, a society that guarantees "full employment" must offer some new positive incentives after this "negative" one—the risk of having no job—no longer operates.

(d) It is understandable that Labour leaders are now devoting time and attention to the "unattractive industries". Referring to the unattractive industries in association with the housing programme Mr. Isaacs said "he believed it would be possible in the next decade to introduce proper bathing facilities, not only for miners, but for all workers in dirty jobs, at their work".[1]

> "The Government was undertaking an exhaustive enquiry into the unattractive industries. Very rarely was it a question of wages. It was cold or damp, heat or dirt, unsatisfactory conditions of manual labour that could be easily overcome if employers were sensible enough to take advantage of the experience and knowledge of the scientific workers and the supervisory staffs."[2]

From these facts and statements certain conclusions follow. It is first of all necessary to ensure that full employment, while improving the productivity of labour and the quality and quantity of the goods produced, does not upset the economic

---

[1] "Statement", p. 5.

[2] Mr. Bevin, according to the *Daily Herald*, has expressed the opinion that the remuneration of workers doing unpleasant or unattractive jobs will have to be reconsidered.

equilibrium. A system guaranteeing full employment must be so organised that neither sufficiency nor a surplus can become a danger, or even be feared as one.

In such system new incentives to work will have to be found. Consideration might be given, for example, to some such methods as (a) increasing the share of the additional product that goes to the individual producer; (b) using part of the additional product for the benefit of the whole group of producers through collective remuneration—e.g., the personnel of a factory might receive part of the value of the increased production to improve its sports grounds, clubs and other amenities, (c) introducing moral rewards for the best workers or teams, as is done in the Soviet Union, and (d) giving publicity to outstanding achievement in the field of labour comparable with that given to those in the scientific fields and in sport.

(g) SOCIAL SECURITY

Some other features of the new situation created by the General Election must greatly influence the tasks and the organisation of the trade unions. The community's acceptance of responsibility for many social services over a wider field must affect, for instance, the insurance and benefit schemes which to-day play such an important part in the activities of many trade unions.

The wage policy of the unions has always had the double purpose of guaranteeing a minimum for the lowest categories of workers, and secondly of providing extra payment for skilled labour. The first function did to a large extent become the responsibility of the State, but has still to be watched by organised Labour and their representatives in Parliament; wages themselves are becoming more and more of the nature of "extra" payment for work done. The lowest wages will tend to rise somewhat above the level of the highest State provisions under a system of social security.

Admittedly, and perhaps unavoidably, the provisions of the various new social insurance Bills—even though some suggestions of the Labour Government were better than those of its predecessor—are still rather low, if measured by standards of social security for everybody.

On the other hand, the new allowances for unemployment, health and similar contingencies compare not unfavourably with the wages of the lowest-paid women workers. Single women get the same allowances as men (26s. per week), though

230

those of married women are a good deal less (20s. and 16s. for unemployment and sickness respectively). A single woman who has a child under her care has a total weekly allowance of 33s. 6d., and the same amount is given to a widowed mother with at least one child of school age, whose husband paid for the insurance.

When comparing these allowances, insufficient as they are, with the wage rates (time rates) for a full working week of the lowest-paid groups of women workers (male workers getting much higher rates) it can be seen that they are only between 10 and 25 per cent. lower than their wages.[1]

These wage-rates are, of course, gross wage-rates. The new insurance contributions will be deducted from the income; and, as they are on a flat-rate basis, the deductions are high compared with the wages. The contributions to be paid by the workers are 4s. 7d. per week for men and 3s. 7d. per week for women. This means, for instance, that a woman in the fur industry, who receives only her wages according to the time-rate, gets out a mere 36s. 5d. per week—that is only 2s. 11d. more than the same woman would receive as her sickness, unemployment, retirement or widow's allowance, provided that she has a dependent child.

Women workers with dependent children, who receive a gross wage for a full working-week of only £2, may be comparatively rare cases to-day, but they certainly exist, and their existence illustrates the fact that there will be comparatively little incentive for women to enter the lowest-paid industries if, and when, they are protected by the "social security" measures of the new Bills. One of the beneficial effects of these will be a sudden upward movement of the lowest wage-rates, first of all the women's, and less directly the men's. Such movements are bound to occur whenever the minimum scales of benefits are raised. These developments, economically and psychologically inevitable, emphasise once again the importance of this problem for the trade unions.

Looked at in more general terms, it will be seen that a new State policy of social services may lead to much readjustment in the wage levels of the lower-paid workers, and to a change of attitude to the importance of the monetary remuneration by wage and salaried workers.

[1] See *Economist*, February 9th, 1946: fur 40s., hat, cap and millinery 41s., furniture making 43s. 1d., made-up textiles 44s., jute 44s. 6d., ready-made and wholesale bespoke tailoring 46s., agriculture 48s. per week.

(h) Changing Tasks

It should occasion no surprise that the economic and social consequences of such fundamentally new facts as nationalisation, planning and a State-guaranteed full employment policy make urgently necessary readjustments of equal importance in the very functions, and consequent strategy, of trade unions. On the one hand, much of the work which unions were created to do—and did—has now been taken over by the State; on the other hand, new problems have to be faced by the unions and new functions assumed, just as happened during the war.

The traditional union activities calling for revision in the light of increased State responsibilities include:—

(a) the unions' past concern to secure stable employment for their members. This would logically render unnecessary the union practices of imposing long years of apprenticeship in order to curtail the supply of craftsmen, and of refusing to admit women and youths to skilled work, etc. It may also result in modifying the traditional demand of some craft unions that only skilled men should be used for certain jobs, and that only a certain volume of work should be done in a given period of time (e.g., the number of bricks laid by a bricklayer during a working day). The justification for all such restrictive practices in the past happily disappears under a policy of full employment.

(b) Similarly, the trade unions will have to transfer to the new state insurance organisations their former insurance work for health and in other fields.

(c) In education, whether in the technical domain or in the wider field of general human culture, the importance of the work required cannot be over-estimated; and the fact that the W.E.A., the Co-operative Union, the T.U.C. Education Committee and the Workers' Education Trade Union Committee are represented on the Council of the new National Foundation for Adult Education, "in which all substantial interests are nationally focused", is incidentally of happy omen. Nothing more perpetuates class consciousness of the wasteful type than inequality of cultural and therefore professional opportunity.

In a planned economy technical education will *ipso facto* come into its own and contribute to national prosperity, both in the volume and quality of goods and services released and in the happiness of each worker who is properly trained for the job best suited to his or her capacities and temperament.

The "Citizenship" curriculum under a Labour Minister of Education should accord due place to the study of the trade union and Co-operative movements. These and the Labour Party with its affiliated bodies should supplement the education of the citizens in the science and art of politics, provided by the national education system, in whatever ways may be required to make them good trade unionists, good co-operators and good members of the Party. In Scandinavia, for instance, the democratic influence of the People's High Schools in according residential education to young men and women after experience in agriculture, industry or at sea is an example deserving examination in a Labour Britain. Nor must it forget in its training for democratic Socialism the sound old educational principle, learn by doing. The trade union, the Co-operative and the Labour movements can severally and jointly afford at every level, national, regional and local, more opportunities to their ordinary members for doing something significant: methods have been suggested at appropriate places in other chapters. In so doing they will counteract the tendency inherent in all large-scale organisations and administrations to set up irrelevant hierarchic patterns in groups which ought to be co-operative; the insidious eternal tendency to accord to the executive and the permanent official a power out of proportion to the service rendered—a power that too often discourages or stultifies the rank and file.

The goal of the educational work of the movement must again be inspired by the words William Morris put in the mouth of John Ball: "Verily, brethren, fellowship is life, lack of fellowship is death".

(i) Voluntary Organisation

Finally, the policy of the closed shop, which had many supporters in the past, requires a completely new examination by the unions. The experience of other countries, and especially that gained inside the Soviet Union, shows how essential it is that trade unions remain voluntary organisations during the period of transition from capitalist to socialist economy. Only by remaining voluntary, by not identifying themselves with the State machinery, and by leaving the worker free to become or not to become a trade union member can they canalise the spontaneous energy of the wage- and salary-earners and render them the greatest service.

It is not difficult to argue that when the worker is guaranteed work by the State he has no right, without State permission, to leave his job or go on strike. It may be logical, but this form of logic does not carry conviction when applied to social relations. There is, however, no justification in a State with full employment for the unions demanding or insisting upon the closed-shop policy.

Once the State recognises trade unions as voluntary organisations, and leaves the worker free to be a member or not, then it is hardly defensible to insist on a man not being employed because he is not a member of a union. The closed-shop policy was primarily directed against the employment of blacklegs who took the place of workers in strikes and lock-outs, but in a democratic State guaranteeing full employment what need is there to enforce it?

It must be evident that the right to strike will also be modified under full employment. The modifications may well resemble those introduced during the war, when machinery of conciliation and arbitration had to be invoked before a strike could legally take place.

There is need, too, for a much more reliable, self-imposed, internal trade union discipline if the unions wish to be as effective as they can in a planned and organised economy. If, and when, trade unions enrol a majority of the working men and women in a certain industry, the State ought to, and probably would, accord the right to trade unions, in any field where their functions are officially recognised, to take decisions by majority vote, and a minority of workers in an industry that tried to act against such a decision would not be entitled to invoke against it the protection of public authority. That principle is of paramount importance in the case of public utilities and nationalised industries, where democratic practice and procedure in Labour matters should be the rule, just as it is in ordinary civil life.

Changes in those trade union functions which may be called defensive, as well as the abandonment or curtailment of certain militant tactics and other practices, are among the developments called for by the existence of a Labour Government. The main ones have been dealt with in earlier pages.

(j) POSITIVE FUNCTIONS

There remains an important sphere of positive readjustment where trade unions may well assume new functions and obligations. Those are participation in the control of labour, in planning and in production. It is of the utmost importance that the Ministry of Labour, which in future will be responsible for the distribution of labour, should fulfil such responsibilities in the closest co-operation with the trade unions. Only by such co-ordination can friction and consequent loss be avoided. The vital interest which the unions must take in recruiting, training, distribution and control of labour in their own industries will be great within any planned economy, and it will necessarily increase in proportion as the movement towards industrial unionism extends. They should therefore claim, and be granted, opportunity to co-operate fully with the Ministry of Labour in these matters at every stage and level of the appropriate industrial process.

Not less important is the collaboration at every level of the trade unions with the planning organisation. If planning is to become democratic throughout, then the right machinery must be found to enable the whole mass of wage- and salary-earners to study and give their opinions on the whole, or the parts, of plans upon which they will have to work. Their own organisations offer the best instrument for the introduction and development of such democratic assistance in planning on all levels. The shop stewards in the shop, the industrial union branch in the factory, the Trades Councils in the area, the industrial unions in each national industry and the T.U.C. for the whole country, will be able to express the attitude and the wishes of their membership and of the mass of the workers concerning the plans put forward by the planning authorities. Further, as Soviet experience has shown, planning can benefit immensely by the simple procedure of having two draft plans, one made by the planning authority and the other by the producing unit: these should "meet" and be discussed together. In this way the mass of wage- and salary-earners take a lively interest, and assume their due active share and responsibility, in planning the economy of the country—a democratic procedure of mass planning which has proved its beneficent effects in practice.[1]

Finally, in a planned economy the trade unions will have to assume increased responsibility for the success of the productive effort. This they have been doing to some extent during the war through the Joint Production Committees; it becomes evident, however, that if Production Committees are really to

[1] See N. Barou in "Our Soviet Ally", pp. 136–39. Also "Co-operation in the Soviet Union", pp. 18–22.

be effective, they must include not only the manual workers but also the technical, managerial and clerical forces of the industry. Not only in the nationalised industries, in which the wage- and salary-earners will probably have to provide a considerable part of the management by recommending to the appropriate body those of their members who can undertake managerial jobs, but also in non-nationalised industries, labour will still have to do all it can to increase and improve production.

Apart, however, from the nationalisation or democratisation of industry, the whole economic health of the country depends on rapidly increasing the productivity of labour, without which all our plans will be in vain. Such increase will largely depend on improved conditions of work, on improving methods and machinery, and on having done with the out-of-date methods of the selfish and monopolistic capitalism of the inter-war period. It will also greatly depend, however, on the utmost active participation by the mass of the workers in speeding up and improving production, and that improvement can best be effected through modern industrial trade union organisations.

To do that job well, the trade unions would be wise to forget a lot and to learn a lot more. They would do well to forget that for many decades they have necessarily served only as defence and benefit organisations and have taken no interest whatsoever in the active organisation of production. They have to learn a lot about their own industries and trades, about technological processes, about economic conditions, about markets and about foreign competition. The trade unions will have to create a first-class general staff of their own, both technical and economic. Only then will they be able to play the part which the peaceful British revolution of 1945 so wonderfully and so fatefully assigned to them. It has conferred on them magnificent yet difficult human problems to solve—problems which can be happily solved, but only with the courageous self-confidence and intelligent help of organised and integrated forces of all the country's labour organisations.

APPENDIX I

THE MINEWORKERS

THE National Union of Mineworkers came into existence—the latest of the important trade unions to become a fully national one—as recently as January 1st, 1945. In the case of the miners it was, no doubt, difficult to achieve national unity in organisation, but the conditions obtaining in that industry, with its previously strong but unco-ordinated local and regional unions, are significant of difficulties that still stand in the way of national organisation in other industries.

The coal-miners were, of course, already well-organised trade unionists before the national union came into existence. There were about 710,000 wage-earners on the colliery companies' books throughout 1944, while the then Mineworkers Federation of Great Britain, which catered for all colliery workers, had a membership of 602,863 in the same year. This indicates a ratio of trade union membership of practically 85 per cent. of the coal-miners throughout the country.

The Mineworkers Federation was, however, no more than is indicated by its name—a loose federation of autonomous unions. Most of these unions —twenty in number—were based on a specific coalfield; though some of the ancillary workers, such as the Power Group and the National Federation of Enginemen, were organised on different principles.

The individual districts differ greatly in strength and importance. Numerically the strongest groups were, in 1944, those in Yorkshire with 115,000 members, Durham with 106,472, South Wales with 100,000, Scotland with 51,000, and Lancashire with 40,000. At the other end of the scale were Leicestershire with 4,000, Somerset with 2,600, and Bristol with 400. Still more important is the great difference in policy and in bases of organisation prevailing in the different districts. These were the more difficult to overcome in that they reflected differences in the history, regional customs and technical outfit of the coalfields—not to mention the language of the miners, which varies enormously in different parts of the United Kingdom. One important difference between two of the most important regional organisations is, for instance, that whereas the Yorkshire mineworkers have built up, in the course of time, a complete system of insurances against every contingency, the South Wales Miners Association has always held that the State should be responsible for the workers' insurance and the trade unions concern themselves with industrial and political matters alone. It naturally follows that the contributions in an association such as Yorkshire were much higher than in South Wales.

The central machinery of the Federation was extremely weak. Only three, or quite occasionally four, officers were employed by this great Federation, with its well over half a million members and its strong representation in Parliament. There were annual national conferences of the Federation, but the national officers had no power to carry on a national policy. The National Secretary, for instance, was not entitled, without special authorisa-

237

tion from the local association, to look after working conditions in a special pit or district. It occurred even during the war, when a certain centralisation had already been achieved, that the national officers learned only from the newspapers about a large-scale dispute going on in a certain district. The decision on the payment of strike benefits exclusively concerned the districts, and there was, therefore, no need to inform the national organisation of any actual or impending dispute. It goes without saying that there was almost no national machinery for such activities as research or education.

The power of the Federation was at its lowest after 1926, when the employers steadfastly refused to have any contact with a national organisation. It was only ten years later, in 1936, that the Federation and the employers formed together an Advisory Board for the Mining Industry, on a national basis; but this Board was not supposed to deal with wages and labour conditions, and up to the outbreak of war the employers were very strict indeed in limiting the discussions in this organisation to questions which were not primarily the concern of the trade unions.

Many mineworkers were critical of the organisational structure of their Union during the whole period since 1926, and it is quite probable that a majority always favoured unification. On the other hand, there was no special inducement to re-organise until the beginning of the Second World War, and the officials of the district association were as a rule less enthusiastic about a change in the organisational structure than the rank and file of the union membership. Above all, the substantial divergences of practice and custom between different districts made it impossible to arrive at a national unification except when there was a strong impulse to overcome these divergences. This impulse developed only in the course of the war.

During the war it became necessary to have definite national machinery for the settlement of labour questions in the mining industry. The employers themselves saw the necessity for national agreements, and the Minister of Labour was also active in creating unification of machinery on the national plane. Thus, the advantages of a national organisation became obvious to the average mineworker and its creation ceased to be an academic question. The Annual Conference of the Mineworkers Federation of 1942 instructed the Executive Committee "to draft proposals for a change in the form of our Miners' organisation"; and after some delay, which was partly due to the war situation, a Special Conference met in Nottingham in August 1944 and accepted most of the recommendations of the Executive Committee for the formation of a national union.

At the same time, the divergencies between the districts were too real to admit any sudden complete dissolution of the district organisations. The twenty individual associations which used to form the Mineworkers Federation remained in existence even after January 1945, and the principle was accepted that in respect of contributions and benefits, apart from normal industrial benefits, there should be as little interference as possible with this particular aspect of the work of the district associations. At the same time, however, the whole of the *industrial* activities of the twenty district associations were wholly centralised as from January 1945 onwards. A minimum contribution of 5*d.* per member per week is being collected and remitted to the centre, and in return the national union assumes responsibility for what had been the liabilities of the district associations in respect of industrial activities, including salaries of full-time officials and staffs, expenses of Council and Committee members and delegates attending authorised meetings of the area or national organisation, legal and other charges in respect of workmen's compensation, negotiations, etc., and allowances to branches to meet authorised branch expenditure.

The collection of contributions in excess of 5d. per member per week, for purposes of benevolent benefits, is still possible for any area association, and the National Executive Committee and officers have no jurisdiction in this matter. In general, it is recommended that local rules and customs should be altered only if absolutely necessary in the interest of national and industrial efficiency. It may perhaps be hoped that further unification will be reached in the course of a longer period, but the essential step has been taken by the acceptance of national jurisdiction in *industrial* matters, and divergencies with regard to schemes of benevolent benefits, and so forth, may continue to exist without injuring the main purpose of a national union.

APPENDIX II

The following table shows the distribution as between the different trades and industries of the membership of the trade unions affiliated to the T.U.C., and also the changes which took place in this distribution between 1937 and 1945.

	1937.		1943.		1945.	
	No. of unions.	No. of members.	No. of unions.	No. of members.	No. of unions.	No. of members.
1. Mining and Quarrying	8	544,705	5	627,944	6	568,359
2. Railways	3	448,779	3	560,835	3	568,208
3. Transport Workers	9	605,893	10	1,191,457	11	1,088,781
4. Shipbuilding	4	77,541	4	125,309	4	125,302
5. Engineering, etc.	27	449,222	31	1,215,147	28	1,079,571
6. Iron and Steel and Minor Metal Trades	19	119,178	20	173,454	20	164,556
7. Building, Woodworking and Furnishing	18	326,619	20	437,549	20	460,846
8. Printing and Paper	13	168,793	14	186,084	14	191,692
9. Cotton	7	185,385	8	143,229	8	144,047
10. Textiles (other than Cotton)	17	104,551	19	90,987	20	96,816
11. Clothing	8	91,792	8	130,412	5	151,779
12. Leather and Boot and Shoe	6	101,995	6	108,192	6	109,411
13. Glass, Pottery, Chemicals, Food, Drink, Tobacco, Brushmakers and Distribution	18	275,472	19	455,557	18	496,639
14. Agriculture	1	32,000	1	87,100	1	104,400
15. Public Employees	5	60,429	5	211,206	4	166,727
16. Non-Manual Workers	3	74,310	13	165,111	13	165,103
17. General Workers	3	341,773	4	732,744	4	610,863
18. Civil Service	—	—	—	—	7	378,020
Total	169	4,008,437	190	6,642,317	192	6,671,120

APPENDIX III

1930

London Society of Lithographic Music Printers (169 members) amalgamated with Amalgamated Society of Lithographic Printers and Auxiliaries thereto of Great Britain and Ireland (7,495 members).

1931

Huddersfield Branch of the Leeds and Huddersfield Federated Cloth Pressers Society (367 members) and Leeds Branch of the Leeds and Huddersfield Federated Cloth Pressers Society (127 members) amalgamated to form Leeds and Huddersfield Cloth Pressers Amalgamation (now Cloth Pressers Society).

1932

Amalgamated Society of Tailors and Tailoresses and Kindred Workers (10,493 members) and the Tailors and Garment Workers Trade Union (40,132 members) amalgamated to form National Union of Tailors and Garment Workers.

1933

Amalgamated Society of Operative Lace Workers (1,440 members), Auxiliary Society of Female Lace Workers (membership unknown) and Auxiliary Society of Male Lace Workers (membership unknown) amalgamated.

1934

United Order of General Labourers (1,500 members) and "Altogether" Builders Labourers and Constructional Workers Union (16,000 members) joined the Transport and General Workers Union.

1935

National Union of Asphalte Workers (1,481 members) and Northern Asphalte Workers' Union (202 members) amalgamated to form Amalgamated Union of Asphalte Workers.

1936

(1) Amalgamated Society of Dyers, Bleachers, Finishers and Kindred Trades (20,779 members), National Union of Textile Workers (40,531 members), and Operative Bleachers, Dyers and Finishers Association (Bolton Amalgamation) (6,984 members—unregistered union), amalgamated to form National Union of Dyers, Bleachers and Textile Workers.

(2) Liverpool and District Painters Society (63 members) amalgamated with National Amalgamated Society of Operative House and Ship Painters (46,871 members).

1937

(1) Nottinghamshire Miners Association (9,790 members) and Nottinghamshire and District Miners Industrial Union (17,179 members) amalgamated to form Nottinghamshire and District Miners Federated Union.

(2) Amalgamated Society of Paper Makers (5,267 members) amalgamated with National Union of Printing, Bookbinding and Paper Workers (72,612 members).

(1) The Association of Officers of Taxes (11,694 members), The Valuation Office Clerical Association (unregistered—membership not available) and the National Association of the Taxes Assessing and Collecting Service (unregistered—membership not available) amalgamated to form the Inland Revenue Staff Federation (15,592 members).

(2) Cutlery Union (589 members) and Amalgamated Scissors Workers Trade Society (unregistered—membership not available) amalgamated to form National Cutlery Union (602 members).

(3) The Association of Floor Constructors (unregistered) and the Northern Association of Reinforced Concrete Engineers and Contractors (unregistered) amalgamated to form Association of Constructional Floor Specialists (19 members).

(1) Northumberland Colliery Enginemen and Firemen's Mutual Protection Association (1,389 members) and the Northumberland Winding Enginemen's Association (140 members) amalgamated to form Northumberland Colliery Winders, Enginemen and Firemen's Association.

(2) United Ladies Tailors Trade Union (3,924 members) with National Union of Tailors and Garment Workers (90,315 members).

(3) South Wales Miners Industrial Union and Benefit Society (589 members) amalgamated with South Wales Miners Federation (121,062 members).

Nil

National Union of Clerks (18,478) and Association of Women Clerks and Secretaries (12,500) combined to form the National Union of Clerical and Administrative Workers.

Nil

Nil

Scottish Brassmoulders Union (1,068 members) and the Associated Iron, Steel and Brass Dressers of Scotland (unregistered—membership not available) amalgamated with Amalgamated Union of Foundry Workers of Great Britain and Ireland (43,818 members).

(1) The National Union of Mineworkers (membership 604,978) replaces the Miners Federation of Great Britain, which operated as a federation of a number of district unions.

(2) The Metropolitan Box and Packing Case Manufacturers Federation (23 members) and the Export Packing Case Manufacturers Association (unregistered—membership unavailable) amalgamated to form London Case Manufacturers Association (59 members).

(1) United Metal Founders Society (396 members), Amalgamated Union of Foundry Workers of Great Britain and Ireland (45,987 members), and Ironfounding Workers Association (8,799 members) amalgamated to form Amalgamated Union of Foundry Workers of Great Britain and Ireland.

(2) Mental Hospital and Institutional Workers Union (23,366 members) and Hospital and Welfare Services Union (14,428 members) amalgamated to form Confederation of Health Service Employees.

(3) The National Union of Distributive and Allied Workers (271,861 members) and the National Union of Shop Assistants, Warehousemen and Clerks (97,268 members) amalgamated to form the National Union of Shop, Distributive and Allied Workers.

TRANSFERS OF ENGAGEMENTS

1941

No. 1632 T
(2,509 members).

Association of Women Clerks and Secretaries transferred engagements to National Union of Clerks and Administrative Workers (now Clerical and Administrative Workers Union) (18,478 members).

1942

No. 173 T (S).

Building and Monumental Workers Association of Scotland transferred engagements to Amalgamated Union of Building Trade Workers of Great Britain and Ireland (70,161 members).

1943
Nil

1944

No. 528 T
(129 members).

Furness Iron Miners and Quarrymen's Union transferred engagements to National Union of Blastfurnacemen, Ore Miners, Coke Workers and Kindred Trades (19,736 members).

No. 966 T
(179 members).

Amalgamated Society of Glass Works Engineers transferred engagements to Amalgamated Engineering Union (908,893 members).

1945

No. 158 T
(5,783 members).

Amalgamated Society of Vehicle Builders, Carpenters and Mechanics transferred engagements to Amalgamated Engineering Union (898,508 members).

1946

No. 880 T
(240 members).

Edge Tool Trade Society transferred engagements to National Union of General and Municipal Workers.

No. 1294 T
(7,943 members).

Journeymen Butchers Federation of Great Britain transferred engagements to National Union of Distributive and Allied Workers (266,467 members).

No. 161 T (S).

Scottish Bankers Association transferred engagements to Bank Officers Guild (now National Union of Bank Employees) (26,096 members).

APPENDIX IV

	No. of members.
1. Transport and General Workers Union	1,089,000
2. Amalgamated Engineering Union	825,418
3. National Union of General and Municipal Workers	726,487
4. Mineworkers Federation (now National Union of Mineworkers)	602,863
5. National Union of Railwaymen	405,758
6. National Union of Distributive and Allied Workers	268,038
7. Amalgamated Society of Woodworkers	168,000
8. Electrical Trades Union	124,889
9. National Union of Tailors and Garment Workers	104,218
10. Railway Clerks Association	87,645
11. National Union of Agricultural Workers	87,100
12. Fire Brigades Union	85,000
13. National Union of Public Employees	85,000
14. National Union of Boot and Shoe Operatives	84,924
15. United Boilermakers and Iron and Steel Shipbuilders Society	83,293
16. Iron and Steel Trades Confederation	82,840
17. Amalgamated Weavers Association	72,391
18. Associated Society of Locomotive Engineers and Firemen	67,432
19. National Amalgamated Union of Shop Assistants, Warehousemen and Clerks	65,719
20. Amalgamated Union of Building Trade Workers of Great Britain and Ireland	65,000
21. National Union of Printing, Bookbinding and Paper Workers	62,638
22. National Union of Dyers, Bleachers and Textile Workers	62,577
23. National Union of Seamen	52,000
24. National Society of Painters	45,678
25. Amalgamated Union of Foundry Workers	41,764
26. National Union of Engineers, Firemen, Mechanics and Electrical Workers	41,759
27. National Union of Sheet Metal Workers and Braziers	39,692
28. Typographical Association	39,108
29. Plumbers, Glaziers and Domestic Engineers Union	38,533
30. Amalgamated Association of Card, Blowing and Ring Room Operatives	38,427
31. National Amalgamated Furnishing Trade Association	36,211
32. Clerical and Administrative Workers Union	33,900
33. Association of Engineering and Shipbuilding Draughtsmen	33,616
34. National Society of Brass and Metal Mechanics	31,750

	No. of members.
35. National Union of Vehicle Builders . . .	30,000
36. Ship Constructors and Shipwrights Society . .	28,938
37. Bank Officers Guild	28,830
38. National Society of Operative Printers and Assistants .	28,023
39. National Federation of Insurance Workers . .	27,156
40. Amalgamated Union of Operative Bakers, Confectioners and Allied Workers	25,502

APPENDIX V

UNIONS WITH 25,000 AND MORE MEMBERS (IN 1943) AFFILIATED TO THE T.U.C. (WITH BRANCH FIGURES).

	No. of Branches (1945).
1. Transport and General Workers Union . . .	4,136
2. National Union of Agricultural Workers . . .	2,466 [1]
3. Amalgamated Engineering Union	2,229
4. National Union of General and Municipal Workers .	2,200
5. National Union of Railwaymen	1,605
6. National Union of Distributive and Allied Workers .	1,401
7. National Federation of Insurance Workers . .	1,398 [2]
8. Amalgamated Society of Woodworkers . . .	1,276
9. Amalgamated Union of Building Trade Workers of Great Britain and Ireland	791
10. National Union of Public Employees . . .	777
11. British Iron Steel and Kindred Trades Association .	625
12. Fire Brigades Union	612
13. National Society of Painters	521
14. Associated Society of Locomotive Engineers and Firemen	456
15. Electrical Trades Union	451
16. Railway Clerks Association	439
17. United Boilermakers and Iron and Steel Shipbuilders Society	390
18. Amalgamated Union of Operative Bakers, Confectioners and Allied Workers	380
19. Plumbers, Glaziers and Domestic Engineers Union .	361
20. Clerical and Administrative Workers Union . .	281
21. National Amalgamated Union of Shop Assistants, Warehousemen and Clerks	242
22. National Union of Tailors and Garment Workers .	241
23. Typographical Association	217
24. National Union of Engineers, Firemen, Mechanics and Electrical Workers	205 [1]

	No. of Branches (1945).
25. National Amalgamated Furnishing Trade Association	202
26. National Union of Printing, Bookbinding and Paper Workers	200
27. National Union of Bank Employees	176 [1]
28. Amalgamated Union of Foundry Workers	174 [1]
29. Ship Constructors and Shipwrights Society	171
30. National Union of Vehicle Builders	148
31. Association of Engineering and Shipbuilding Draughtsmen	139 [1]
32. National Union of Dyers, Bleachers and Textile Workers	95
33. National Union of Sheet Metal Workers and Braziers	78
34. National Society of Brass and Metal Mechanics	77
35. National Union of Boot and Shoe Operatives	63
36. National Union of Seamen	52
37. Mineworkers Federation (now National Union of Mineworkers)	37 [3]
38. Amalgamated Association of Card, Blowing and Ring Room Operatives	15

[1] 1944 figures.

[2] This Federation comprises 7 registered unions and 1 unregistered. The returns of the registered unions show a total of 1,398 branches; no particulars of branches are available in respect of the unregistered union.

[3] "Constituent Associations."

APPENDIX VI

TRADE UNION MEMBERSHIP AND THE TRADE CYCLE.

Year.	Economic characteristics.	Total membership of trade unions in Great Britain and Northern Ireland (in 1,000's). (Figures relate to the end of the year.)	Percentage of increase (+) and decrease (−) of trade union membership compared with previous year.
1892	Crisis	1,576	—
1893	,,	1,559	− 1
1894	Economic upswing starts	1,530	− 2
1895	,, ,,	1,504	− 2
1896	,, ,,	1,608	+ 7
1897	,, ,,	1,731	+ 8
1898	,, ,,	1,753	+ 1
1899	,, ,,	1,911	+ 9
1900	,, ,,	2,022	+ 6
1901	Crisis	2,025	—

Year.	Economic characteristics.	Total membership of trade unions in Great Britain and Northern Ireland (in 1,000's). (Figures relate to the end of the year.)	Percentage of increase (+) and decrease (−) of trade union membership compared with previous year.
1902	Crisis	2,013	− 1
1903	Depression . . .	1,994	− 1
1904	,, . . .	1,967	− 1
1905	Upswing . . .	1,997	+ 1
1906	,, . . .	2,210	+11
1907	,, . . .	2,513	+14
1908	Crisis . . .	2,485	− 1
1909	Depression . . .	2,477	—
1910	Upswing . . .	2,565	+ 4
1911	,, . . .	3,139	+22
1912	,, . . .	3,416	+ 9
1913	,, . . .	4,135	+21
1914	Change over to war .	4,145	—
1915	War	4,359	+ 5
1916	,, . . .	4,644	+ 6
1917	,, . . .	5,499	+18
1918	,, . . .	6,533	+19
1919	Post-War Boom . .	7,926	+21
1920	,, ,, .	8,346	+ 5
1921	Crisis . . .	6,631	−20
1922	Depression . . .	5,624	−15
1923	Upswing . . .	5,428	− 3
1924	,, . . .	5,543	+ 2
1925	Recession . . .	5,505	− 1
1926	General Strike . .	5,218	− 5
1927	Upswing . . .	4,917	− 6
1928	,, . . .	4,806	− 2
1929	,, . . .	4,858	+ 1
1930	Crisis . . .	4,842	—
1931	,, . . .	4,624	− 5
1932	,, . . .	4,444	− 4
1933	Improvement . .	4,392	− 1
1934	Upswing . . .	4,590	+ 5
1935	,, . . .	4,867	+ 6
1936	,, . . .	5,295	+ 9
1937	,, . . .	5,842	+10
1938	Recession . . .	6,053	+ 4
1939	Change over to War .	6,244	+ 3
1940	War	6,558	+ 5
1941	,, ...	7,109	+ 8
1942	,, ...	7,810	+10
1943	,, ...	8,117	+ 4
1944	,, ...	8,026	− 1
1945	,, ...	7,803	− 3

APPENDIX VII

THE RELATIVE DENSITY OF TRADE UNIONISM

Before we proceed to any actual calculations of the density of trade unionism in this country, we shall outline the main factors which make it very difficult, if not impossible, to arrive at reliable estimates.

(1) The main difficulty is in the organisational structure of British trade unionism, with its variety of industrial unions, craft unions, general workers' unions, etc. The general unions, in particular, comprise workers belonging to all kinds of trades, especially quite a number of agricultural, metal, textile, building, chemical, etc., workers, in addition to the great majority of the organised workers in the public utilities, road, dock and harbour transport, etc.; some of the craft unions also contain workers belonging to various industries and trades; and in no case do the classifications used by the unions tally exactly with the classifications of either the insurance or census statistics.

(2) The number of workers in unions of different descriptions may be compared either with the numbers of workers in comparable trades, according to the census statistics, or with the number of workers insured against unemployment. In general, the latter comparison is preferable, partly because employers, managers and persons working on their own account are not included among the statistics of insured workers, and partly because the last census was carried through in 1931, while the insurance statistics are compiled annually. It must be pointed out, however, that a great number of workers who are available for organisation in trade unions are outside the insurance statistics; for instance, the number of insured workpeople in July 1939 was approximately 15·4 millions in Great Britain, while the number of all wage- and salary-earners (including Civil Servants) was probably not very short of 19 millions. Outside the numbers of "insured" workpeople are all the Civil Servants and teachers, the bulk of the domestic workers, all highly paid white-collar employees, most employees in the railway service, in gas, water and electricity supply, and in banking and insurance.

(3) There are, furthermore, various minor difficulties, of which may be mentioned the fact that a number of members of British trade unions are situated in Ireland or otherwise outside Great Britain, and the duplication of trade union membership in a certain number of cases.

It might well be argued that in these circumstances one should rather resign oneself to acknowledging that no satisfactory estimate can be given with regard to trade union density in various trades. Indeed, we have found it impossible to give a valid estimate in most of the trades where the bulk of the organised workers are catered for by the general workers' unions, or where there exist some special difficulties, as in the case of the Government employees. Those industries and services where no reasonable estimate can be given include three with a fairly satisfactory standard of trade union organisation, namely:—

    (i) Road, dock, harbour transport;
    (ii) Gas, water, and electricity supply, and
    (iii) Government (national and local).

Other industries (including food, chemicals, leather, bricks and mining other than coal) and services (including professional, domestic, catering, and laundries) for which no estimate has been offered, are known to contain a comparatively small number of organised workers.

For fifteen different economic branches (industries and services) we have, however, offered a tentative estimate of the percentage of organised workers, even though we are aware of the shortcomings of any such statistical account. We believe that these estimates, though crude, are somewhat better than a mere guess, and we would be grateful for any constructive criticism aiming at an improvement of this method of computation. Most of the computations have been made by comparing the numbers of workers organised in trade unions of a certain group (for instance, agriculture, forestry, gardening) with the number of insured workers belonging to the same group; but the percentage figures for the groups "railways" and "education" have been arrived at by comparing the number of organised workers in 1939 with the number of workers according to the industrial census of 1931. Practically all the wage-earners and the moderately paid salary-earners belonging to the other thirteen groups for which computations have been made are included in the statistics of insured workpeople, the only exception being the group "commerce, etc.", where a great number of employees belonging to the banking and insurance branches are outside the general insurance scheme and where, therefore, the actual percentage of trade unionists is probably slightly smaller than it is computed in our table. A not inconsiderable number of workers belonging to some of the fifteen "groups" for which we have made calculations are organised in general workers' unions, and if these had been included in our computations the percentage figures would be somewhat higher, particularly in agriculture, metal, etc., "other textile industries", and building, etc.

APPENDIX VIII

TENTATIVE ESTIMATE OF TRADE UNION DENSITY AMONG MALE AND FEMALE WORKERS IN 1939.[1]

(No conclusion should be drawn from this table before the qualifying remarks and explanation in Appendix VIII have been read.)

Percentage of all workers organised in trade unions.	Among all workers.	Among male workers.	Among female workers.[2]
In agriculture, forestry, gardening [3]	% 7	% 7	% (2)
Coal-mining	82	81	(59)
Pottery and glass manufacture	17	18	14
Metal, engineering, etc., industry [3]	37	43	25
Cotton industry	63	64	62
Other textile industries [3]	25	33	18
Boot and shoe making	68	77	53
Other clothing industries	23	31	21
Paper and printing trades	46	59	27

Percentage of all adult workers organised in trade unions.	Among all workers.	Amond male workers.	Among female workers.[2]
Building, woodwork, furniture, public contracting [3]	26	27	(12)
Railways	85	85	(55)
Water transport	58	60	(13)
Commerce, distribution, banking, insurance [4]	16	19	10
Education	60	65	57
Entertainment and sport	23	29	15
Road, dock, harbour transport. Gas, water, electricity supply National and Local Government	A considerable proportion of the workers is organised though the percentage cannot be ascertained.		
Other manufacturing industries (including food, chemicals, leather, bricks, etc.) Mining other than coal mining. Other services (including professional, domestic, catering, laundries, etc.)	Trade union organisation is known to be weak.		
All trade unionists in percentage of *all* workers	28	36	15

[1] Basis of computation: trade union membership for individual industries at end of 1939 compared (excluding for railway and education) with number of insured workers age 14–64 in July 1939; railway employees (excluding persons employed in hotel and catering, docks, shipping, etc., depots of railway companies) and teachers according to 1931 Census. For computation of all trade unionists in percentage of all workers see text.

[2] Figures are put in brackets where less than one-tenth of all workers in the industry are females.

[3] The percentages of workers in these industries are probably computed slightly too low, since a considerable number of workers are organised in general labour unions and are not included in the statistical sections of organised workers in their own industry.

[4] Many employees (especially in banking and insurance) are outside the general insurance scheme; if these were included in the calculation, the percentage figure for the unionists would be slightly lower.

APPENDIX IX

Year.	No. of disputes. (1)	No. of workpeople (1,000's) involved.[2] (2)	Working days (1,000's) lost. (3)	No. of workpeople involved per dispute. (4)	Working days lost per dispute. (5)	Working days lost per dispute per man. (6)
1890	1,040	393	7,317	385	7,315	19
1891	906	267	6,809	295	7,530	25
1892	700	357	17,249	510	24,690	48
1893	615	634	30,468	1,003	49,500	49
1894	929	325	9,529	350	10,250	29
1895	745	263	5,724	353	7,690	22
1896	926	198	3,746	214	4,500	19
1897	864	230	10,346	267	1,990	45
1898	711	254	15,289	357	21,500	60
1899	719	180	2,516	250	3,500	14
1900	648	189	3,153	292	4,870	17
1901	642	180	4,142	280	6,450	23
1902	442	257	3,479	581	7,870	14
1903	387	117	2,339	303	6,040	20
1904	355	87	1,484	245	4,180	17
1905	358	95	2,470	265	6,900	26
1906	486	218	3,029	448	6,250	14
1907	601	148	2,162	246	3,600	15
1908	399	296	10,834	743	27,190	37
1909	436	301	2,773	691	6,360	9
1910	521	514	9,867	987	18,950	19
1911	872	952	10,155	1,091	11,630	11
1912 [3]	834	1,462	40,890	1,755	49,100	28
1913	1,459	664	9,804	456	6,720	15
1914	972	447	9,878	459	10,150	22
1915	672	448	2,953	667	4,400	7
1916	532	276	2,446	520	4,600	9
1917	730	872	5,647	1,196	7,730	6
1918	1,165	1,116	5,875	958	5,050	5
1919	1,352	2,591	34,969	1,915	25,800	13
1920	1,607	1,932	26,568	1,200	16,500	14
1921	763	1,801	85,872	2,370	114,300	48
1922	576	552	19,850	960	34,440	36
1923	628	405	10,672	645	17,000	26
1924	710	613	8,424	865	11,860	13
1925	603	441	7,952	733	13,220	18
1926	323	2,734	162,233	8,460	503,000	60
1927	308	108	1,174	352	3,810	11
1928	302	124	1,388	410	4,600	11

Year.	No. of disputes. (1)	No. of workpeople (1,000's) involved.[2] (2)	Working days (1,000's) lost. (3)	No. of workpeople involved per dispute. (4)	Working days lost per dispute. (5)	Working days lost per dispute per man. (6)
1929	431	533	8,287	1,240	19,200	15
1930	422	307	4,399	730	10,400	14
1931	420	490	6,983	1,165	16,600	14
1932	389	379	6,488	975	16,680	17
1933	357	136	1,072	381	3,000	8
1934	471	134	959	285	2,040	7
1935	553	271	1,955	490	3,540	7
1936	818	316	1,829	386	2,240	6
1937 [4]	1,129	610	3,413	540	3,020	6
1938	875	275	1,334	314	1,520	5
1939	940	337	1,360	359	1,450	4
1940	922	299	940	324	1,020	3
1941	1,251	362	1,079	288	860	3
1942	1,303	457	1,527	351	1,170	3
1943	1,785	559	1,810	313	1,010	3
1944	2,194	826	3,710	376	1,690	4
1945	2,293	532	2,835	238	1,240	5
1918–26 Average	859	1,354	40,268	1,580	46,900	30
1927–45 Average	903	371	2,765	411	3,600	9

[1] Excluding disputes involving fewer than ten workpeople and those which lasted less than one day, except when the aggregate duration exceeded 100 working days.

[2] Including those indirectly involved—*i.e.*, those thrown out of work at the establishment, but not themselves parties to the dispute. Duplications in numbers involved arising through the fact that the same workers were involved in more than one dispute, were estimated for various years as follows:—

1919, 150,000; 1920, 300,000; 1921, 100,000; 1931, 57,000; 1932, 70,000; 1935, 59,000; 1936, 66,000.

[3] High figures due to one coal dispute in that year in which about one million workers were involved and over 30 million days lost.

[4] From 1937, the numbers of workpeople involved are computed on a slightly different basis.

APPENDIX X

PERCENTAGE OF WORKERS DIRECTLY AFFECTED BY DISPUTES CAUSED
BY CONFLICT:

Year.	Wages.	Hours of labour.	Employment of particular person.	Other working arrangements.	Recognition of trade unions.	Sympathetic action and other causes.
	%	%	%	%	%	%
1891	48·6	5·0	2·8	25·5	6·9	11·2
1892	58·1	0·8	5·2	18·9	5·2	11·8
1893	90·8	0·7	1·5	1·9	3·5	1·6
1894	78·3	1·7	7·0	5·8	5·1	2·1
1895	56·6	2·7	5·7	30·5	2·6	1·9
1896	64·9	1·6	15·4	11·8	3·6	2·7
1897	44·1	23·4	8·9	17·4	3·8	2·4
1898	87·9	0·4	4·6	5·8	1·1	0·2
1899	68·6	2·8	5·9	13·0	3·7	6·0
1900	61·4	0·5	7·7	14·0	14·5	1·9
1901	52·8	3·8	9·4	20·8	10·4	2·8
1902	48·6	2·6	9·8	17·0	21·8	0·2
1903	53·0	4·4	8·4	14·5	18·8	0·9
1904	58·1	3·5	10·8	13·5	14·1	—
1905	57·2	4·6	9·5	8·2	13·9	6·6
1906	55·7	4·5	3·0	4·1	32·2	0·5
1907	55·7	2·1	13·6	11·7	16·3	0·6
1908	78·5	3·7	4·9	5·6	5·5	1·8
1909	24·7	51·3	7·9	5·2	7·6	3·3
1910	19·9	23·9	29·8	16·1	8·5	1·8
1911	46·2	1·6	4·0	8·3	39·6	0·3
1912	82·8	0·7	2·8	3·4	9·8	0·5
1913	56·4	2·7	10·7	4·0	21·2	5·0
1914	62·0	3·3	9·4	4·4	15·2	5·7
1919	70·1	19·2	5·4	2·5	1·1	1·7
1920	81·5	0·7	9·9	2·5	1·6	3·8
1921	96·3	0·6	1·3	0·8	0·4	0·6
1922	40·2	1·3	4·5	51·3	2·0	0·7
1923	42·9	1·8	6·9	12·4	30·7	5·3
1924	75·6	0·4	6·2	4·7	3·3	9·8
1925	68·6	2·2	14·2	5·6	7·7	1·7
1926	39·9	—	0·6	0·3	0·5	58·7
1927	34·4	14·6	32·5	5·8	6·7	6·0
1928	47·8	1·0	15·8	8·2	1·6	25·6
1929	89·4	0·7	5·0	1·4	3·0	0·5
1930	54·1	33·8	6·1	4·1	1·8	0·1
1931	56·4	5·8	3·7	33·0	1·1	0·0
1932	86·5	1·4	4·7	5·0	1·7	0·7
1933	40·2	0·2	29·8	22·6	4·7	2·5
1934	42·1	2·1	29·6	14·1	7·9	4·2

Year.	Wages.	Hours of labour.	Employment of particular person.	Other working arrangements.	Recognition of trade unions.	Sympathetic action and other causes.
	%	%	%	%	%	%
1935	24·6	2·0	17·3	15·0	8·7	32·4
1936	32·0	3·0	22·1	14·3	8·4	20·2
1937	46·4	10·4	13·9	6·0	5·6	17·7
1938	31·3	3·3	28·3	16·3	16·4	4·4
1939	39·8	3·5	26·8	10·4	12·7	6·8
1940	44·4	3·3	16·4	12·8	4·4	18·7
1941	52·8	4·4	19·7	12·6	5·5	5·0
1942	65·3	3·8	16·4	9·6	1·5	3·4
1943	53·7	2·4	14·3	10·9	2·6	16·1
1944	70·0	1·5	8·5	14·5	1·4	4·1
1945	49·0	7·6	11·2	24·1	3·8	4·3

APPENDIX XI

DISPUTES ACCORDING TO METHODS OF SETTLEMENT, IN PERCENTAGE
OF PARTICIPATING WORKERS.

Year.	Direct negotiation.	Conciliation and arbitration.	Return to work on employers' terms without negotiations.	Otherwise.
	%	%	%	%
1893	30·0	52·3	16·9	0·8 [1]
1894	71·2	7·1	17·8	3·9
1895	47·9	30·8	17·9	3·4
1896	68·7	11·1	15·7	4·5
1897	81·3	8·9	6·5	3·3
1898	81·6	8·7	7·1	2·6
1899	87·3	6·1	3·9	2·7
1900	82·0	8·5	4·8	4·7
1901	79·4	10·0	5·0	5·6
1902	87·0	4·2	6·6	2·2
1903	69·6	20·7	7·6	2·1
1904	77·3	8·8	7·0	6·9
1905	70·7	16·1	8·8	4·4
1906	82·3	5·7	10·8	1·2
1907	74·7	13·2	9·1	3·0
1908	25·0	70·5	3·1	1·4
1909	44·5	46·7	7·0	1·8
1910	49·9	45·0	4·5	0·6
1911	33·8	63·9	1·9	0·4

Year.	Direct negotiation.	Conciliation and arbitration.	Return to work on employers' terms without negotiations.	Otherwise.
	%	%	%	%
1912	23·2	5·9	1·8	69·1 [2]
1913	72·5	22·3	4·6	0·6
1914	52·8	40·9	5·4	0·9
1919	70·5	8·7	11·2	9·6 [3]
1920	89·6	6·9	3·2	0·3
1921	97·1	1·2	1·6	0·1
1922	93·1	1·9	4·6	0·4
1923	66·7	17·0	15·8	0·5
1924	56·7	37·1	5·9	0·3
1925	45·6	50·0	2·4	2·0
1926	41·4	0·2	0·4	58·0 [4]
1927	77·3	13·2	5·8	3·7
1928	68·6	7·0	23·4	1·0
1929	16·1	80·4	3·3	0·2
1930	60·7	31·7	7·0	0·6
1931	48·5	39·4	11·2	0·9
1932	15·3	40·1	43·4	1·2
1933	61·5	3·9	32·7	1·9
1934	73·7	9·5	14·8	2·0
1935	74·3	5·5	12·7	7·5
1936	53·6	11·8	33·6	1·0
1937	46·3	9·2	44·0	0·5
1938	61·9	6·4	30·1	1·6
1939	64·8	5·5	28·9	0·8
1940	64·1	6·5	29·0	0·4
1941	65·8	13·1	20·5	0·6
1942	46·7	12·2	39·1	2·0
1943	44·8	7·7	33·5	14·0
1944	58·3	2·7	37·7	1·3
1945	—	—		

[1] The figures for 1893 to 1902 refer to all affected workers; later figures for directly involved workers only.

[2] Large number due to special legislation in settlement of coal dispute.

[3] Large number due to Government intervention in two large-scale coal strikes.

[4] Large number due to "calling-off" of General Strike.

APPENDIX XII

DISPUTES GROUPED BY TRADES.

(No. of workpeople affected, 1,000's.)

Beginning in:	Building trades.	Mining and quarrying.	Metal, engineering, shipbuilding.	Textile trades.	Clothing.	Transport.	All others.	Total.
1891	19	51	61	47	39	30	20	267
1892	16	120	40	103	36	13	29	357
1893	15	505	30	45	11	15	13	634
1894	14	218	28	40	6	11	8	325
1895	10	84	46	64	50	4	5	263
1896	33	67	48	34	4	3	9	198
1897	15	49	97	37	7	13	12	230
1898	17	177	21	25	4	3	7	254
1899	31	47	21	61	2	13	5	180
1900	19	75	20	24	2	23	26	189
1901	10	113	22	17	4	3	11	180
1902	6	209	16	17	3	2	6	257
1903	4	64	32	9	3	2	3	117
1904	9	46	12	13	1	2	4	87
1905	7	45	13	16	4	2	8	95
1906	1	84	42	75	9	2	5	218
1907	1	53	20	47	12	9	6	148
1908	3	87	58	133	5	5	5	296
1909	1	272	10	7	3	5	3	301
1910	1	297	55	131	5	20	5	514
1911	3	141	93	221	9	443	42	952
1912	6	1,107	83	56	31	154	25	1,462
1913	40	214	153	93	15	84	65	664
1914	38	273	51	22	7	13	43	447
1915	16	298	46	33	6	25	24	448
1916	6	64	75	61	16	28	26	276
1917	7	281	429	65	12	26	52	872
1918	36	383	242	268	25	59	103	1,116
1919	22	925	403	488	28	571	154	2,591
1920	42	1,411	179	80	34	65	121	1,932
1921	26	1,256	63	380	5	25	46	1,801
1922	10	124	369	5	3	10	31	552
1923	21	189	61	37	4	58	35	405
1924	115	137	71	11	5	245	29	613
1925	6	136	24	172	5	29	69	441
1926[1]	3	1,091	14	17	1	20	8	2,734
1927	8	67	16	5	9	2	1	108
1928	3	82	8	25	1	2	3	124
1929	3	80	39	400	1	7	3	533
1930	4	149	10	127	1	5	11	307

Beginning in:	Building trades.	Mining and quarrying.	Metal, engineering, shipbuilding.	Textile trades.	Clothing.	Transport.	All others.	Total.
1931	12	281	12	163	1	5	16	490
1932	3	53	4	300	2	12	5	379
1933	1	72	15	7	2	27	12	136
1934	8	74	15	16	4	11	6	134
1935	3	194	17	14	3	24	16	271
1936	8	181	47	13	12	26	29	316
1937[2]	8	393	108	23	10	53	15	610
1938	14	174	44	7	7	15	14	275
1939	35	207	56	9	6	12	12	337
1940	26	190	40	10	9	5	19	299
1941	11	155	154	7	6	16	13	362
1942	13	257	142	10	5	16	14	457
1943	13	296	171	6	3	54	16	559
1944	5	571	197	7	3	32	11	826
1945	3	244	124	4	9	128	20	532

[1] The total includes workers involved in the General Strike who were not added to their respective trades.

[2] From 1937, the computations are made on a slightly different basis.

APPENDIX XIII

RESULTS OF LABOUR DISPUTES.

(In percentage according to workpeople directly involved.)

Year.	In favour of workpeople.	In favour of employers.	Compromises.
	%	%	%
1891	25·6	34·8	39·6
1892	27·5	19·9	52·6
1893	64·3	26·5	9·2
1894	21·0	59·1	19·9
1895	23·6	29·8	48·6
1896	43·5	28·0	28·5
1897	24·2	40·7	35·1
1898	22·6	60·1	17·3
1899	26·7	43·7	29·6
1900	30·1	24·8	45·1
1901	27·5	34·7	37·8
1902	31·8	31·8	36·4

Year.	In favour of workpeople.	In favour of employers.	Compromises.
	%	%	%
1903	31·2	48·1	20·7
1904	27·3	41·7	31·0
1905	24·7	34·0	41·3
1906	42·5	24·5	33·0
1907	32·7	27·3	40·0
1908	8·7	25·7	65·6
1909	11·2	22·3	66·5
1910	16·3	13·8	69·9
1911	6·6	8·7	84·7
1912	74·5	14·4	11·1
1913	32·4	18·8	48·8
1914	19·8	14·9	65·3
1919	14·0	23·9	62·1
1920	10·6	10·6	78·8
1921	1·5	5·6	92·9
1922	4·4	12·5	83·1
1923	24·8	23·1	52·1
1924	9·7	18·0	72·3
1925	53·1	16·1	30·8
1926	1·8	94·7	3·5
1927	28·1	30·6	41·3
1928	5·1	39·3	55·6
1929	4·7	6·9	88·4
1930	6·2	77·8	16·0
1931	36·4	15·6	48·0
1932	6·9	47·9	45·2
1933	12·5	42·0	45·5
1934	30·3	32·7	37·0
1935	49·3	27·2	23·5
1936	22·9	49·6	27·5
1937	11·0	63·6	25·4
1938	21·2	53·6	25·2
1939	26·8	51·2	22·0
1940	No information for later years available.		

APPENDIX XIV

End of year.	Labour Party's membership.		Trade union membership.		Co-operative membership.		
	Total.	Trade union membership.	Total.	Affiliated to the T.U.C.	Consumers societies.	Co-operative party's membership.	
							%
1913	—	—	4,135,000	2,232,446	2,878,296	—	—
1914	1,612,147	1,572,391	4,145,000	—	3,053,770	—	—
1915	2,093,365	2,053,735	4,359,000	2,682,357	3,264,211	—	—
1916	2,219,764	2,170,782	4,644,000	2,850,547	3,520,227	—	—
1917	2,465,131	2,415,383	5,499,000	3,082,352	3,788,490	—	—
1918	3,013,129	2,960,409	6,533,000	4,582,085	3,846,531	—	—
1919	3,511,290	3,464,020	7,926,000	5,283,676	4,131,477	—	—
1920	4,359,807	4,317,537	8,346,000	6,505,482	4,504,852	—	—
1921	4,010,361	3,973,558	6,631,000	6,417,910	4,548,557	—	—
1926	3,388,286	3,352,347	5,218,000	4,365,619	5,186,728	2,009,240	39
1931	2,358,066	2,024,216	4,624,000	3,719,401	6,590,020	3,522,566	53
1936	2,444,357	1,968,538	5,295,000	3,614,551	7,807,942	5,250,000	67
1937	2,527,672	2,097,071	5,842,000	4,008,647	8,084,990	5,340,000	66
1938	2,630,256	2,158,076	6,053,000	4,460,617	8,404,688	5,565,698	66
1939	2,663,067	2,214,070	6,244,000	4,669,186	8,643,233	5,883,082	68
1940	2,571,163	2,226,575	6,558,000	4,886,711	8,716,894	6,161,875	71
1941	2,485,306	2,230,576	7,109,000	5,432,644	8,772,255	6,305,017	72
1942	2,453,392	2,206,209	7,810,000	6,024,411	8,924,868	6,773,443	76
1943	2,503,240	2,237,307	8,117,000	6,642,000	9,082,218	7,071,225	78
1944	2,672,845	2,375,381	8,026,000	6,576,000	9,217,739	7,392,242	80
1945	3,038,697	2,510,369	7,803,000	6,671,120	9,400,000	7,511,072	80

Note: Trade union membership Total column percentages: 1914 (97), 1915 (98), 1916 (98), 1917 (98), 1918 (98), 1919 (99), 1920 (99), 1921 (99), 1926 (99), 1931 (86), 1936 (80), 1937 (83), 1938 (82), 1939 (83), 1940 (87), 1941 (90), 1942 (90), 1943 (89), 1944 (88), 1945 (82). Affiliated to the T.U.C. percentages: 1913 (54), 1915 (61), 1916 (61), 1917 (56), 1918 (70), 1919 (67), 1920 (78), 1921 (97), 1926 (84), 1931 (80), 1936 (68), 1937 (69), 1938 (74), 1939 (75), 1940 (75), 1941 (77), 1942 (77), 1943 (82), 1944 (82), 1945 (85).

APPENDIX XV

Rates of Contribution.

Set out below are details of the rates of contribution contained in the Rules of a number of unions, being the rates payable by adult members. It is not possible to draw any hard-and-fast distinction between general unions and industrial unions, or between industrial unions and craft unions. Where, for example, does the National Union of Clerks come; is it general or craft? or the Association of Scientific Workers? or, for that matter, the A.E.U. which is general in the sense that it embraces many trades all covered by the omnibus heading of "engineering", is industrial in that it is confined to the "engineering industry" (whatever that may be), and yet has very many of the traditions and still retains much of the outlook of the craft unions from which it sprang? The same problem arises, though less acutely, in the case of the E.T.U., A.U.B.T.W., and N.A.F.T.A., which are essentially craft unions, but which, by the force of economic pressure, are absorbing a greater degree of unskilled workers and, hence, are becoming increasing industrial unions.

Subject to these factors, the following list follows, roughly, the order general, industrial, craft.

Transport and General Workers Union.

Scale A.—6d. per week, 3d. quarterage and 3d. per quarter political levy.
Scale B.—9d. per week, 3d. quarterage and 3d. per quarter political levy.

In addition there are special scales for agricultural workers and optional scales for various classes of workers.

National Union of Distributive and Allied Workers.

Scale 1	.	.	1s. 3½d. industrial,	½d.	political per week.
,, 2	.	.	11½d.	½d.	,,	,,
,, 3	.	.	7½d.	½d.	,,	,,
,, 4	.	.	5½d.	½d.	,,	,,

National Union of Clerical and Administrative Workers.

9d. per week men, 7d. per week women, save where women work under agreements providing for equal rates for men and women.

Association of Scientific Workers.

21–25 years, 8d. per week; over 25, 10d. per week.
Varying rates for student members (5s. a year).

National Union of Railwaymen.

5½d. per week. Political levy ½d. per week.

Amalgamated Engineering Union.

Section 1 . . . . 2s. per week } full members.
,, 2 . . . . 1s. 6d. ,,

Varying other rates for youths, apprentices, industrial section members, etc.

Electrical Trades Union.

Full benefit section members	.	.	.	1s. 2d. per week.
Trade protection section	.	.	.	9d. ,,
Auxiliary	.	.	.	.	8d. ,,
Apprentice	.	.	.	.	4d. ,,

Amalgamated Union of Building Trade Workers.

Section 1.	Trade benefits	9d. per week.
,, 2.	Trade and funeral benefits . .	11d. ,,
,, 3.	Trade and superannuation benefits .	1s. ,,
,, 4.	Trade, funeral and superannuation benefits	1s. 2d. ,,
,, 5.	Trade and sickness benefits . .	1s. 3d. ,,
,, 6.	Trade, sickness and funeral benefits .	1s. 5d. ,,
,, 7.	Trade, sickness and superannuation benefits	1s. 6d. ,,
,, 8.	Trade, sickness and funeral benefits .	1s. 8d. ,,

National Amalgamated Furnishing Trade Association.

Section 1 . . . . . . 1s. 6d. per week.
,, 2 . . . . . . 1s. ,,
,, 3 (industrial) . . . . . 6d. ,,
,, 4 (industrial) . . . . 9d. ,,

British Iron, Steel and Kindred Trades Confederation.

Section 1—trade benefits and services.
A grade . . . . . 2s. per week.
B ,, ... 1s. 6d. ,,
C ,, ... 1s. ,,
DX ,, ... 8d. ,,
D ,, ... 6d. ,,

(Grades are based on member's earnings.)

Section 2—friendly society section.
A grade . . . . 9d. per week.
B ,, ... 7d. ,,
C ,, ... 5d. ,,
DX ,, ... 4d. ,,
D ,, ... 3d. ,,

(These rates will vary with financial conditions of friendly society fund.)

Plumbers Union.

Table A . . 1s. 9d. for trade union and friendly society activities.
10d. industrial only.
,, B . . 1s. 7d. for trade union and friendly society activities.
6d. industrial only.
,, C . . 1s. 3d. for trade union and friendly society activities.
,, D . . 1s. 2d. ,, ,, ,, ,,

Amalgamated Society of Woodworkers.

Section 1 . . . . 1s. 7d. per week.
,, 2 . . . . 9d. ,,
,, 3 . . . . 3d. ,, (apprentices).

Amalgamated Society of Operative Bakers.

Scale 1 . . . . 1s. 5d. per week.
,, 2 . . . . 1s. 2d. ,,
,, 3 . . . . 11d. ,,
,, 4 . . . . 7d. ,,

National Union of Sheet Metal Workers.

Section 1 . . . . . . 2s. per week.
,, 2 . . . . . . 1s. 8d. ,,
,, 3 . . . . . . 1s. ,,
Lower rates for juniors.

National Society of Brass and Metal Mechanics.

Section A . . . . : .	1s. 7d. per week.
„ B	1s. 3d. „
„ C	1s. „
„ D	10d. „
E (industrial only)	6d. „

National Union of General and Municipal Workers.

Entrance fee: men 1s., women 6d.
Full members: 7d. per week + 4 annual payments of 3d.
Half „ 4d. „ + 4 „ „ 2d.
Reduced rates in special circumstances.

National Union of Journalists.

Full members: 6s. contribution . . . .
        6d. death benefit contribution . . ⎫ per month.
        Varying unemployment contribution (at ⎬
          present 3s. 6d.) . . . . ⎭

Probationers: 2s. 6d. per month plus half unemployment contribution
        if 20 years and over.

Associate members: 3s. plus, in some cases, half unemployment con-
        tribution and 6d. death benefit contribution.

The varying scales call for some explanation. They carry with them either
varying types of benefit—as shown in the particulars given for the
A.U.B.T.W.—or, more often, varying rates of pay for the same types of
benefit. The members can chose which scale he will subscribe to, though
there is usually some limitation on his free choice. Thus, an age limit is
sometimes imposed, sometimes a certain qualifying period of membership
is necessary for a high-benefit scale, a certificate of health is usually called
for when moving up from one grade to another.

The above is the general basis of scaling. In view of the practicability of
stating the general principles involved, no exact details have been got out
for each union, as they are, in some cases, excessively lengthy and complicated, and would only serve to confuse rather than enlighten the reader.

APPENDIX XVI

Trade Union Funds (1890–1942)

End of year.	Funds in:	Funds per member approx.			Membership (1,000's).
	£	£	s.	d.	
1890 [1]	1,002,687	2	2	0	483
1891	1,179,354	2	6	0	509
1892 [2]	1,619,502	1	16	0	905
1893	1,381,813	1	10	0	910
1894	1,579,229	1	14	0	924
1895	1,747,740	1	18	0	915

End of year.	Funds in:	Funds per member approx.			Membership (1,000's).
	£	£	s.	d.	
1896	2,187,923	2	5	0	962
1897	2,272,273	2	3	0	1,064
1898	2,698,422	2	12	0	1,043
1899	3,282,922	2	19	0	1,117
1900	3,732,900	3	2	0	1,210
1901	4,129,927	3	8	0	1,216
1902	4,415,669	3	13	0	1,213
1903	4,598,867	3	16	0	1,202
1904	4,667,043	3	18	0	1,197
1905	4,815,044	3	19	0	1,215
1906	5,201,215	4	0	0	1,299
1907	5,642,652	3	17	0	1,462
1908	5,178,216	3	12	0	1,438
1909	5,054,631	3	11	0	1,425
1910	5,121,529	3	10	0	1,460
1911	5,594,603	3	1	0	1,821
1912	5,001,505	2	10	0	2,000
1911 [3]	6,294,456	2	14	0	2,321
1912	5,589,492	2	6	0	2,547
1913	6,471,199	2	0	0	3,205
1918	14,948,094	2	17	0	5,259
1919	15,956,195	2	9	0	6,516
1920	15,860,804	2	6	0	6,929
1921	10,814,903	2	0	0	5,454
1922	9,861,317	2	1	0	4,506
1923	10,752,213	2	9	0	4,369
1924	11,434,414	2	10	0	4,458
1925	12,556,453	2	16	0	4,448
1926	8,478,371	2	1	0	4,148
1927	9,709,538	2	10	0	3,903
1928	10,602,403	2	16	0	3,765
1929	11,361,112	3	0	0	3,779
1930	11,651,159	3	2	0	3,764
1931	11,285,347	3	3	0	3,577
1932	11,192,222	3	6	0	3,405
1933	11,760,465	3	10	0	3,347
1934	12,892,847	3	13	0	3,513
1935	14,167,202	3	15	0	3,795
1936	16,032,000	3	16	0	4,214
1937	18,141,000	3	17	0	4,695
1938	20,013,963	4	2	0	4,867

[1] 1890–1891 figures relate to biggest 20 unions.
[2] 1892–1912 figures relate to biggest 100 unions.
[3] 1911–1913, 1918–1938 figures relate to all *registered* unions.

Sources: for 1890–1937—Abstracts of Labour Statistics and Ministry of Labour Gazette.

APPENDIX XVII

IMPORTANT UNOFFICIAL STRIKES, 1940–1946

1940

1. Scottish collieries. 26,000 hold one-day token strike on wage question.
2. Maple's depository, Camden Town. Short strike against employment of non-unionist.
3. Yorkshire collieries. 20,000 lose 130,000 days in strike for war additions to wages.
4. De Havillands. 450 workers have an "extended holiday" until the transfer of a shop steward is rescinded.
5. Scottish aero engine works. 600 in short strike for right to organise women in the Transport and General Workers Union, the company having proposed a company union for them.
6. Montague Burton's at Swinton and Walkden, Lancs. 4,000 out for a week.

1941

1. Napiers. Half-hour strike for canteen to be provided. January.
2. Handley Page, North London. 4,000 on strike for two days in January in dispute over bonus times and piecework prices.
3. Durham miners. 2,000 in short strike on wage dispute.
4. London meat porters. 3,000 in sit-down strike against unfair dismissal of thirty men.
5. Belfast engineers. 3,770 out for reinstatement of two fitters.
6. Manchester docks. Demand for canteen facilities refused by employers; consequential refusal to work overtime leads to two-day lock-out. June.
7. Glasgow engineers. 12,500 in short strike over the alleged incapacity of a charge hand.
8. Welsh tinplate clerks. 8,000 lose 27,000 days over suspension of a clerk and recognition of the Trade Union. N.B.—Very doubtful if this was an unofficial strike in any sense of the word.
9. At varying times and for different periods 25,000 engineering and ship-building apprentices in Scotland, Belfast, Barrow and Manchester district lost total of 220,000 days between end-February and beginning-April in a whole series of spasmodic and largely un-correlated strikes. The primary cause was a demand for increased wages but in different places different local issues came to the fore. This was the largest series of unofficial strikes during the war.

1942

1. Bettershanger colliery, Kent. Three weeks strike over wages, culminating in prison sentences for the leaders of the strike committee, which in itself became a fresh issue.
2. Blackhall Colliery, Durham. 2,000 idle for a fortnight over dispute as to manner of weighing coal.
3. South Wales collieries. 10,000 idle for 28,000 days over wages to be paid to youths.
4. Lancashire collieries. Two disputes in May and June, both over wages. In the first 15,000 men lost 80,000 days, and in the second 13,000 lost 60,000 days.

5. Cumberland collieries. 5,000 lost 60,000 days because of rejection by arbitrator of men's application for a wage increase.

6. Belfast engineers. 9,000 lose 120,000 days. Demand for reinstatement of dismissed shop stewards. October.

7. Tyneside shipbuilders. 20,000 lose 135,000 days as result of objection to employers' rearrangement of the working- and pay-week.

8. A Yorkshire colliery. 1,500 lose 40,000 days in December.

1943

1. Road transport. Very widespread, spasmodic strikes. Prime cause rejection by arbitrator of their demand for increased wages, and local demands became superimposed in different places. Some 12,000 passenger transport workers involved and loss of 50,000 days.

2. Liverpool and Birkenhead dockers. 16,000 men lose 55,000 days in demand to rescind an order suspending men for refusing to work overtime.

3. Barrow engineers. 7,000 lose 100,000 days in dispute as to the meaning and interpretation of an award of the National Arbitration Tribunal relating to wages. This strike was interesting because, although quite unofficial as far as the National Executive Committee of the A.E.U. was concerned, it received the official—but quite irregular—backing of the local District Committee who acted in defiance of Head Office, and very strong disciplinary action was subsequently taken by the E.C. against members of the District Committee, not for participating in a strike but for doing so contrary to the definite orders of the Union.

4. Notts collieries. 24,000 lose 80,000 days in September in protest strike against the imprisonment of a surface worker for refusing to obey the direction of a National Service Officer to work underground.

5. Scottish collieries. 10,000 out 45,000 days in protest strike against the arrest of a number of miners who had refused to pay the fines imposed at a Police Court in respect of an earlier stoppage.

6. Annam and Swansea collieries. 7,500 lose 35,000 days. Strike over youths' wages.

7. A Yorkshire colliery. 2,000 men out 55,000 days.

8. Lancashire collieries. Two disputes involve 12,500 men in loss of 97,500 days.

9. West of Scotland engineers. 16,000 lose 90,000 days in October and November because of their objection to the terms of an agreement negotiated by the union on women's wages.

1945

1. London docks. 15,000 workers in five-day strike in March. Cause was the moving of the calling-on stand from the outside to the inside of the dock gate at the Royal Albert Dock, and it spread to other districts for other reasons.

2. Three A. V. Roe factories in the Manchester area. 10,000 directly involved in demand for revision of wage rates, 16,000 in two-day token strike in sympathy.

3. London Docks. Closed the London docks from May 28th to August 10th caused by employers' ending a piecework agreement, known as the "Western Front Agreement", and became coupled with a demand for an increase in the basic wage. The most solid and lengthy unofficial strike of the war.

264

4. 5,000 aircraft engineers of one firm in Lancashire and Cheshire on strike in April for a fortnight against piecework rates and for a guaranteed bonus of 100 per cent. on basic time rates. During last two days number of strikers rose to 9,200.

5. London Transport. 6,230 tram and bus drivers and conductors on four-day strike in May. Cause: New time schedules.

6. 50,000 dock-workers in various ports (London, Liverpool, Glasgow, Hull, etc.) on strike for about six weeks in October for wage increase and improved working conditions.

1946

1. Coventry. 3,000 engineering workers on three weeks' strike for joint negotiating machinery for the firm's three factories.

2. Coventry. 4,000 engineers in three weeks' strike about piece-work rates.

3. Dagenham. 11,000 engineers on strike for eight days for wage increase and union recognition.

4. 3,000 shipbuilding workers at the Clydeside and East Scotland yards on strike for two weeks for wage increase.

INDEX OF TRADE UNION
ORGANISATIONS

266

267

GENERAL INDEX

269

52
147

$P/_2$

$(9/_6)$ $3/_6$